Welcon

THE

EVERYTHING

PROFILES SERIES ®

Welcome to the EVERYTHING® Profiles line of books—an extension of the bestselling EVERYTHING® series!

These authoritative books help you learn everything you ever wanted to know about the lives, social context, and surrounding historical events of fascinating people who made or influenced history. While reading this EVERYTHING® book you will discover two useful boxes, in additional to numerous quotes:

Fact: Definitions and additional information
Question: Questions and answers for deeper insights
They Said: Memorable quotes made by others about this person
He Said: Memorable quotes made by this person

Whether you are learning about a figure for the first time or are just brushing up on your knowledge, EVERYTHING® Profiles help you on your journey toward a greater understanding of the individuals who have shaped and enriched our lives, culture, and history.

Visit the entire Everything® series at *www.everything.com*

The
EVERYTHING®
Martin Luther King Jr. Book

Dear Reader,

For many years now, I have considered Martin Luther King Jr. one of the most fascinating people in American history. He was a gifted orator, a passionate crusader for justice, and a leader adored by many, and yet he remained humble. He wanted neither to be worshipped nor held up as a saint. He constantly questioned his own abilities and leadership. Instead of praise for his awards and prizes, he sought nothing more than the remembrance of his work as a "drum major for justice" and as a person who served humanity. If he were alive today, a humble King would probably voice his shock over the heroic praise given his life.

Nevertheless, to gain a better understanding of America, it is necessary to explore the centrality of his role in the Civil Rights movement. His contribution to creating a society more just and equitable is certainly something to be remembered. With the wealth of resources about his struggles, failures, and successes, one can take a glimpse into the life of America's most renowned civil-rights leader. I hope this book moves you to explore more about Martin Luther King Jr.

Jessica McElrath

THE

EVERYTHING®
MARTIN
LUTHER
KING JR.
BOOK

The EVERYTHING Series

Editorial

Director of Innovation	Paula Munier
Editorial Director	Laura M. Daly
Executive Editor, Series Books	Brielle K. Matson
Associate Copy Chief	Sheila Zwiebel
Acquisitions Editor	Brielle K. Matson
Development Editor	Katie McDonough
Production Editor	Casey Ebert

Production

Director of Manufacturing	Susan Beale
Production Project Manager	Michelle Roy Kelly
Prepress	Matt LeBlanc
	Erick DaCosta
Interior Layout	Heather Barrett
	Brewster Brownville
	Colleen Cunningham
	Jennifer Oliveira
Cover Design	Erin Alexander
	Stephanie Chrusz
	Frank Rivera

Visit the entire Everything® Series at *www.everything.com*

THE

EVERYTHING®

MARTIN
LUTHER
KING JR.
BOOK

The Struggle. The Dream. The Legacy.

Jessica McElrath
The About.com Guide to African-American History

Foreword by Rev. Dale P. Andrews, Ph.D.

To my husband and children

An Everything® Series Book.
Everything® and everything.com® are registered
trademarks of F+W Publications, Inc.

Published by Adams Media, an F+W Publications Company
57 Littlefield Street, Avon, MA 02322 U.S.A.

www.adamsmedia.com

ISBN 10: 1-59869-528-2
ISBN: 13: 978-1-59869-528-1

Printed in Canada.

J I H G F E D C B A

Library of Congress Cataloging-in-Publication Data

McElrath, Jessica.
The everything Martin Luther King Jr. book / Jessica McElrath.
p. cm. — (An everything series book)
Includes bibliographical references.
ISBN-13: 978-1-59869-528-1 (pbk.)
ISBN-10: 1-59869-528-2 (pbk.)
1. King, Martin Luther, Jr., 1929-1968. 2. King, Martin Luther, Jr., 1929–
1968—Influence. 3. African Americans—Biography. 4. Civil rights
workers—United States—Biography. 5. Baptists—United States—Clergy—
Biography. 6. African Americans—Civil rights—History—20th century. 7. Civil rights movements—United States—History—20th century.
8. United States—Race relations—History—20th century. I. Title.

E185.97.K5M355 2007
323.092—dc22
2007030987

This book is available at quantity discounts for bulk purchases.
For information, please call 1-800-289-0963.

Contents

Foreword

This book is vastly different from what I have grown accustomed to when studying the life and vocation of Martin Luther King Jr. I am usually drawn to texts that serve the university or seminary classroom, the world in which I serve by vocation. Studying the Civil Rights era is a spiritual or religious venture for me, as well as an indispensable enterprise into social or political ethics. While our culture may often find these pursuits disparate, I believe King found in them an indivisible vocation, a ministry, or perhaps most accurately, a way of faithful living. This text allows us a glimpse into King's very human struggle on the road to becoming a contemporary prophet. Jessica McElrath brings to this work her gift for creating public and personal access to African American history. Reading this text caused me to pause in critical reflection on the struggles within the movement, to ponder the moral dilemma or crisis within various events, and at times to contend with some claims embedded in the author's assertions. In essence, I trust you too will "experience" this intriguing venture into King's legacy.

My own view of King's legacy is wrapped up in his role as prophet. Prophetic consciousness cannot neatly distill spiritual faith and the exigencies of justice and ethics. King could preach to the Church and address the nation from the same platform because he held both worlds together. To serve God is to serve humanity. To seek justice in what he called a "revolution of values" (that is, to resist "racism, materialism, and militarism") is to liberate both the oppressed and the oppressor from the chains of human evil. Perhaps the greatest tragedy today is that our nation, culture, and global community have yet to gain much ground in this revolution. Instead, we discover the revolution of values must add a couple of "isms" as we continue to struggle for justice within our social regression into cultural racism, economic exploitation, and militarism as an article of faith. I am not sure we should regard it as growth, but at least we have since unearthed the need for justice in resisting sexism and our phobic-laden heterosexism. The struggles seem relentless. No less today than during the Civil Rights era, we should be astonished at the invocation of God's name in our pursuits of dominance, privilege, conquest, and subjugation of another.

In fact, alongside our national campaign to sustain the socio-political legacy of this historic figure, I believe the Church should call for an ecumenical council to consider expanding the biblical canon to include proclamation from Christian prophets. And we can start the deliberations with Martin Luther King Jr.'s *Letter from the Birmingham City Jail*. This letter weaves the counsel of a pastoral epistle and the outcry of prophetic consciousness. Justice and reconciliation are the goals; love is the mission. I suppose it will take a lifetime or two for us to resolve how even King's humanity needed a revolution of values and reconciliation before we will be able to discern that he still was a prophet to an age in desperate need of that revolution and reconciliation. But I believe you too may want to pause, to ponder, and even to contend with *The Everything® Martin Luther King Jr. Book*, but it will serve you well in the discernment.

Dale P. Andrews, Ph.D.

Introduction

Martin Luther King Jr. holds a unique place in American history. He was a controversial figure in his own time; adored by some and hated by others. His harshest critics called him an Uncle Tom, while others referred to him as militant and extremist for his views on equality, poverty, and the Vietnam War. Yet, today his life and work is often revered and romanticized, and he is considered the Civil Rights movement's greatest martyr.

Perhaps it is more important to look at King's own view of his legacy. King considered himself a man and a sinner. By his own admission, he was neither a saint nor a martyr. He wanted to be viewed as an ordinary man, who would be remembered for his commitment to justice and righteousness.

King was clearly one of the most gifted orators of his time. He is most remembered for his eloquent speech "I Have a Dream," which he delivered at the March on Washington for Jobs and Freedom. While King's speech aptly summed up some of his goals, his views were hardly limited to just the recitation of his dream for America. While equality was the goal, it was through the use of nonviolent resistance that King sought the ultimate objective of reconciliation between whites and blacks and the creation of a beloved community.

Still, far more controversial than his dream of equality was his view on the evil of the Vietnam War and poverty. It was this later stance on the war that set him apart from many Americans and from other black leaders in the Civil Rights movement. At the time, his opinion was the minority rather than the majority, and his popularity suffered a chilling blow. Adding fuel to the fire, King took his crusade for equality to the economic realm. He envisioned a society where jobs and income were guaranteed for all. His new goals of peace and economic equality were met with an intensified resistance.

With the emphasis on King's work in the Civil Rights movement, it is sometimes easily forgotten that he was a reverend with a strong faith in God. It was to this faith that King attributed his commitment to the cause of equality. King was a man who relied on the might of God to give him courage, solace, and companionship. Left to his own devices, King admits that he would have left the Civil Rights movement to pursue more ordinary endeavors.

Recent scholarship shows that King had serious battles with more than just a desire to leave the movement. He had extramarital affairs, and it has been discovered that King was neither accurate about citing his academic work correctly nor careful to avoid plagiarism in his writings. These failings are perhaps the biggest mystery of his life. How could a man of God, America's civil-rights crusader, a moral compass for right, have justified such acts of dishonesty? More than anything else, however, it is the humanness of Martin Luther King Jr. that makes his life story so fascinating.

Due to the release of the FBI files on King, the extensive research done by leading King scholars, and the wealth of information from those who worked with him, the details of his life from the trivial to the personal have been uncovered. This book is the product of careful research and is intended to explore King's role in the Civil Rights movement, his philosophical beliefs, and the personal struggles that he faced.

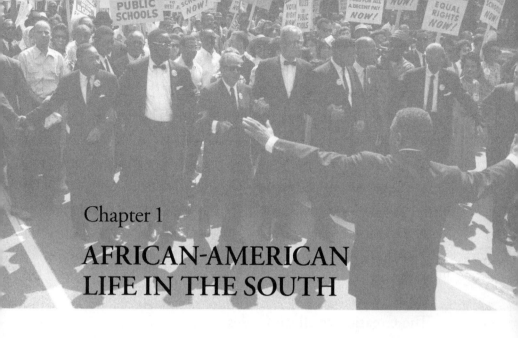

Chapter 1

AFRICAN-AMERICAN LIFE IN THE SOUTH

IN ORDER TO UNDERSTAND why the United States became a country divided by race, it is necessary to explore the history of race relations in the South. The enslavement of blacks was the determining factor that set the stage for segregation. After the Civil War, though freedom from enslavement had been won, freedom of citizenship and equality remained unrealized. Early on, blacks and whites worked together toward the elimination of segregation laws, but it was not until the 1950s that mass protest was targeted at the system of segregation.

The Aftermath of Slavery

The segregation in the South that existed during King's time was a direct result of America's history of enslaving its black population. After slaves were freed in 1865, the nation embarked upon a long journey toward equality for all of its citizens. From the beginning, however, white Southerners were far from ready to give up their way of life. While blacks were free, whites found it difficult to adjust to this new reality. During the early stages of Reconstruction, Southern whites temporarily gained control over local provisional governments. With this power, they set out to recreate the old ways of the South.

The Creation of Black Codes

White southerners were mostly interested in ensuring that they had a labor force. To that end, they enacted Black Codes. Black Codes served as a way to control the black population through the law. The laws restricted all areas of life: Blacks were denied the right to own property, were forced to work in agriculture or as a domestic, vagrancy laws were imposed, speech was restricted, curfews were established, and the possession of firearms was prohibited. The Black Codes in their harshest form were short-lived, but after 1866 some state legislatures passed revised codes that were less severe.

FACT

In the city of Opelousas, Louisiana, in order for blacks to enter the town, a note from an employer was necessary. The note had to relate such specifics as the reason for their visit and how long they intended to stay. If in town without a note, imprisonment was the penalty.

The Freedmen's Bureau

In order to implement structure in the South, Congress created the Bureau of Refugees, Freedmen, and Abandoned Lands, also known as the Freedmen's Bureau. The bureau took charge of providing food and medical services, help with settlement, management of abandoned lands, regulating labor, and establishing schools for former slaves. Education was the biggest challenge for the bureau. They created teacher-training institutions, over 1,000 schools were built, and several colleges were founded. President Andrew Johnson made the job of the bureau especially difficult when he interfered with their efforts. When the bureau gave 850,000 acres of abandoned land to former slaves, Johnson promptly returned the land to its Confederate owners. In 1870, partly due to inadequate funds, all of the efforts of the bureau came to an end when it was terminated.

Gaining Political Power

When Johnson became president after Abraham Lincoln's death, he assured Congress that he planned to follow Lincoln's reconstruction plan. However, when he allowed white Southerners to rule the South as they had done during slavery, it became clear that a battle to restructure the South had been waged. In the fall of 1866, congressional opponents to Johnson's reconstruction plan were voted in overwhelmingly. With the new Congress in place, it was not long before home rule was terminated. The Reconstruction Act of 1867 put an end to the Southern governments that had ruled over black citizens. At the state constitutional conventions black delegates were common, and in some states were even the majority. Every state extended the right to vote to all male residents. In 1868, the 14th Amendment, which was ratified by every state, gave blacks citizenship and established that all laws would apply equally to all citizens. Two years later, the 15th Amendment was enacted. It declared that the right to vote could not be infringed upon due to one's race.

Black state legislators were elected into office in sweeping numbers. Blacks also occupied seats in the U.S. Congress. Between the Reconstruction period and the turn of the century, there were two black senators and twenty black House of Representative members. In no way did blacks at any time have complete control of the government, but it was a sign that blacks had made gains in politics during this time.

Democrats Regain Control

Although African Americans had made substantial political gains, white Southerners continued to work to regain power. In 1877, when President Rutherford B. Hayes took office, he withdrew troops from the South. This was the end of Reconstruction. Southern Democrats quickly seized control, but with the 15th Amendment firmly in place, they were forced to seek other means to prevent blacks from voting. In addition to the intimidation exercised by the Ku Klux Klan (KKK), Democrats thought of new ways to disenfranchise black voters. Poll taxes were created, polling places were changed without warning, reading requirements were implemented, and gerrymandering was practiced. Before long, although blacks were free, they once again had few rights in the South.

Q: **Why did President Hayes withdraw troops from the South?**
Although Hayes was a Republican, based on political motivations, he decided to withdraw troops so that local governments could regain control. He anticipated that this action would lead to the creation of a stronger Republican party.

Jim Crow Laws

Southern Democrats were interested in more than just eliminating black political rights. They also wanted to have a stronger hold on black freedom. While the Black Codes had come to an end by 1868, Southern whites wanted to renew the effort to control the black populace by using the law. In 1870, Tennessee enacted a law preventing intermarriage between whites and blacks. Five years later, Tennessee turned its attention to segregation laws, enacting the first Jim Crow law. Other Southern states soon followed suit.

It was not long before the U.S. Supreme Court took an active role in condoning discrimination. In 1883, the Court made the decision that the Civil Rights Act of 1875 was unconstitutional. The Act protected access to public accommodations regardless of race. This ruling paved the way for discrimination. States began implementing segregation in every area of life: African Americans were banned from whites-only restaurants, barber shops, hospitals, parks, and hotels.

FACT

The phrase Jim Crow emerged in 1828, when minstrel performer Thomas Dartmouth Daddy Rice popularized it with his performance as a crippled slave named Jim Crow. As Jim Crow, Rice covered his face with charcoal paste or burnt cork and danced and sang for the audience.

As southern states enacted various versions of Jim Crow laws, the Supreme Court made another favorable ruling for segregationists. In 1896, it ruled in *Plessy v. Ferguson* that as long as railway cars were equal, separate facilities for whites and blacks were constitutional. This doctrine of "separate but equal" would remain in place for nearly sixty years. By the time of Martin Luther King's birth in 1929, the United States was a nation divided by race.

African Americans and Education

With the enactment of Jim Crow laws in the South, education was one of the only options blacks had for betterment. Many of the schools created by the Freedmen's Bureau still existed, and whites, with their newly created separate community, had little interest in monitoring or interfering with black schools. For blacks, some of whom were former slaves, the education of their children was extremely important.

HE SAID...

" Education should equip us with the power to think effectively and objectively. . . . Education should cause us to rise beyond the horizon of legions of half truth, prejudices and propaganda. Education should enable us to 'weigh and consider,' to discern the true from the false, the relevant from the irrelevant, and the real from the unreal. *"*

Philanthropic Support of Black Education

While white southerners remained uninterested in the education of blacks, northern philanthropists and churches took on the cause of education. Blacks benefited immensely from the financial contributions of churches. Methodists, Episcopalians, Catholics, and Baptists were instrumental in the creation of secondary schools and colleges. Philanthropists joined the churches in the effort. From 1865 until 1914, such organizations as the Peabody Education Fund, the General Education Board, and the Julius Rosenwald Fund contributed to the establishment of educational institutions for blacks. By 1900, black teachers numbered 28,560, thirty-four black college-level institutions were created, 1.5 million children were attending school, and many blacks migrated north to attend college.

Booker T. Washington and the Tuskegee Institute

Among the benefactors of philanthropy was Booker T. Washington, a graduate of Hampton Normal and Agricultural Institute. At Hampton, Washington had come under the direction of its founder, Samuel Chapman Armstrong, who believed that physical labor and vocational skills were practical ways for blacks to achieve financial success. Washington was a quick convert, and a few years after he graduated, with the support of Armstrong, he set out to establish the Tuskegee Normal and Industrial Institute in Tuskegee, Alabama in

1881. The Institute focused on preparing blacks for skilled trades, and also emphasized economic independence and self-determination.

Separate and Unequal Schools

In addition to the increased number of students and the creation of educational facilities for blacks, at the turn of the century, the legalization of separate schools was condoned by the Supreme Court. In 1899, the Court ruled in *Cumming v. School Board of Richmond County, Georgia* that a county was not obligated to provide blacks with comparable educational opportunities to whites.

THEY SAID...

*" *Martin King appealed constantly for school integration as a part of his vision for the 'beloved community.' His own life was a testimony to the importance he attached to education and his commitment to education dedicated to the service of God and the community. *"*

—Noel Leo Erskine, *King Among the Theologians*

One year later, with the codification of segregation in public schools, every southern state had enacted laws providing for separate schools for whites and blacks. The inequality between the education of whites and blacks could be seen in the differences in the facilities and by the inequity in the distribution of money spent on each student. By the time of King's birth in 1929, on average, for every $2 spent on a black pupil, $7 was spent on a white student.

Economic Opportunities

After emerging from slavery, blacks in the South found that employment opportunities outside of farming were limited. Many now worked for wages, but found that the wages that had previously been paid to a hired slave were more than they could earn as a free citizen. As former slaves worked toward economic freedom, the South quickly recuperated, thanks to the combination of cheap labor and the increased production of cotton. By 1880, 75 percent of blacks still lived in the South and worked in agriculture. Purchasing land was often not a choice, since capital was needed and whites were reluctant to sell to blacks. Thus, many blacks worked under the sharecropping system, which often left them penniless due to the cost of maintenance.

Black Exodus North

As a result of the inequitable economic conditions, thousands of blacks left the South to go north and west, where industrialization had already taken root. At the same time, industrialization finally came to the South and blacks took advantage of the new opportunities. They were employed in sawmills, cottonseed-oil mills, machine shops, and furniture factories. Despite the fact that they were often hired to work in the least-desirable jobs, blacks flocked to southern urban centers. In 1910, black factory workers numbered 350,000.

By the time of the black exodus, Booker T. Washington had emerged as a black leader. He believed that it was paramount for blacks to establish themselves economically. Less important to him were intellectual endeavors, which he regarded as impractical. In an attempt to address the exodus of southern blacks to the North and to counter the competition for the new jobs between the races, he encouraged them to strive for economic independence with the creation of black-owned companies. In 1900, Booker T. Washington created the Negro Business League in Boston. If blacks established businesses in which they sold products cheaper, argued Washington, they could achieve prominence in the business market. Many blacks did as encouraged by opening grocery stores, drugstores, bakeries, cotton mills, and lumber mills.

Economic Decline for Blacks

After World War I, black businesses increased, while black retail dealers were on the decline. Blacks continued to flee the South as boll weevils plagued farmers, forcing them to discontinue farming and subjecting farm laborers to unemployment. Foreign competition in cotton, tobacco, and sugar plunged the farming industry even lower. The stock market crash in October 1929 only furthered the economic despair of blacks. After the Depression, blacks still faced economic challenges.

The Importance of the Church

Even before the Civil War separate black churches had been established, but this was more common in the North. In the South, it was customary for whites and black slaves to attend the same church. Nevertheless, separate black churches did exist. In 1779, in Savannah, Georgia, black resident George Liele established a Baptist church. After Liele left the area, Andrew Bryan continued the effort. His church was later a central part of the organization of other Baptist churches in the state. Southern Baptist churches sprung up throughout Virginia, and congregations boomed. The Colored Methodist Episcopal church congregation surged from 75,000 in 1856 to more than 200,000 in 1876. The black Baptist church, whose congregation numbered 150,000 in 1850, had increased to 500,000 by 1870.

The black church served the community in important ways. In the past, slave preachers were easily controlled by laws regulating their behavior. With the establishment of their own churches, ministers had substantial freedom from white suppression. The church was a place where the unskilled, especially if a powerful orator, could become a well-respected leader in the community. The Baptist church, in particular, was very appealing to blacks, since the denomination was open to even the most illiterate ministers.

HE SAID...

" Every minister of the gospel has a mandate to stand up courageously for righteousness, to proclaim the eternal verities of the gospel, and to lead men from the darkness of falsehood and fear to the light of truth and love. *"*

Black ministers were often turned into leaders. They provided the community with social, political, and economic direction. The church was instrumental in the creation of credit unions, benevolent societies, and helped with other financial needs. It was a place where the news of the community was spread and political activity was encouraged. It was typical for ministers to take a leadership role in influencing the black community to challenge segregation. For instance, Martin Luther King Jr. was preceded in his commitment to equality by his father and grandfather, ministers who were actively involved in leading protest.

The Early Civil Rights Movement

By 1900, America's racial tension was apparent. The lynching of blacks had become a notable problem: By the start of World War I, more than 1,100 blacks had been lynched since 1900. Lynching did little to help race relations. Outbreaks of rioting took root across the country. There were riots in Statesboro and Atlanta, Georgia, and in Brownsville, Texas. Riots commonly began when blacks were accused of crimes against whites. White mobs were known to kidnap black defendants from police custody and beat or kill them. Blacks often responded with their own kind of similar justice. When it was all over, both sides had to bury their dead or tend to their injured.

The Leadership of W.E.B. Du Bois

The riots and the general dissatisfaction in the black community caught the attention of W.E.B Du Bois. In 1903, he had published his most notable work, *The Souls of Black Folk*. At the time, the book's assertion that the problem in the nation was "the color line" was forward thinking. In addition, Du Bois also criticized Booker T. Washington's promotion of black economic equality at the expense of education. Washington had stated in his 1895 speech, "The Atlanta Compromise," that separation in social matters was acceptable, while at the same time segregation was unacceptable in economic matters. Although Washington's public stance on equality appeared to serve whites more than blacks, after his death in 1915, it was uncovered that he secretly financially supported the elimination of lynching, segregation, and disenfranchisement.

THEY SAID...

" Since King believed that oppressed people have a moral obligation to resist any system that refuses to treat them as persons…he rejected Booker T. Washington's method of the passive acceptance of segregation…Nor could he accept W.E.B. Du Bois's method of resistance because it depended mainly upon the efforts of a 'Talented Tenth.' *"*

—John J. Ansbro, *Martin Luther King, Jr.: Nonviolent Strategies and Tactics for Social Change*

The Creation of the NAACP

While Washington publicly refused to support black causes, in 1905, W.E.B. Du Bois was fed up with the inequity. He called a meeting in June 1905 in Niagara Falls, Canada to organize progress toward the acquirement of full citizenship rights for blacks. Their cause became known as the Niagara Movement. The group's resolution included the demand for male suffrage, freedom of speech, the elimination of racial categorization, and humane treatment. The group continued to meet over the next four years.

In 1909, the organization received an invitation to meet with an interracial caucus to discuss the struggle for civil rights. Du Bois accepted the invitation, and at the meeting was joined by professors, judges, bishops, educators, and such notables as Jane Addams, Ida B. Wells, and John Dewey. By the conclusion of the meeting, the National Association for the Advancement of Colored People (NAACP) had been formed.

Its official start was in May 1910. Du Bois, the only black on staff, served as the director of publicity and research. The goals of the organization were male suffrage, the elimination of segregation, equality in education, and the enforcement of the 14th and 15th Amendments. In November 1910, their magazine, the *Crisis*, set out to attack the evils of lynching and mob violence. In its first month, it sold thousands of copies, and the success of the magazine was recognized when by 1918, 100,000 copies were sold per month. By 1921, 400 local branches of the organization had spread throughout the nation.

FACT

The NAACP was committed to keeping blacks informed about lynching. In 1919, they published *Thirty Years of Lynching in the United States, 1889–1918*, which explored the causes of lynching. The NAACP also kept New York City blacks informed by displaying a banner out their office window when a lynching occurred. It announced, A man was lynched yesterday.

The NAACP also established a legal committee. In 1915, they received a victory with the Supreme Court ruling in *Guinn v. United States* that the grandfather clauses of Maryland and Oklahoma were unconstitutional. Two years later, the NAACP emerged the victor with the Court's declaration in *Buchanan v. Warley* that a Louisville ordinance segregating black residences to specified sections of town was unconstitutional. They even won the 1923 case *Moore v. Dempsey*, where they argued that a black man in Arkansas had not been given a fair trial. The group's biggest victory came with the ruling in *Brown v. Board of Education* in 1954. The Court struck down the *Plessy* decision of "separate but equal" with its ruling that segregation in public schools was impermissible.

Formation of the National Urban League

While the NAACP took their causes to the courts and attacked lynching, other organizations sought economic equality for blacks. Two groups, the Committee for Improving Industrial Conditions of Negroes and the National League for the Protection of Colored Women, were created in the early 1900s. Contributing to their cause was black graduate student George Edmund Haynes, who produced a study reciting the economic inequality of black residents in New York City. When the two organizations reviewed his study, they formed a coordinating agency to take on community programs.

As knowledge increased about the conditions for New York's blacks, in 1911, the organizations merged and created the National League on Urban Conditions, which became known as the National Urban League. Like the NAACP, the Urban League expanded their grasp throughout the nation with the creation of local branches. They focused on helping migrants adjust to city life, acted as an intermediary between employee and employer, and provided training for those planning to enter the field of social work.

The work of the NAACP and the National Urban League set the stage for the Civil Rights movement of the 1950s and 1960s. By slowly carving out gains in the legal arena and in economic areas, black leaders and organizations were able to move the nation closer to equality. It was in this era of segregation that Martin Luther King Jr. was born. He would benefit from the work of these groups, and would join forces in the struggle for equality by taking the movement beyond its early beginnings. His leadership would take the nation to the next stage of equality.

Chapter 2
EARLY LIFE

MARTIN LUTHER KING WAS born into the racially segregated system of the South. It was the quiet strength of his mother and the powerful personality of his father that would play a vital role in the formation of King's personality. Although he experienced a relatively comfortable childhood, just like other southern blacks, he also experienced the pain of racism. This pain, which eventually served a purpose, lingered with him from elementary school through college.

Growing up in Atlanta

On January 15, 1929, Michael Luther King Jr., later named Martin Luther King Jr., was born in Atlanta, Georgia. While the neighboring cities enjoyed slave-toiled plantations, Atlanta was originally formed as a railroad crossing. It wasn't long, though, before it became a slave territory itself. Even though Atlanta's early history was much like a frontier town, its post–Civil War way of dealing with the black population was in step with other southern cities.

FACT

Auburn Avenue was at its height of vitality from the 1920s through the 1940s. Ebenezer Baptist Church, the birthplace of Martin Luther King Jr., and the Odd Fellows Building were located on this popular street. By the 1960s, as desegregation took effect, its function as the center of the black community declined. Today, Auburn Avenue is home of the Martin Luther King Jr. National Historic Site.

By the time of King's birth, Atlanta's segregation of black residents was a well-established tradition. Schools, swimming pools, parks, lunch counters, movie theaters, and waiting rooms were just some of the segregated facilities in Atlanta. In 1919, the city gave its black residents its first park, and converted Ashby Street School from a white to a black school. To counteract the economic effects of segregation, blacks opened their own businesses. Auburn Avenue, also called Sweet Auburn, was a mile-and-a-half stretch of black businesses that offered the black community restaurants, nightclubs, churches, barbershops, and hotels. While the communities remained somewhat separate, when the races did encounter one another, strict rules guided their interactions. As was common in the South, whites often referred to adult black men and women as "boy" and "girl," and required blacks to respond with "Yes, Sir" and "Yes, Ma'am."

It was in this environment that King grew up. Although he was subjected to segregation on occasion, most of his time was spent in the black community. He was by all accounts an average child, and had a happy childhood. He played on YMCA basketball teams, he had a newspaper route delivering the *Atlanta Journal*, and as most children do, he got into his fair share of trouble. Even though King seemed quite ordinary, he had one quality that stood out; he was highly articulate, and on more than one occasion was able to talk his way out of trouble.

King's Parents

King's parents, both strong critics of the system of segregation, attempted to protect him from its harsh realities. He grew up under the firm hand of his father and the loving care of his mother. He had an older sister, Christine, and a younger brother, Adam Daniel, or A.D. Despite the economic challenges of the Great Depression, the King family never suffered financially. King's parents, both dedicated to the proper upbringing of their children, provided a stable home.

His Mother's Quiet Strength

King's mother, Alberta Williams, was the daughter of Adam Daniel Williams, the pastor at Ebenezer Baptist Church. An only child, Alberta grew up in relative comfort. After she graduated from high school, she attended Spelman College, an all-black women's school. While she was somewhat protected from the cruelty of racism, she was surrounded by the political activity of her father. A.D. Williams, as he was often called, was an advocate for equality. He was a member of the Georgia Equal Rights League and served as president of the Atlanta chapter of the National Association of Colored People.

Just like her father, Alberta believed in the equality of African Americans. She often told King as a child that even though the system of segregation promoted the idea that blacks were inferior, he should not consider himself less than whites. She also emphasized that segregation was a social structure and not a reflection of nature. Using her calm and even-keeled way, Alberta King successfully instilled a sense of self-worth in her son.

His Father's Courage

Michael Luther King Sr. was the son of a sharecropper outside Stockbridge, Georgia. King Sr. later changed his name and his son's to Martin, after traveling to Germany, home of the monk Martin Luther. King Sr.'s father, a heavy drinker, struggled to provide for his family. King Sr. left home for Atlanta when he was sixteen years old, with only a sixth-grade education. He vowed that he would be financially successful one day, and began working odd jobs while attending night school. He eventually became the pastor at two small churches near Atlanta, and it was during this time that he met Alberta Williams. They married in 1926. Shortly thereafter, Reverend A.D. Williams asked King Sr. to serve as assistant pastor at Ebenezer, and he accepted. When Williams died of a heart attack in 1931, King Sr. replaced him.

King Sr., or Daddy King as he was often called, was a large man who possessed a forceful and powerful demeanor. Daddy King made sure that the King children knew that he was the boss, and enforced his position with frequent whippings. King Sr. held a strict standard of conduct for his children. Just as he required of himself, he believed that his children should be moral and ethical. As a teenager, King was not immune from a whipping. Like many young boys of the time, King Jr. was afraid of his father.

While King Sr. had strict control over his family, in the outside world he demonstrated a staunch advocacy for equality. As the pastor at Ebenezer, he was influential in the black community and respected by many whites. Like his father-in-law, King Sr. took his role in the community beyond the religious sphere. He believed that the church had a responsibility to take part in the Civil Rights movement. He was president of the Atlanta chapter of the NAACP and the Atlanta Civic and Political League, and the Chairman of the

Committee on the Equalization of Teachers' Salaries. He led voter-registration drives and a march to City Hall, enjoying a reputation in the community as an activist.

HE SAID...

" I have rarely ever met a person more fearless and courageous than my father, notwithstanding the fact that he feared for me. He never feared the autocratic and brutal person in the white community. If they said something to him that was insulting, he made it clear in no uncertain terms that he didn't like it. *"*

King was most influenced by his father's refusal to accept the system of segregation. Daddy King was not afraid to challenge this unique southern system forced on blacks. When it came to remaining quiet in the face of injustice, Daddy King was unable to do so. When King was just a boy, while in the car with his father, they were pulled over by a police officer. The officer referred to his father as "boy," to which King Sr. responded that he was a man, and would not answer unless addressed properly. The officer, shocked by the unlikely response, just gave him a ticket and left.

This was not the first time King witnessed his father's courage. King recalled going to the shoe store with his father as a small child. As they sat at the front of the store waiting for service, the salesman asked them to move to the back of the store where he could help them. Daddy King responded that if he was refused service in front, then he would not buy shoes. Not surprisingly, King Sr. and Jr. left the store without shoes. King remembers that it was these acts of defiance to the unjust system of segregation that helped shape his own conscience. The strength and courage of his father would later serve as an example to King of the courage he himself would need in order to stand up to the injustice of segregation and discrimination.

Primary and Secondary Education

Education was important in the King household. At an early age, King's parents quickly noticed his advanced intellect. When his older sister began elementary school, his parents enrolled five-year-old King Jr. Like other children his age, he was unable to keep a secret. Thus, he quickly disclosed his age, and was promptly sent home.

THEY SAID...

" As to Daddy King, of course he loved all his children—but he adored Martin. Shortly after Martin's death he said, 'There was always something special about M.L. Even before he could read, he kept books around him. He just liked the idea of having them. He learned to recite the Scriptures before he was five, years before he could read the Bible for himself.' *"*

—Coretta Scott King, *My Life with Martin Luther King, Jr.*

When King was old enough, he started Yonge Street Elementary, later changing to David T. Howard Elementary. When he was in seventh and eighth grade, he attended the experimental Atlanta University Laboratory School. When the school closed after he finished eighth grade, he began attending Booker T. Washington High, a segregated school. In high school, he was quite advanced, and easily skipped ninth and twelfth grades.

Influence of the Church and Religion

While Daddy King was molding King's conscience and Alberta King was instilling confidence, the Christian religion served as reinforcement for these values. With his father serving as pastor of Ebenezer Baptist Church, religion was always a key component in King's life. At the age of five, mostly out of competition with his sister, he became a member of the church. Despite his early motives, his faith eventually gave him comfort after his grandmother died when he was twelve years old.

His maternal grandmother had lived with the family for most of his childhood, and King had a close relationship with her. When she died, he found it difficult to cope with the loss. In response to the news of her death, he jumped off the second story of a building. To comfort their distraught young son, his parents introduced him to the doctrine of spiritual immortality. This was a great comfort to King, and the beginning of his serious exploration of Christianity.

As King grew older, he began to question some of the tenets of the Christian faith. At thirteen, an inquisitive King told his Sunday-school teacher that he was unsure whether Jesus was really resurrected from the dead. By the time he was in high school, he had become uncertain about the literal interpretation of the Bible. Years later, in college, King would again question Christianity and some of the traditions of the black church.

 What is the doctrine of spiritual immortality?
Spiritual immortality is a belief incorporated by many religious faiths. Christians, in general, believe that upon death, each person will either live forever with God or will be separated from God and eternally punished for their sins.

Experiencing Segregation

Just as Alberta Williams's parents had done, the King parents attempted to protect their children from the harsh realities of segregation. Despite the efforts of King's parents, he was keenly aware of the racism and injustice against African Americans. While his contact with whites was limited, he was cognizant of Ku Klux Klan violence and police brutality, and he knew that justice for most blacks wasn't usually achieved through the court system.

With all of this knowledge, as King grew older, he became less surprised at the mistreatment directed toward him because of his race. However, resentment and dislike of whites increased with each experience. One of the most painful childhood memories occurred when he was six years old. For several years, he had played with a white child whose father owned a grocery store near his home. When both boys started school, they played less often. One day, the friend told King that his father had forbid him from playing with him anymore. King, confused, asked his parents about the reason. After it was explained, he began to understand the concept of racism. This incident left a lasting impression, and caused him to begin to hate white people. Regardless of his parents' urging that as a Christian he must love all people, his hatred grew as he became older.

HE SAID...

" My parents would always tell me that I should not hate the white man, but that it was my duty as a Christian to love him. The question arose in my mind: How could I love a race of people who hated me....This was a great question in my mind for a number of years. *"*

His experiences under segregation during high school furthered his resentment toward the system. Every morning he traveled by bus across town to Booker T. Washington High School. The buses were segregated, so he had to sit in the back of the bus. According to King, this was one of the most difficult experiences of his life. To deal with the pain, he assured himself that while his body was sitting in the back, his mind remained in the front of the bus. He imagined that one day he would sit in the front.

He would be reminded of the pain of racism when he was fifteen years old. In April 1944, King won a local speech contest. The win entitled him to compete at the national level. King and his teacher traveled to Dublin, Georgia by bus to compete. After coming in second, they boarded the bus to return home to Atlanta. Soon, the bus became crowded. As was the southern custom, the driver asked King and his teacher to give their seats to white passengers. King refused, and only moved after his teacher convinced him to do as requested. They stood for the remainder of the 90-mile journey. This experience elicited intense anger in King, and he remembered it as the angriest he had ever been.

Off to College

When King was fifteen years old, he received a rare opportunity. As the need for soldiers increased during World War II, the number of college students declined. Dr. Benjamin Mays, a friend of Daddy King's and the president of Morehouse College, implemented a bold new plan. To increase student ranks, he created a program that recruited top black high school students. King was one of the privileged students selected to attend Morehouse under this new program. Without hesitancy, he accepted the offer. His father and maternal grandfather had both graduated from Morehouse, and he was excited to attend the same college.

FACT

Morehouse College, today recognized as a Historically Black College, was established in 1867 in the basement of Springfield Baptist Church in Augusta, Georgia. Its goal was to prepare black men for the ministry and teaching. By the time King enrolled it had expanded its curriculum, and eventually, under the leadership of Benjamin Mays, earned an international reputation for excellence.

Prior to entering Morehouse, King had his first experience outside of the segregated South. To earn extra money for college, he took a summer job in Simsbury, Connecticut. Accustomed to the ways of the South, King was surprised that he could eat at any restaurant and attend an integrated church. It was not until his train

trip back to Atlanta that he was reminded of the pain of segregation. On the train, he could sit anywhere he wanted from New York
to Washington, D.C. When he reached D.C., he had to change to a
segregated car. The scars of racism had made him increasingly bitter,
and this experience on the train furthered his resentment.

Settling into College Life

King began his studies at Morehouse College in September 1944.
His education at segregated schools had provided him with a less-
than-average preparation for college, so by the time he began, he
was only reading at an eighth-grade level. King continued to live
at home and ride the bus to school. He took full advantage of his
college opportunity, participating in numerous activities outside of
his studies. He joined the glee club, the NAACP chapter, the student-
faculty discipline committee, and competed in oratorical contests.

It was also the first time that he was able to participate in open
discussions about racism in an academic setting. Without the restric-
tions of state funds, Morehouse professors engaged their students
in discussions about racism and solving racial problems. Benjamin
Mays was especially influential during this time, and King would
later describe him as one of the most influential people in his life.
Each week, Mays held Tuesday-morning meetings where he urged
students to stand up against segregation and to serve their communities. Over the objections of his father, King joined an interracial
college organization, where he saw that whites could be allies with
blacks in the fight against racism. His built-up resentment toward
whites began to soften as he contemplated the unification of blacks
and whites working toward a solution to end racism.

Enjoying a Social Life at Morehouse

With the heavy hand of his father no longer the overriding factor in his life, King slowly pulled away from the strict Baptist doctrine regarding sinful behavior. King made friends with students that
were like him. Many were from families with a long line of preachers.

However, like King, they struggled to stay in line with Baptist morality, and to the dismay of their families, considered careers outside of the ministry. One good friend of King's was Walter McCall, an army veteran. King, along with McCall, experimented with his new freedom by playing cards and gambling, two activities condemned by the Baptist faith. King also became known as a lady's man. McCall and King soon earned the nickname "The Wreckers," due to the fact that they "wrecked" girls.

King's reputation as a social, fun-loving guy increased after he went back to Simsbury, Connecticut to earn some extra money during the summer before his fourth year. It was there that King encountered his first brush with the law. Beer was always readily available, and the behavior of the less-than-hardworking King ended with a run-in with the police. Fortunately, the incident didn't lead to his incarceration; however, King did make an important decision. His spiritual growth in Simsbury had a profound effect on his future plans. He had delivered the weekly sermons, and enjoyed it. Years before, the same opportunity to give the sermons had been met with hesitancy. King decided that he was ready to enter the ministry. While it would come as a surprise to some of his friends, his decision pleased Daddy King. Now with the blessing of his father, King entered his final year at Morehouse.

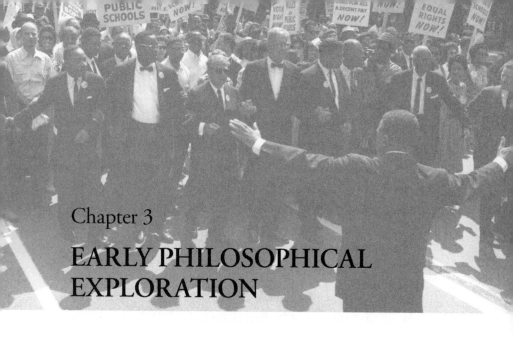

Chapter 3
EARLY PHILOSOPHICAL EXPLORATION

KING, DESCRIBED BY HIS college friends as funny, social, and stylish, enjoyed the social perks of college. As he matured, he enjoyed the intellectual and philosophical challenges offered by Morehouse College and Crozer Theological Seminary even more. He revisited some of his childhood religious skepticism and expanded his exploration to such issues as sin, social justice, Communism, and the effectiveness of the church. It was a time of immense growth, and the early stages of the formation of King's philosophical beliefs.

Questioning Christianity

The decision to enter the ministry didn't come easily for King. Initially, he thought about becoming a doctor, but biology had been challenging. When a good friend told him of his plans to practice law, King was easily persuaded to consider the same. His father expected him to follow in his footsteps and become a minister, but King was unsure whether the ministry was right either. His experiences at Morehouse College had been more than just fun and games. They had opened up new ways of thinking, and as his knowledge increased, so did his skepticism about the religious teachings he had grown up with and the traditions of the black church.

At Morehouse, just as he had done as a child, he questioned the Christian faith. He was troubled with how science and religion were at odds. Besides this emerging doubt, he was concerned about the teaching method of black churches. Most black pastors were uneducated, and King was unsure whether a career in the ministry would be satisfying. Many teachings in the black church were based on emotion instead of ideas. King opposed the emotionalism of the black church, and was embarrassed by it. Furthermore, sermons in the black church often focused on teaching about the afterlife, rather than on using its influence as an instrument for improving society. He believed that the emotionalism of the church failed the black community.

In spite of his misgivings about the church, by his senior year at Morehouse he was able to resolve these conflicts. After taking a course in the Bible, King realized that beyond the myths and legends, as he phrased it, the Bible was filled with many inescapable truths. In addition, he concluded that religion and the intellect could fuse. Morehouse president and minister, Benjamin Mays, served as an example of the type of minister King wanted to be. He decided that he would preach from the pulpit by combining an intellectual approach with his pastoral role.

Studying for the Ministry

In the summer of 1947, King received his first opportunity to preach to a church congregation. His trial sermon at Ebenezer Baptist Church earned him a license to preach from the board of deacons, and he was made assistant pastor. On February 25, 1948 he was ordained at Ebenezer, with Daddy King, Benjamin Mays, and two professors from Morehouse presiding. On June 8, 1948, King received his Bachelor of Arts in Sociology from Morehouse College.

HE SAID...
" I had felt the urge to enter the ministry from my latter high school days, but accumulated doubts had somewhat blocked the urge. Now it appeared again with an inescapable drive. My call to the ministry was not a miraculous or supernatural something; on the contrary, it was an inner urge calling me to serve humanity. *"*

King's first choice of schools was Crozer Theological Seminary in Chester, Pennsylvania, to which he applied in 1948 for the fall term. King had been an average student at Morehouse; therefore, the recommendations that accompanied his application reflected this. Benjamin Mays referred to King as less-than brilliant, and another recommendation stated that King's 2.48 GPA was a result of an inadequate high school education and the lack of effort he displayed during the first couple of years in college. King's father, on the other hand, described his son as conscientious, likeable, and scholarly. King himself wrote on his application that he possessed "an inescapable urge to serve society." Despite these less-than-stellar reviews and a low GPA, King was admitted to Crozer.

Settling into Crozer

Crozer was a small school with a student populace of less than 100. The goal of Crozer's president, Edwin Aubrey, had been to keep it small and attended by elite scholars. However, by 1948 the dwindling student population threatened the extinction of the school. Crozer's liberal religious leaning had become less popular as religious conservative seminaries were on the rise. In an attempt to prevent the school's closure, Aubrey made a bold move. He decided to diversify the seminary's racial makeup. King, who began attending Crozer on September 14, 1948, benefited from this decision. Upon his arrival, he found that in his class of thirty-two, there were ten blacks, three Chinese, a few Indians, a Japanese student, and several southern whites.

FACT

Even though Crozer relaxed its standard of admittance in order to attract more students, it did not relax its academic standards. Aubrey expected that many of the students in the incoming class would not graduate. His prediction was correct. In 1951, less than half of the 1948 class remained, and only six of the eleven blacks graduated.

King, now more accustomed to being around white people, was able to adjust to the white culture at Crozer that included an all-white teaching staff, racially mixed dorms, and the white maids that cleaned the rooms. King found that the adjustment was easy, and he had become quite comfortable around whites by this time. So comfortable, in fact, that he began dating Betty, the white daughter of the cook at the cafeteria. Initially, it started as a competition between King and his white professor for the attention of Betty, but King soon fell in love. He became so enamored with Betty that he contemplated marrying her. The relationship lasted for six months until King, through the help of friends, decided that an interracial marriage would jeopardize his future as a pastor in the black community. Reluctantly, King ended the relationship.

King's Social Life at Crozer

Although King took his studies seriously, he did find time to have fun. Crozer Seminary encouraged its students to interact with each other outside of the classroom. Below the chapel was a recreation room with three pool tables. Despite the initial misgivings King and his classmates had about pool-playing being an activity engaged in by low-life degenerates, their perception quickly changed as they settled into the freethinking environment of Crozer. As King adjusted to his newfound hobby, Daddy King was skeptical. Whenever he visited, he witnessed his son's new vices of smoking, drinking, and playing pool. To Daddy King, these behaviors were sinful, but King, now fully enthralled with Crozer's liberal Christian teachings, was convinced that sin only came from within oneself and was not part of the environment. King's new behaviors would remain a sore point between him and Daddy King during his time at Crozer.

In addition to billiards, he also found time to visit Reverend J. Pius "Joe" Barbour, a family friend and a Morehouse and Crozer graduate who lived nearby. Barbour's house became a popular hangout for many of Crozer's students, including King. The lively discussions at Barbour's home provided King the opportunity to develop and strengthen his philosophical viewpoints on politics and race.

Taking Academic Success Seriously

King was aware of white stereotypes of blacks as loud, messy, and dirty, and he sought to disprove these assumptions. He was always on time to class, was prepared, and took pride in his attire. Well aware of the superior college education of many of the white students, King wanted to show that he could excel academically. While his grades at Morehouse left an imprint of mediocrity, this time his academic ability was impressive. By his second year, he earned nothing below a B, and in his third year he earned straight As.

THEY SAID...

" When he got there, he really applied himself to his studies. Now he knew what he wanted to do with his life, and he was a serious student....Perhaps the call had been standing in Martin's way, and now that his searching for it was over, he could move forward more surely. *"*

—Coretta Scott King, *My Life with Martin Luther King Jr.*

King's academic success was due in part to his ability to accept the unorthodox environment of Crozer. The seminary prided itself on its classical liberalism, as opposed to the more popular conservative religious view. Liberals believed in the ultimate goodness of man, that the Bible shouldn't be taken literally, and that the attention should be on loving one's neighbor as opposed to focusing on salvation. Religious conservatives, on the other hand, accepted that human nature was prone to sinful ways. It was in this environment of freethinking that King began his studies.

King's religious skepticism in high school and college was revived by Crozer professors, who held uncommon beliefs about the Bible, Christianity, and Jesus. Two of his first-year courses challenged commonly held beliefs of religious scholars. In his New Testament class with linguist M. Scott Enslin, many of the quotations credited to Jesus were disputed by the instructor. Enslin, a biblical critic, boldly asserted that John the Baptist never met Jesus. Another radical instructor and linguist was James B. Pritchard, who alleged that Moses was possibly a legendary figure, and that the Exodus was a much smaller symbolic event. For King, this skepticism revived familiar memories of his own previous questions, and he embraced this method of thought.

Regardless of his strong academic record and his interpersonal skills, he failed to impress Reverend William E. Gardener, who served as his pastoral mentor. To fulfill a class requirement, King served as a student pastor at Rev. Gardener's First Baptist Church in New York. In Gardener's end-of-the-term evaluation, he assessed King's overall ability as "below outstanding." While he noted that he was liked by many members of the church, he sensed that King was aloof. In his opinion, this was due to King's above-average intellect and his inability to relate to regular people. Thus, King, he decided, deserved a B.

FACT

In the 1920s, liberal Christian theology took over academic institutions, but their hold declined as conservatives created their own more-popular seminaries. When King entered the seminary, the liberalism that espoused the belief that the Bible was full of errors, the virgin birth was mythical, and Jesus was a moral teacher, had increasingly declined in popularity.

At Crozer, King was able to sharpen his already well-developed oratory style. He took at least nine classes on oratory skills, and through these courses he was able to fine-tune his preaching ability. Under the guidance of Professor Robert Keighton, King learned the art of public persuasion by using the methods of proving, painting, and persuading the audience. King was also introduced to Saint Augustine's use of clichés, and he read works by English poets, some of which he would later quote in his speeches. King, considered one of the best student preachers at Crozer, was able to draw a crowd of his peers when he gave the weekly student sermon. His classmates looked forward to his sermons, or as King called them, "religious lectures." Of all the things remembered by his peers, the biggest was his ability to present a powerful sermon that was formal in style yet entertaining.

Studying the Great Theologians

Professor George W. Davis served as King's faculty advisor and mentor and played a major part in his intellectual development. Davis was a proponent of the Social Gospel movement, a follower of the theologian Walter Rauschenbusch, and a pacifist who admired

Gandhi. King, though not a pacifist at this time, took many of his courses from Davis, and was consequently influenced by him. Davis encouraged King to explore such subjects as the Social Gospel, sin, and Gandhi's nonviolent resistance.

Embracing the Social Gospel

During King's first year at Crozer, he began his studies by reading the writings of Walter Rauschenbusch, a key figure in the Social Gospel movement. Social Gospel advocates deemphasized salvation and instead focused more on the teaching of Jesus that advocated helping the poor. Rauschenbusch, a German Lutheran who converted to a Baptist, laid out several ideas in his book, *Christianity and the Social Crisis,* that intrigued King. Rauschenbusch had two beliefs that stuck out in King's mind: He was optimistic about social change and he believed that religion was relevant to the real world. Ultimately, according to Rauschenbusch, a classless and stateless society and the Second Coming were related and at the center of biblical religion. Rauschenbusch's optimism about social change was appealing to King, and until his third year, he would remain a loyal convert of Rauschenbusch and the Social Gospel movement.

The Influence of Reinhold Niebuhr

During his last year at Crozer, King studied the writings of another theologian, Reinhold Niebuhr, who held opposite beliefs to Rauschenbusch and the Social Gospel movement. Niebuhr was a former pacifist who had served as president of the Fellowship of Reconciliation for several years and taught at Union Theological Seminary in New York. By the time that King finished reading his 1932 book *Moral Man and Immoral Society,* he began to question whether his belief in the Social Gospel had been misguided. King was strongly affected by Niebuhr's assertion that because the Social Gospel was incapable of challenging evil in the world, it was not moral. Furthermore, Niebuhr argued that the failure of the Social Gospel movement was its emphasis on good works at the expense of emphasizing salvation. According to Niebuhr, Social Gospel preachers falsely benefited and spread false hope to their congregations.

For King, Niebuhr held many other powerful beliefs. He asserted that Christian love could not promote social justice because man was selfish. Niebuhr believed that power in society was disproportioned, which was the cause of social injustice. In addition, he argued that individuals were capable of responding to reason and justice, while large social groups such as corporations, nations, and labor unions would always respond in a selfish way.

HE SAID...

" The prophetic and realistic elements in Niebuhr's passionate style and profound thought were appealing to me, and made me aware of the complexity of human motives and the reality of sin on every level of man's existence. I became so enamored of his social ethics that I almost fell into the trap of accepting uncritically everything he wrote. *"*

Up to this point, the Social Gospel had influenced King's belief that his contribution to society could be achieved through helping people. King's drinking and smoking had been a reflection of his belief in the Social Gospel's primary focus on good works as opposed to salvation. Reading Niebuhr caused King to question his prior motivation in pursuing a doctorate for prestige, rather than for a loftier goal. Thus, Niebuhr's writings caused King to rethink his beliefs.

King teetered between the theories of both men. Rauschenbusch's liberal view of man and Niebuhr's view of human nature both had appealing elements. The appeal of liberalism, he realized, was its optimism about human nature and its continuous search for the truth. Niebuhr's view, on the other hand, was appealing because the racism King experienced while growing up in the South could be explained through this view. King began to lean more toward Niebuhr's view, because the liberal view was too idealistic and failed to accept that human nature was complex, with a potential for evil. As King's optimistic outlook lessened, he no longer believed in the natural goodness of man.

Sin and Man

King also explored Niebuhr's concept regarding man's sinfulness. King was most convinced by Niebuhr's assertion that not only was man sinful, but collective evil in society existed. He arrived at the conclusion that this evil had to be taken into account before social reform could be achieved. From Niebuhr, King also came to realize that the government was essential in the control of man's sinfulness. To counteract this, according to Niebuhr, because man would rather have his own interests met, the government needed to control man's inclination for selfishness. King agreed with this analysis, but he did take one exception. He strongly felt that the government should never be perceived as divine. King's perception of man's sinfulness was instrumental in his later understanding of the most effective way to bring about change in America.

Exploring Communism and Capitalism

In December 1949, King spent the Christmas holiday at home in Atlanta. To his father's dismay, he began studying *Das Kapital* and *The Communist Manifesto* by Karl Marx. King found Communism appealing in several ways. He admired the intense passion that Communists had for the creation of a society that was socially just. He believed that Communists provided Christians with an example of the kind of zeal that was needed to generate change. Most impressive to King was the Communist ideal of a classless society that rejected any distinction of race. In a time when segregation was condoned by society and the church, this was especially appealing to King.

What is Communism?
According to Karl Marx, communism is an economic theory that promotes the idea that society should control the production of goods. Ideally, it was a classless society without a government structure.

King also found truth in one aspect of Marx's analysis of capitalism. Capitalism's failing was the gap between the rich and the poor, according to Marx. Communism's concern for the poor and underprivileged was in line with King's view that there was an unfair disparity between the classes. King believed that although social reform in capitalism had successfully reduced that gap, more reform was needed. As opposed to Communism, Capitalism, according to King, was concerned with the individual's focus on the acquisition of wealth, instead of focusing on serving others. Capitalism, believed King, promoted selfish ambition rather than relationships with others.

Despite his agreement with Marx on many points, King ultimately decided to reject Communism. First, Communism excluded God; history was not merely about economic forces. Furthermore, its materialistic interpretation of history failed to incorporate his belief that history was guided by the spirit rather than by matter and motion. According to King, the spirit's works in history is to provide salvation. Since man was sinful, salvation was necessary.

Secondly, Communism failed to embody a moral order. Without moral principles, any type of behavior or action was acceptable. The Communist stance that a classless society should be achieved through any method was unappealing to King. This type of ethical relativism, which promoted achieving a goal at any cost, could not justify destructive means. Thirdly, the political totalitarianism was objectionable to King. In this way, Communism was similar to segregation, because it took away such freedoms as voting, the right to assemble, and the freedom of the press. Because a Communistic state eliminated liberty, it controlled the individual.

The Church and the Individual

King's education at Crozer led him to believe that the ministers' role in the church was to use the pulpit for the good of society and the individual. According to King, ministers needed to do more than just elicit emotion with a sermon. He found that in his experience with the black church, the pastor relied on emotion when delivering a sermon, and failed to present a useful message that was relevant to living a moral and decent life. Parishioners, in turn, judged the message by the level of emotion and not by the content. The minister, he argued, should be intelligent, possess spiritual power, and be in tune with the needs of the congregation. Educated ministers should present their lessons in a way that was understandable to the congregation. Ultimately, it was the job of the minister to both change the individual, and at the same time, to try to change society. King believed that by eliciting change, both society and the individual would benefit.

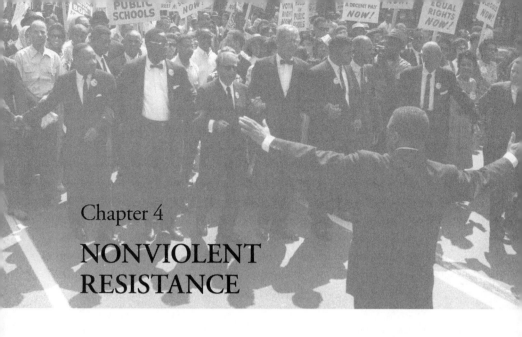

Chapter 4
NONVIOLENT RESISTANCE

KING NEITHER SET OUT to become a leader in the Civil Rights movement, nor did he expect to embrace nonviolent resistance. In fact, while he admired Gandhi and his implementation of the method, he discarded the approach as an unlikely source of success for desegregation. However, King's knowledge of nonviolent resistance lingered with him through his college years, long enough for him to adopt the technique after witnessing its powerful effect in the Montgomery bus boycott.

Henry David Thoreau's View on Civil Disobedience

While at Morehouse, King studied the work of nineteenth-century Transcendentalist Henry David Thoreau. He was immediately impressed with Thoreau's concept of civil disobedience and especially intrigued with Thoreau's essay "Civil Disobedience," which was motivated by Thoreau's own act of rebellion. Thoreau disagreed with the war against Mexico and with slavery, so in an act of defiance against a government that he believed was unjust, he refused to pay his poll taxes. According to Thoreau, his refusal was an act of protest. The cost of his insurrection was a night in jail.

Q: **What was the philosophy of Transcendentalism?**
Transcendentalism emerged in the early 1800s in New England as a reaction against the strict rituals of many religions. Transcendentalists believed that there was a connection between an individual's soul and the universe. According to Transcendentalism, truth could be discovered through nature.

While at Morehouse, King read Thoreau's essay several times and was struck by the possibilities that this method of resistance offered. In the essay, Thoreau declared that it was better to break the law than to participate in the injustice directed toward another person. Thus, Thoreau encouraged abolitionists to withdraw their monetary and personal support from the government in protest of slavery. He argued that it wasn't necessary to wait until they had achieved a majority, because the government would have to choose a side. Accordingly, if they withdrew their support from the government, slavery would be abolished.

Thoreau also alleged that a peaceful revolution could be waged by refusing to pay taxes. Paying taxes supported the state's immoral actions; therefore, it was wrong to pay them, since to do so would wound one's conscience. To prevent the injury to oneself and others, a revolution should be waged, he argued. However, it did not require the shedding of blood. Instead, it was the simple act of refusing to cooperate. It was the just men, Thoreau argued, who belonged in the prisons of a government that imprisoned individuals unjustly. It was there that the just could battle injustice most effectively.

Thoreau's Influence on King

After reading Thoreau's essay, King came to the conclusion that just as there was an obligation to cooperate with good, there was also a moral obligation to not cooperate with evil. The influence of Thoreau's "Civil Disobedience" was at the center of King's belief in disobeying unjust laws. Civil disobedience was practiced by Christians in the Bible, by Socrates, in Hitler's Germany, and even by early Americans who participated in the Boston Tea Party. For King, all of these acts reflected historical support for defying unjust laws using civil disobedience.

HE SAID...

"I became convinced that noncooperation with evil is as much a moral obligation as is cooperation with good. No other person has been more eloquent and passionate in getting this idea across than Henry David Thoreau. As a result of his writings and personal witness, we are the heirs of a legacy of creative protest."

King justified civil disobedience by defining the difference between just and unjust laws. Unjust laws, according to King, could be described in both a religious way and a secular way. Through Christianity, an unjust law could be described as one that was opposed to God's law and was not in harmony with moral law. King further described unjust laws as those that the majority required the minority to obey without requiring the obedience of one's self. It was a law that the majority inflicted on the minority even though

41

the minority wasn't a participant in its enactment, such as in cases where an individual was not entitled to vote. Consequently, by not submitting to unjust laws, one didn't seek to evade or defy laws as an anarchist would.

On the other hand, a just law was a law that was moral. It uplifted humanity. In other terms, it was "saneness made legal." A just law was one that the majority enacted despite the disagreement of the minority. However, the difference between the majority enforcing an unjust law and the majority enforcing a just law was the willingness of the majority to submit to the just law. King concluded that a just law should be obeyed because there was a moral obligation, whereas an unjust law could be disobeyed using the long-established tradition of civil disobedience.

Although King was impressed with Thoreau's concept of civil disobedience and the distinction between obeying just and unjust laws, several years would pass before he would have the opportunity to implement Thoreau's method of civil disobedience. King's own understanding of nonviolent resistance would incorporate Thoreau's ideas on civil disobedience. As King later reflected, the Civil Rights movement was an outgrowth of Thoreau's advocacy of resisting evil. Years before King would encounter the opportunity to use nonviolent resistance, Gandhi would use it successfully in India.

Gandhi's Example

While Thoreau's essay planted the seeds of nonviolent protest in King's mind, Mohandas Gandhi put the method into action. King's real interest in Gandhi came as a result of hearing Howard University president, Dr. Mordecai Johnson, deliver a Sunday sermon about him. Dr. Johnson had just returned from India, and spoke about the life of Gandhi. King was fascinated and impressed with Gandhi and his accomplishment of effecting social change in South Africa and India through nonviolent resistance. King admired Gandhi for being the first person to use the love ethic of Jesus beyond the personal level, and for using the love ethic as a tool to effect social change on a larger scale.

Gandhi's Concept of Satyagraha

Gandhi was born in British-controlled India in 1869. After finishing high school, he lived in England while attending law school. He returned to India to practice law, but had trouble sustaining his practice due to his extreme shyness. Thus, the twenty-four-year-old Gandhi jumped at the opportunity to practice law in South Africa. While prejudice existed in India, especially toward those who practiced the Hindu religion, in Durban, South Africa, Gandhi experienced the profound effects of prejudice. Immediately upon his arrival in 1893, he found that the strict code of segregation that applied to the native blacks also applied to Indians. Gandhi was disturbed by the treatment he received. The injustice of segregation motivated this shy lawyer to form organizations that worked to change laws that perpetuated discrimination against Indians in Africa.

FACT

The social structure in Durban was similar to many of the colonies in South Africa. Durban was broken up into colonies that were controlled by British or Dutch rule. These colonies were plagued by divisions of color, class, and religion. Although whites were a minority, they were the privileged class.

After spending years in South Africa working to end discrimination against Indians, Gandhi became a well-known leader. When the Boer War and the Zulu rebellion took place, Gandhi, having grown up under British rule, lent his support to the British in both causes. During the Zulu rebellion, however, he witnessed the British brutality against the Zulu rebels. His deep commitment to nonviolence was formed due to this experience. Violence, according to Gandhi, failed to solve social ills. Through this experience, Gandhi came to believe that passive resistance could challenge violence and win.

Gandhi's term for passive resistance was *satyagraha*. According to Gandhi, satyagraha was "the force of truth and love." Over time, satyagraha came to incorporate civil disobedience as well. Gandhi was strongly influenced by Henry David Thoreau's essay "Civil Disobedience," and believed that civil disobedience should be used to challenge unjust laws. This, according to Gandhi, should be done in a civilized way that would win the opponent's respect. Utilizing the Christian doctrine of loving thy neighbor and turning the other cheek, Gandhi asserted that the ultimate goal was to change the heart of the oppressor and to love one's enemy as a friend.

Gandhi Uses Nonviolent Resistance

Gandhi's first use of the method of satyagraha was during his opposition to the 1907 Black Act. The Black Act required that all Indians register and have fingerprints on file with the government. Failure to do so would result in fines and jail time. Believing that this act was unfair, Gandhi urged Indians to oppose it. Gandhi and his supporters refused to register and instead picketed government offices. By July, his idea received widespread support with only a small number of Indians registering. The British government was finally fed up with Gandhi and the protestors, and arrested them. Gandhi was sentenced to two months hard labor. This was the first time he had been arrested. The protest of the Act persisted for several years. During this time, Gandhi continued to lead nonviolent protests and submitted to numerous arrests. Protestors were often subjected to violent attacks by the police. This brutality brought attention to the movement and made Gandhi into an international figure. In June 1914, Gandhi's hard-fought and lengthy battle finally paid off when the Black Act was repealed.

After spending twenty years in South Africa, Gandhi turned his attention to India. It was still under British rule, and now that his method of nonviolent resistance was well developed, he sought to make changes in his home country. After he saw the severity of the inhumane living conditions of India's peasants, he decided that he too would live like a peasant. For sixteen years he dressed and lived like an Indian peasant in a small room.

Gandhi emerged again when his assistance was requested by farmers forced to agree to higher rents by landowners. This time, Gandhi appealed to the landowners' sense of morality and fairness. He decided that by fasting, his appeal would be more effective. His calculation was correct. The landowners, not wanting to be responsible for the death of a leader admired and glorified by thousands of Indians, after seven months of pressure, agreed to his conditions. This method of appealing to the moral conscience of his opponent through fasting became a common nonviolent approach for Gandhi.

HE SAID...

II My study of Gandhi convinced me that true pacifism is not nonresistance to evil, but nonviolent resistance to evil. Between the two positions, there is a world of difference. Gandhi resisted evil with as much vigor and power as the violent resister, but he resisted with love instead of hate. *II*

After World War I, Gandhi's next goal was to win India's independence from British rule. To that end, he supported the use of nonviolent noncooperation and boycotts. The first attempt to gain independence ended with violent outbursts across India. The second attempt at independence began in December 1929. This time, just as Thoreau had attempted to effect change, Ghandi's noncooperation was in the form of refusing to pay taxes. When the British government failed to meet the deadline for independence, Gandhi led protestors on a two-hundred-mile march to the coast of the Arabian Sea in protest of the law that prohibited Indians from making their own salt or from purchasing it from nongovernmental entities. This became known as the Salt March, and Gandhi's act became a powerful symbol of Indian defiance against British rule.

FACT

The British began their rule of India's 200 million people in 1858. Most of India's territory was under British control, but there were still some regions that were ruled by Indian princes. However, most princes served as figureheads while British leaders were in command.

This act instigated marches and the beginning of salt making throughout the country. This time the protest didn't end in violent eruptions. Instead, resisters subjected themselves to the violent blows of the police without responding with violence. This brutality was publicized, and Britain felt compelled to make a deal. Although it failed to lead to the immediate granting of independence, it set the stage for the lengthy fight that ended on August 15, 1947 when India achieved its independence. Gandhi once again showed that through nonviolent resistance, gains for social justice were possible.

Gandhi's Influence on King

Gandhi put Thoreau's civil disobedience into action, and his leadership provided King with concrete examples of nonviolent resistance. Gandhi refused to cooperate with evil, he was willing to accept punishment for his noncooperation, he appealed to the moral conscience of his opponent, and he never reacted to violence with violence. King didn't adopt every method that Gandhi practiced. For instance, he declined to use the practices of the nonpayment of taxes and the taking over of private property, and he contemplated, but never implemented, fasting. Despite these differences, King would later adopt Gandhi's overall philosophy of nonviolent resistance.

Niebuhr on Nonviolent Resistance

King also studied Reinhold Niebuhr's position on nonviolence. In Niebuhr's *Moral Man and Immoral Society*, he asserted that Gandhi's nonviolent method could be useful to an oppressed minority group, like blacks in America. Blacks, wrote Niebuhr, had failed to achieve political and economic freedom, but had made some gains in schools and sanitation. These gains had led well-meaning blacks to conclude that the moral conscience of white America would eventually change. According to Niebuhr, white America would never grant blacks equal rights unless forced to do so; thus, attacking the moral conscience of white Americans was not enough. Neither was a violent revolution the answer, since it would create hostility and prejudice. On the other hand, nonviolent resistance, while not a complete solution for black Americans, if used in the manner of Gandhi, could lead to some amount of justice that was unattainable by moral persuasion.

HE SAID...

" ...Niebuhr has extraordinary insight into human nature, especially the behavior of nations and social groups. He is keenly aware of the complexity of human motives and of the relation between morality and power. His theology is a persistent reminder of the reality of sin on every level of man's existence. *"*

At the time King read Niebuhr, even though he was heavily influenced by him, he rejected the immediate acceptance of Gandhi's nonviolent resistance, or pacifism. Months before he heard Mordecai Johnson's lecture about Gandhi, he also learned about the concept of pacifism at a lecture given by A.J. Muste. Contrary to Niebuhr's beliefs, King thought that the evil of human nature created the need for an armed revolt to cure segregation. In a paper at Crozer, King wrote that the pacifist nature of Gandhi's method was not viable everywhere. He asserted that the pacifist approach failed to consider the sinfulness of man, and since man was sinful, he must be forced to not hurt others. King concluded that pacifism was an ineffective way to eliminate social injustice because it tolerated rather than resisted injustice. During the time that King studied at Crozer, he would never come to accept the pacifist approach.

King would only consider the viability of nonviolent resistance after his involvement in the Montgomery bus boycott in 1955. It was only then that, to his surprise, the method he had learned about in college quite naturally emerged during his leadership of the bus boycott. It became a strong and central tool in the fight to end bus segregation. It was through this experience that King became a convert to the method of nonviolent resistance as a practical solution to attacking segregation. However, his complete commitment to the method wasn't realized until after his visit to India in 1959.

THEY SAID...

" Although the Niebuhr influence went to the heart of the public and private King and affected him more deeply than did any modern figure, including Gandhi, the connection between King and Niebuhr would be obscured by complicated twists of time, race, and popular imagery. "

—Taylor Branch, *Parting the Waters*

It is commonly believed that the greatest influence on King was Gandhi. According to scholar Taylor Branch, although Gandhi did influence King's movement toward nonviolent resistance, Reinhold Niebuhr would have a greater impact on King's overall philosophy. Once King became a public figure in the Civil Rights movement, he realized that Gandhi's appeal to mainstream America was greater than the appeal of Niebuhr. While Niebuhr was a central influence on his beliefs, Gandhi's nonviolent method, he explained, was "a Niebuhrian stratagem of power."

King's Interpretation

Throughout King's leadership in the Civil Rights movement, he spoke and wrote about his interpretation of nonviolent resistance on numerous occasions. He believed that the method of nonviolent resistance consisted of specific characteristics. King believed these characteristics included that the method was not cowardly; it should be used to gain the opponent's friendship; the battle was against evil, not people; retaliation with violence was prohibited; agape love was a necessary component of the resistance; and the universe was on the side of justice, therefore, on the side of nonviolent resistance.

Displaying Courage

Nonviolent resistance, according to King, was a method that required courage in the face of a violent attack. King believed that while injustice was capable of eliciting a number of different reactions such as violence or submission, the nonviolent method required that the protestor resist the urge to respond with violence. Even though it took time for King to become completely convinced of the power of nonviolent resistance, when he did, it became clear that violence failed to solve any of society's social ills. Violence, according to King, was not only futile, but once violence was used as a means to combat injustice, it created chaos for successive generations. According to the philosophy of nonviolent resistance, the end did not justify the means. Instead, the means should be just as pure as the end.

According to King, nonviolent resistance required the body to remain passive while the mind worked to persuade the resister that he was wrong. Nonviolent resistance attacked the moral conscience by drawing attention to the wrong not through violence, but through persuading the mind of the opponent. It was a method of resistance where the participants were just as passionate as the violent protestor. The fact that the nonviolent resister was willing to risk his life in an attempt to persuade the opponent through nonviolent means as opposed to persuasion through a violent uprising was evidence that it was not a cowardly method.

HE SAID...

" If the American Negro and other victims of oppression succumb to the temptation of using violence in the struggle for justice, unborn generations will live in a desolate night of bitterness, and their chief legacy will be an endless reign of chaos. "

Gaining the Opponent's Friendship

The second characteristic of nonviolent resistance was its focus on gaining the friendship of the opponent. Although King was not a proponent of the idea that human nature was good, he believed that there was a potential for goodness in all human beings. King understood that man could be both good and evil, but the overriding feature of human beings was the ability to respond to goodness. The nonviolent resister, therefore, must appeal to the natural inclination of human nature's goodness. While there would always be those who would follow an evil dictator like Hitler, for black Americans, hope of bringing about change in white segregationists should remain a steadfast belief. Thus, friendship with the opponent would be gained by appealing to human nature's goodness instead of seeking to humiliate the opponent.

Battling Evil

The third approach of nonviolence was to attack the evil force itself as opposed to the people who carry out the evil. The evil was the unjust system and not the individuals, concluded King. Individuals within the system were misguided into promoting the injustice. Like a child who was taught to misbehave in early childhood, the judgment of the misled was clouded. By attacking the system, the misled could be guided away from the evil system. The focus should be placed on defeating the system instead of defeating the individuals who are victimized by the evil. According to King, as a consequence, the battle was not between blacks and whites, but between justice and injustice. A win against the system of segregation would be for justice and democracy, not just for blacks.

Retaliation Not Allowed

The fourth characteristic of nonviolence was that the resister had to accept the consequences of their behavior. If subjected to violence, the resister must not use violence in response. In the same vein, if arrested and put in jail, that was a consequence that must be accepted. Suffering was believed to be a powerful tool of the nonviolent resister. While the violent protestor attempts to inflict suffering on others, the nonviolent protestor readily accepts the violence against oneself. Suffering was at the center of the nonviolent method. Because of its redemptive quality, it could serve to transform social injustice in a way that reason was unable to.

Agape Love

King believed that love was a powerful tool in changing the opponent, but the love King referred to was not the affectionate type. He distinguished between three types of love, all derived from Greek words: *eros, philia*, and *agape*. Eros was a romantic love and philia was a reciprocal love expressed to those such as friends. Agape love, the type of love King referred to, was a love that sought nothing in return for its goodwill toward others.

Although Niebuhr influenced many of King's philosophical viewpoints, the power of agape love was where he diverged from Niebuhr's analysis. In Niebuhr's *Interpretation of Christian Ethics*, he had asserted that while agape could possibly be used to regulate injustice, human imperfection ultimately prevented it from affecting the evil in society. He stressed that because of this imperfection, agape was impossible. King, however, believed that redemption could be achieved by committed people. Further, he noted that the power of agape love combined with nonviolent resistance could successfully be used to combat evil in society.

Love, according to King, was a powerful tool in changing humanity, as long as it was at the center of an individual's life. King believed that individuals loved each other not because the other was likeable, but because God loved them. It was not the kind of love that distinguished between people who were worthy and unworthy; it was the kind of love that was concerned for all individuals, both friends and enemies. In loving one's enemy, love in return should never be expected. In fact, in its place, one should anticipate hostility.

Agape love also seeks to fulfill the need of the other person. King compared this analysis with the Samaritan who stopped to help the Jew on the road. He stopped not because he expected something in return, but because his help was needed. White segregationists were like the Jew on the road in need of help, and blacks should love the white man whose soul has been scarred by the repercussions of segregation. The act of loving whites would help soothe their fears and insecurities, argued King.

THEY SAID...

" The third kind of love was agape....This was the kind of love Martin aspired to give his enemies. If, because of the defect in the English language, he sometimes sounded mild, just remember that his was a militant life and a militant love. *"*

—Coretta Scott King, *My Life with Martin Luther King Jr.*

King described agape love as a love of action; it was a love that wanted to preserve community. The reaction to answer hate with hate would fail to change society, and would only create a community that was even further divided. Instead, to preserve community, agape love required that one would go to any lengths. Thus, forgiveness should be offered an unlimited number of times.

Justice Will Prevail

Lastly, the nonviolent resister should hold the belief that the universe is on the side of justice. The resister garners strength from the belief that through one's suffering, justice will come. King held the Christian view that God is on the side of justice and truth, and that God's force will prevail. The belief in universal justice was not restricted to believers in God. King strongly felt that all resisters, regardless of whether they held religious beliefs, resisted because they ultimately believed that the universe was on the side of justice and that a force worked to bring harmony to the world.

King felt strongly about this last characteristic of nonviolent resistance. His leadership role in the Civil Rights movement eventually validated his own personal belief that God was on the side of justice. Over time, he had come to believe in a personal God, but in an abstract way. As the pressures of his leadership role intensified, he began to feel frustrated, tired, and at times even hopeless. These feelings were met with a calm and hope that came over him. King began to believe that God was with him every day. This experience convinced him that God was in control of the universe and was on the side of justice. Thus, King put his faith in the belief that God will prevent the reign of injustice.

Chapter 5

WORK, SCHOOL, AND FAMILY LIFE

THIS WAS A TIME of big change for Martin Luther King Jr. His decision to earn a doctorate degree put his career choice on hold, but not for long. And there was still the matter of finding a wife. Luckily, Boston put him in the right place. It was there that his romance with Coretta Scott began. While it was a happy time for King, it was also plagued by bouts of his father's anger. However, King emerged with a newfound independence when he secured a position as a minister.

Graduate Studies at Boston University

On May 8, 1951, King, the Valedictorian of Crozer Theological Seminary, received his Bachelor of Divinity. Daddy King was finally happy, and anticipated the return of his son to assist him in his ministry at Ebenezer Baptist Church. However, King was again considering other prospects beyond the ministry. A professor urged him to earn a doctorate, an idea that displeased Daddy King. King was able to persuade his father of the necessity of continuing his education, and Daddy King agreed to pay for graduate school. He even bought King a new green Chevrolet.

Deciding on a Graduate School

King was financially set for graduate school. With the financial assistance of his father and the $1,200 he was awarded from Crozer for his scholarship, graduate school was paid for. Now he had to decide on a school. Unlike his mediocre recommendations to Crozer, this time his intellectual aptitude stood out. The dean at Crozer wrote in his recommendation that King was "one of the most brilliant students we have had at Crozer." King made clear in his application that he wanted to teach theology with the statement, "In a word, scholarship is my goal." King was accepted to both Edinburgh in Scotland and to Boston University. He chose Boston University because of the presence of Edgar S. Brightman, an expert in the theology of Personalism. King was very familiar with his work, having read it extensively while at Crozer. Boston University had a long history with the theology of Personalism; it was the home of Borden P. Browne, the founder of the philosophy.

 What was the philosophy of Personalism?
Personalists, like Brightman, believed that the meaning of reality was found in personality, and thus, the individual held intrinsic value in the world.

Driving from Atlanta to Boston in his new car, King started classes on September 13, 1951. King, an eager student of Brightman's, took most of his courses from him, and from Personalist L. Harold DeWolf. King was a good student, earning the respect of DeWolf for his intellectual abilities. Throughout King's time at Boston, his relationship with DeWolf blossomed, especially when DeWolf became his faculty advisor after Brightman died in 1953.

Adjusting to Life at Boston University

The environment at Boston University was much different than at Crozer. It was a larger school, and King lived off campus in an apartment. King's social life was also different at Boston. Instead of smoking, drinking, and playing pool, King took on a more restrained social life. He organized a philosophical club for other black graduate students. The group met once a week to eat and discuss that week's paper presented to the group by a member. Through the cigar-smoke-filled room, the members then critiqued the paper, arguing in favor of it or against it.

King's preaching classes at Crozer had provided him with ample preparation for the pulpit. Therefore, although he enjoyed pulpit oratory immensely, he eliminated preaching classes from his curriculum. King did continue to develop sermons, inspired by classes or books that he was reading. King's sermon "Three Dimensions of a Complete Life" was inspired by an epistemological theory that asserted there were three levels of human development. These three elements were length, breadth, and height. Length was the concern for oneself; breadth was the concern for others; and height was one's faith and love for God, the source of existence. Each dimension needed to work in concert with the other. For example, living a life only involving the dimension of length would lead to self-centeredness. Without breadth, life was meaningless. On the other hand, practicing only the first two without God would lead to the experience that one's accomplishments were worthless.

Strengthening Philosophical Viewpoints

At Boston, King still debated the merits of Rauschenbusch and Niebuhr. In the face of the discrimination he experienced as a child and its contradiction to human goodness, he still leaned toward Niebuhr. King, however, began reflecting on Niebuhr's focus on sin, and came to the conclusion that his pessimism failed to allow room for optimism.

THEY SAID...

II Theology...was resorting to more and more elaborate shrugs. King himself shared this propensity to vagueness on the crucial questions, but, in much the same way that a doubting preacher fell back from the afterlife to morality, he embraced Personalism's teaching that there was rich, empirical meaning in religious experience. *II*

—Taylor Branch, *Parting the Waters*

King's study under Drs. Brightman and DeWolf also had an impact. In personalist theology, King found the answers for many of his questions. Brightman believed that though God was perfect, God didn't hold infinite power over the actions of people. Therefore, while God could guide the world toward good, his power failed to prevent destruction. This, according to Brightman, was why pain, suffering, and catastrophes occurred. From Personalism, King came to believe that there is worth in all people, and that a personal God exists.

Studying the Work of Hegel

King began to study the works of G.W.F. Hegel. He read Hegel's *The Phenomenology of Mind*, *The Philosophy of History*, and *The Philosophy of Right*. These works gave him insight into social justice. From Hegel, King came to the important conclusion that without a struggle, growth could never be achieved. While Hegel failed to convince King of the soundness of absolute idealism, from Hegel's work King adopted the Hegelian dialectical method of logical deduction.

FACT

Hegel's dialectical method of deduction entailed the exploration of two opposite ideologies. According to Hegel, since an idea by itself was incomplete, it gave rise to an opposite idea. These two ideas together formed a synthesis, which resulted in a new premise.

Hegel's dialectical method shed new light on King's philosophical exploration. He attempted to reach a conclusion that synthesized the ideology of Niebuhr and the Social Gospel. In a paper, King asserted that both Rauschenbusch's ethical love and the political power focused on by realists were necessary to become a balanced Christian who was both loving and realistic. King felt that the love ethic could not work by itself outside of a direct relationship. Instead, the combination of the love ethic with coercive power was the only way to increase social justice. Because men were controlled by both power and the mind, the Social Gospel and liberalism were misled in their focus on love as a cure for society's evil, asserted King. In the end, he was unable to merge the two theories of thought. He concluded that Niebuhr's analysis of society was correct and that the Social Gospel's concept of love was incapable of being used alone to coerce society.

Hegel's dialectical method stayed with King beyond graduate school. During his leadership in the Civil Rights movement, he often attempted to synthesize two ideologies. According to Hosea Williams, who worked closely with King, his strength lay in his ability to listen to various opinions and attempt to merge them. King's leadership style welcomed varied opinions, especially extreme ones. He regularly relied on this method of discussion to formulate a new premise. King believed that through this process the truth would emerge.

Exploring Concepts of Social Justice

Although King rejected communism, he began to develop a passion for social justice. He was heavily influenced by Niebuhr's concept of economic power. According to Niebuhr, injustice was the result of economic power placed in the hands of the few who controlled the wealth. Accordingly, when this power was used in an irresponsible way, injustice was the result. Niebuhr also believed that the only way to improve the plight of the poor was by a direct confrontation between the poor masses and the wealthy. King agreed with both of Niebuhr's points. Near the end of King's life, his passion for social justice would emerge, and just as Niebuhr called for a class conflict, King would attempt to use this method to bring about change for the poor.

Falling in Love with Coretta Scott

By the time King reached Boston University, he had engaged in a fair number of relationships. One relationship, encouraged by his father, was with Juanita Sellers, a girl King had known since high school. She was the daughter of a successful mortician and was raised on the West Side of Atlanta in an elite black neighborhood. In addition to financial clout, she was educated, having attended graduate school at Columbia University while King was at Crozer. While a seminary student, his interest in her was peeked. He traveled to New York to visit Sellers and she visited him at Crozer. Daddy King was excited to for his son to marry, especially someone like Sellers, who was from an affluent family. To the dismay of his father, the relationship soon died out.

Courting Coretta

While at Boston, King soon realized that the time to find a wife had arrived. Coretta Scott entered King's life in early 1952. King and Coretta met through a mutual friend, whom King had told of his desire to find a southern girlfriend. The friend told him about Coretta Scott, and gave him her number. Using humor and poetry and flooding her with compliments to persuade her, King called her and asked for a date. Coretta was so amused by King's audacity in complimenting her even though they had never met, that she agreed to meet him for lunch.

HE SAID...

" She talked about things other than music. I never will forget, the first discussion we had was about the question of racial and economic injustice and the question of peace....I didn't want a wife I couldn't communicate with. I had to have a wife who would be as dedicated as I was. *"*

Coretta was a twenty-five-year-old classical singer and a New England Conservatory student from Marion, Alabama. She was the daughter of Obadiah Scott, a business owner and the owner of several hundred acres of land. Although Coretta and her sisters spent several hours a day picking cotton to help their family, they were able to attend a private school close to Marion. Like her older sister, after graduating from high school, Coretta attended Antioch College in Ohio. After earning her degree she moved to Boston, where she began attending the Conservatory on a scholarship. Life was difficult financially for Coretta. She lived at a Beacon Hill boardinghouse, where she worked as a maid in exchange for her room and board.

When King and Coretta met for their lunch date, she was surprised by his short stature. As she later recalled, she found him unattractive, but as she got to know him, her opinion changed. King was impressed with her looks as well as her ability to talk about race and politics. King told Coretta that he was concerned about the masses, the inequitable distribution of wealth, and the unfairness of the control of wealth by a small percentage of the population.

Coretta was able to keep up with the conversation, and she had strong opinions of her own. King expressed his enthusiasm for Coretta with a surprising proposition of marriage. He told Coretta that she had all of the attributes that he wanted in a woman: intelligence, character, beauty, and personality. Coretta, more sensible than King, agreed to see him again, but ignored his premature talk of marriage.

King and Coretta continued to date, attending concerts and the theater. King, after regaining his senses, considered seriously whether Coretta would make a good preacher's wife. While King romanced Coretta, he also considered whether, as a Baptist preacher's wife, she could fit in with the congregation. Coretta was well-mannered and socially astute. Her cooking ability was put to the test and determined to be adequate. King, now seriously considering marrying Coretta, introduced her to his family.

The Relationship under Attack

While King was impressed with Coretta, Daddy King was uncertain of the match up. He had envisioned his son's marriage to a girl from a prominent family on the west side of Atlanta, not one from the rural South. To the dismay of Daddy King, Coretta Scott arrived at his doorstep in August 1952. Despite the politeness of the welcome she received, she was quite aware of King's parents' lack of support for the relationship. Not only uncomfortable with King's parents, Coretta was also overwhelmed by the lifestyle of the King family. They lived in a large house, belonged to elite black social clubs, and Daddy King was the pastor of the sizeable Ebenezer Baptist Church.

Coretta's Atlanta visit had gone over reasonably well, but doubts of her acceptance emerged. Her fear over the lack of acceptance from King's parents was realized when they visited King that fall in Boston. Coretta, a constant companion to King, was by his side as he entertained his parents. Daddy King, annoyed by King's choice of a potential wife, now openly displayed his objection. He began with references about King's prior girlfriends, and then proceeded to interrogate Coretta about her career in secular music. He suggested that such a career was inappropriate for a Baptist minister's wife. Coretta was unresponsive; however, her stint of silence quickly ended when Daddy King rattled her by declaring that she had nothing to offer in comparison to the potential matches from good families in Atlanta.

King remained silent as his father continued with his objections to the relationship. However, he took his mother aside and informed her that he would marry Coretta. Days later, King was forced to tell his father as well. After another angry outburst from his father, King told him that he planned to marry Coretta after he received his doctorate. Daddy King finally accepted the idea.

Just like Daddy King, King's friends were unsure whether marriage to Coretta was a good idea. King endured harassment by his friends that Coretta was too much of a bourgeois. According to them, the evidence of this lay in the fact that unlike King's other girlfriends, she refused to dance the jitterbug. In addition, she enjoyed classical music and preferred an evening out in a formal gown. Eventually, the important matters regarding her character overrode their opinions on trivial matters. They recognized that she was loyal, ambitious, socially skilled, and intelligent, and finally decided that she was a good match.

The Wedding Day

The wedding took place on June 18, 1953 in the front yard of the Scott home in Marion, Alabama. It was a sizable wedding with members from both sides of the family. Daddy King, determined to the bitter end to thwart the marriage plans of the young couple, took them aside and urged them to forgo marriage unless they felt impelled to do so. Daddy King performed the ceremony, and even agreed to Coretta's request to omit the promise to obey from the vows. After the reception, King and Coretta spent their honeymoon in a funeral parlor owned by a family friend of the Scotts. While it was a less-than-ideal location, it was the only option, since segregation laws prohibited motels and hotels from accommodating blacks. After their honeymoon, they returned to the King home in Atlanta. They spent the summer there before returning to Boston in the fall.

Searching for a Purpose

King was now a year away from graduating from Boston University. He switched from the philosophy department to the School of

Theology. With the passing of Professor Brightman, King worked under the care of his new advisor, Professor DeWolf. With a wife to support, King decided to become serious about a career. Daddy King, however, was certain about a career choice for his son: He expected him to return to his post as assistant pastor at Ebenezer. King had other ideas, and in time would inform his father of his decision to seek a pastorate elsewhere.

King began his job search in December 1953. He was still considering both the ministry and teaching at a university. He returned to the South for one month to explore various opportunities. King inquired with contacts at black universities about job prospects. He considered Morehouse, and contacted Benjamin Mays. Although he was prepared for a teaching position, King leaned toward becoming a pastor, and he believed that it was his mission to serve in a Baptist church. Thus, leaving his options open, he began preaching at various churches. First Baptist Church in Chattanooga, Tennessee was one of the churches that interested him. He preached a trial sermon to the congregation on January 3, 1954.

HE SAID...

" I had had a great deal of satisfaction in the pastorate and had almost come to the point of feeling that I could best render my service in this area. I never could quite get the idea out of my mind that I should do some teaching, yet I felt a great deal of satisfaction with the pastorate. **"**

Meanwhile, Dexter Avenue Baptist Church in Montgomery, Alabama had heard that King was scouting the South looking for a job. Dexter's pastor, Vernon Johns, had recently left, and King had been recommended to them as his replacement. While King was in Atlanta, R.D. Nesbitt, the chairman of the pastor selection committee arrived at the King home. Nesbitt asked King to deliver a trial sermon at Dexter, which King initially declined, but reconsidered and agreed to. The day before the trial sermon, King set out for Montgomery from Atlanta with Vernon Johns, the former pastor of Dexter, at his side.

Becoming Pastor at Dexter Avenue Baptist Church

Dexter Avenue Baptist Church had a reputation for being hard on its pastors, and believed that leadership ran from the deacons to the pulpit, as opposed to from the pulpit to the congregation. Vernon Johns's departure from the church had been messy. Johns was an outspoken pastor who had embarrassed the church by selling watermelon at the wedding of the daughter of a wealthy family, and had even dared to scold a parishioner who murdered his wife and escaped punishment. Finally, after years of dealing with Johns, the church was ready to get rid of him. So, when he submitted his fifth resignation, the board quickly accepted it. Johns, surprised by this, refused to leave the church, despite the disconnection of the water, gas, and electricity.

Considering a Ministry at Dexter Avenue Baptist Church

Johns finally did leave, and Dexter sought a new pastor. Dexter had heard about King, and believed that their refined church, that prided itself on the lack of shouting that was common in many Baptist churches, would be appealing to the graduate student. Ralph Abernathy, the pastor of Montgomery's First Baptist Church, gave King some tips about the church when he arrived in Montgomery. He described Dexter as a church where the mention of Jesus was discouraged; instead, the pastor was encouraged to talk about such topics as Socrates or Plato. For a soon-to-be Ph.D. like King, who was a longstanding opponent of the emotionalism of a typical black church and enjoyed a bit of intellectual jostling, this appeared to be a good match.

As scheduled, King took the pulpit to preach his trial sermon. He delivered the sermon he had perfected at Boston University, "Three Dimensions of a Completed Life." The congregation was impressed. Their enthusiasm was evident when Nesbitt and a group of congregants arrived at the home of King's hosts that afternoon. King was somewhat less enthusiastic when he learned that his Morehouse and Crozer friend, Walter McCall, had also delivered a trial sermon and was scheduled to deliver a second one. Nesbitt put him at ease, and King left the option of a ministry at Dexter open.

Accepting the Call to Dexter Avenue Baptist Church

Weeks later when McCall delivered his second trial sermon, it failed to win over Dexter members. In the meantime, King had received word that First Baptist in Chattanooga had chosen another minister. King, still cautious about Dexter, agreed to give a second trial sermon, but gave Nesbitt no assurances that he would accept the position if offered. Nesbitt, now determined to secure King as the new pastor of Dexter, removed the condition that King deliver a second trial sermon. He offered King the position with a salary of $4,200 a year. Upon acceptance, this would make King the highest-paid black minister in Montgomery.

HE SAID...

" At this time I was torn in two directions. On the one hand I was inclined toward the pastorate; on the other hand, toward educational work. Which way should I go? And if I accepted a church, should it be one in the South, with all the tragic implications of segregation, or one of the two available pulpits in the North? *"*

On April 14, 1954, to the dismay of Coretta and Daddy King, King accepted the offer. Daddy King had convinced his old friend, Benjamin Mays, to offer King a teaching position at Morehouse. This way King could both teach and serve as assistant pastor at Ebenezer.

Coretta, on the other hand, had enjoyed life in the North. The segregation and racism she was familiar with from childhood lacked the appeal of staying in the North, where she had more opportunities to pursue a career as a singer. Despite the misgivings of Coretta and Daddy King, King laid out additional demands to Dexter for regular salary raises and the payment of his traveling expenses from Montgomery to Boston to finish his dissertation. On April 18, the Dexter selection committee quickly accepted.

Settling into Life in Montgomery

On May 2, 1954, King delivered his first sermon as Dexter's minister. He was still working on his dissertation, so his status as full-time pastor began on September 5, 1954. King, aware of Dexter's desire for an intellectual preacher who exercised minimal involvement in the church organization, set out to establish his authority. He issued a document to the church members entitled "Recommendations to the Dexter Avenue Baptist Church for the Fiscal Year 1954–1955." As opposed to Dexter's idea of power, King declared that leadership and authority went from the pastor to the congregation. In the document, King also proposed thirty-four financial and organizational goals. King, with the determination and fortitude of his father, took charge of the church by recommending social and political action committees and even went so far as to assign specific church members to leadership of the committees. The finance plan entailed improvements to the church building and a new way to collect and deposit the money. King also insisted that one committee take charge of promoting membership to the NAACP, and that every church member register to vote. King's ambitious plan for the church worked. Committees were established by excited members, and Dexter's collection baskets filled up.

While King was making significant changes at Dexter, he was still working on his dissertation, comparing the ideas of two Transcendentalists, Paul Tillich and Henry Nelson Wieman. King criticized both theologians' conception of God. He disagreed with Tillich, who argued that God was impersonal, and with Wieman's assertion that God was not personal. He spent early mornings and some late evenings working on it. After completing numerous hours of research and traveling back and forth from Atlanta to Boston, King received his Doctorate of Systematic Theology in June 1955.

THEY SAID...

" This critique not only revealed King's acceptance of the Personalist conception of a provident God but also implied his appreciation of the existential implications of such an acceptance for believers who have both the privilege and the obligation to seek fellowship with a God Whose loving purpose directs them. *"*

—John J. Ansbro, *Martin Luther King, Jr.: Nonviolent Strategies and Tactics for Social Change*

With his dissertation finished, King could finally focus on his full-time ministry at Dexter. When he wasn't working on a sermon or involved in a church activity, King became involved in Montgomery's black community, beginning work with the Alabama Council on Human Relations. The council was an interracial group that focused on equal opportunity for all Alabamians. He also became involved with the NAACP, giving a speech at the local chapter in August 1955. The organization was so impressed with him that they appointed him to the executive committee. King enjoyed his new role in the organization, and contemplated running for president of the local chapter. However, his mother and Coretta urged him to reconsider. On November 17, 1955, his first child, Yolanda Denise King, had been born, and his already-busy schedule occupied most of his time. King agreed to relinquish the idea, but continued his involvement in the organization and the community.

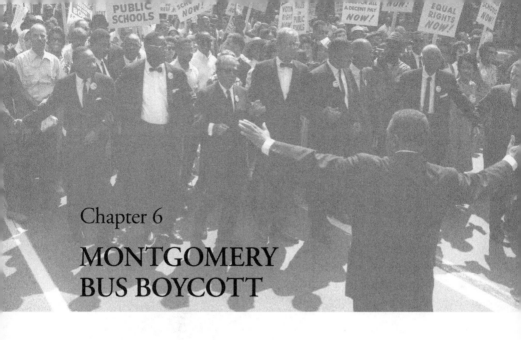

Chapter 6

MONTGOMERY BUS BOYCOTT

AS MARTIN LUTHER KING was settling into his role as pastor at Dexter Street Baptist Church, an unexpected turn of events soon changed the direction of his life. While he had hoped to make a difference in the world, he couldn't have anticipated that Rosa Parks's arrest for violating Montgomery's bus segregation law would put him center stage in a lengthy boycott and legal battle to end segregation on buses. In just over a year's time, the young Martin Luther King would develop into a charismatic leader.

Moving to the Back of the Bus

In 1955, Montgomery, Alabama had a large African American population of 37 percent. Just as other southern cities required of its black residents, Montgomery enforced a strict code of segregation. Separate facilities, such as schools, parks, drinking fountains, and waiting rooms, were provided for blacks. Black employment consisted mainly of manual labor and domestic work. For the average black resident, a car was not an option and instead, the bus was the most affordable mode of transportation. Most middle-class whites, on the other hand, were reasonably comfortable and could afford to drive cars, while lower-class whites rode the bus.

Bus Segregation

Despite the fact that the majority of bus riders were black, a system of segregation on buses was legalized and enforced by white bus drivers. According to long-established custom and the city ordinance, the first ten seats on the bus were reserved for white passengers and the last ten seats were for black riders. Unfortunately for black passengers, the bus engine was located in the back, and in addition to the noise it produced, the heat it generated was a nuisance in the summer months. The sixteen seats in between could be used by either race. While these seats were mostly used by black riders, if the white section was full, black patrons in the middle seats were required to move to make room for one or more white passengers. This color-coded tradition forbid black and white patrons from sitting next to each other on the bus under any circumstances.

FACT

A bus driver held a significant amount of power. Discourteous treatment was quite common and many blacks became accustomed to it. Even Rosa Parks experienced it. Prior to the Montgomery bus boycott, the same driver who had Parks arrested for violating the city segregation ordinance had forced her off the bus several years earlier.

Getting onto the bus proved to be quite an ordeal for black riders. The fare had to be paid at the front of the bus. Once it was paid, regardless of weather conditions, black riders had to get off the bus and re-enter the bus using the rear door. While most of the time this procedure was followed without incident, there were occasions when an ornery bus driver would drive off before the rider could enter the bus at the rear.

Early Signs of Protest

Like other southern cities, Montgomery was susceptible to the growing dissatisfaction of its black residents. A local chapter of the NAACP was active in the community and enjoyed a substantial membership. In 1949, Jo Ann Robinson, a teacher at Alabama State and later a participant in organizing the bus boycott, cofounded the Montgomery Women's Political Council. Its original goals were to advocate voter registration and to help rape victims. As time progressed, the organization became focused on issues such as the improvement of black parks and playgrounds, and on helping to eliminate the mistreatment that blacks encountered on Montgomery buses.

Claudette Colvin's Arrest

In March 1955, segregation on buses was pushed to the forefront in local elections. A candidate's opposition to the desegregation of buses was essential to success. With bus segregation an election topic, fifteen year-old Claudette Colvin, a member of the NAACP Youth Council, decided to test the issue. Acting on her own accord, Colvin refused to give up her seat to a white passenger when asked to move by the bus driver. She was promptly arrested for violation of segregation laws, and for assault and battery because she resisted arrest.

Viewing the situation as an opportunity to discuss the bus segregation issue, Jo Ann Robinson led the appeal to city officials. Following her lead was Martin Luther King, local activist E.D. Nixon, NAACP Montgomery-branch secretary Rosa Parks, and other local leaders. At the meeting with the mayor and other city officials, Robinson put forth the assertion that the ordinance was misinterpreted. According to Robinson, the law did not force a black rider to give up their seat in the middle section unless there was one available in the black section. The city officials disagreed. The meeting ended without a resolution, but with a warning from Robinson that a bus boycott may ensue.

However, a boycott was out of the question—the community was lukewarm in its support of the idea. In addition, it was decided that Colvin's assault charge and her pregnant and unmarried status wouldn't make a good test case. Colvin was found guilty for violating segregation laws and for assault and battery. Her conviction was appealed. The assault charge was upheld, but the violation of the segregation law was thrown out. The judge, aware of the legal implications had he upheld the segregation conviction, made it impossible to challenge bus segregation laws using Colvin's criminal case.

Rosa Parks's Arrest

Despite the failure of Colvin's case to incite a protest, 1955 would still turn out to be a time of change for the nation and Montgomery. On May 31, the U.S. Supreme Court ordered in *Brown II* that desegregation of public schools needed to proceed with "all deliberate speed." Civil-rights activists celebrated another win when the U.S. Fourth Circuit Court of Appeals ruled in *Flemming v. South Carolina Electric and Gas Company* that intrastate bus segregation was unconstitutional.

The time for change was ripe, and as Rosa Parks would prove, Montgomery blacks were finally growing impatient with the second-class treatment they received on buses. While Colvin's case had failed to inspire the community, it did set the stage for another attempt at challenging bus segregation. This time Rosa Parks's arrest would ignite the Montgomery bus boycott.

Forty-two-year-old Rosa Parks was a seamstress and longstanding member of the local chapter of the NAACP. As a regular bus rider, she had always been bothered by the segregation and unfair treatment of blacks. She had resolved long ago that if ever asked to move for a white rider, she would refuse. This belief, combined with the fact that she had just spent two weeks at an interracial workshop at Highlander Folk School in Tennessee, prepared her to take a stand against bus segregation.

 Q: How close was the ruling in *Brown v. Board of Education*?

If the Supreme Court had made a ruling in *Brown v. Board of Education* when it was first heard in 1952, the doctrine of separate but equal would have been upheld. However, the decision was made a year later, after Chief Justice Vinson died, and Justice Warren was appointed in his place. Warren influenced the other Justices to vote to end public-school segregation.

On December 1, 1955, Rosa Parks left her seamstress job at a department store and boarded a Montgomery bus headed for home. Parks sat in one of the sixteen seats available to either race. A man sat next to her by the window, and in the aisle across sat two women. Soon the bus was full and a white man stood in the aisle. The bus driver told Parks and the three others next to her to give their seats to the man. After being told a second time, the two women got up from their seats and Parks moved her legs so the man seated next to her could pass. The driver again asked Parks to move, but she refused. The police were called and Parks was arrested for violating the bus-segregation ordinance.

As Parks was taken to the police station and her arrest was processed, word spread in the community that she had been arrested. When E.D. Nixon heard the news he contacted the police, but was denied information pertaining to her arrest. Since Fred Gray, a local black attorney, was out of town, Nixon called Clifford Durr, a white attorney sympathetic to racial causes. Nixon, Durr, and Durr's wife went to the police station together, and Nixon paid Parks's bond.

The four went back to Parks's house and discussed how to proceed. While Colvin's case was hardly ideal, since she was an unmarried pregnant teenager who had resisted arrest, Parks was a well-respected member in the community and an ideal litigant. The group decided to use Parks's case to challenge Montgomery bus-segregation practices.

The Bus Boycott

With the decision made, Nixon began contacting local black leaders the next day. Fred Gray was back in town, and agreed to take the case. Since the church had always been the center of the black community, next on the list of contacts was Ralph Abernathy, the minister at First Baptist Church. Abernathy, on board with the plan, suggested that Nixon contact the Reverend Martin Luther King. When informed of the plan, King was initially hesitant, and told Nixon to call him back after he thought about it. King's hesitancy stemmed from his concern about his growing family. His first child, Yolanda Denise, had just been born, and such a commitment would require time away from his wife and newborn.

> **THEY SAID...**
> *" Reverend King said, 'Brother Nixon, let me think about it awhile and call me back....' He's a new man in town, he don't know what it's all about. So I said, 'Okay.'...I called him back and he said, 'Yeah, Brother Nixon, I'll go along with it,' and I said, 'I'm glad of that, reverend King, because I talked to eighteen other people, I told them to meet at your church at three o'clock.' "*
>
> —E.D. Nixon, *Voices of Freedom*

Hours later, a somewhat reluctant King agreed to provide his support for the boycott. A meeting got underway for local leaders and ministers at Dexter Church that evening. The gathering concluded with the decision that a boycott would take place on Monday, December 5, the day of Parks's trial. Jo Ann Robinson was put in charge of writing, printing, and distributing leaflets about the boycott and the Monday-night-mass meeting. The ministers were responsible for notifying their parishioners about the boycott at their Sunday services.

The weekend passed with the community successfully notified and on board with the boycott. Monday morning arrived, and except for a few black passengers spotted on the buses, the boycott was a success. In court, as expected, Parks was found guilty and fined $10.

HE SAID...

" The bus protest did not spring into being full grown as Athena sprang from the head of Zeus; it was the culmination of a slowly developing process. Mrs. Parks' arrest was the precipitating factor rather than the cause of the protest. The cause lay deep in the record of similar injustices. *"*

Creating the Montgomery Improvement Association

With the first day of the boycott a success, King, Abernathy, Nixon, and local clergy met that afternoon to discuss whether to continue the boycott. It was decided to let the community decide at the mass meeting that night whether they wanted to carry on with the boycott.

Next on the agenda was the creation of an organization to run the boycott. Abernathy's proposal of the name Montgomery Improvement Association (MIA) was adopted. Fearful of white reprisals, some members of the group wanted to keep the organization a secret. A lone E.D. Nixon reprimanded the ministers for being cowards, and when King arrived, he agreed. Thus, the MIA would operate openly and its members would withstand the worst of any retaliation.

The meeting turned to the issue of a leader. After discussing potential leaders, even though E.D. Nixon was a likely candidate, King was nominated for the position. While Nixon was known in Montgomery, he lacked ties to the religious black community. To gain the support of the churchgoers and the more wealthy blacks, King appeared to be the best candidate. The combination of strong oratory skills, being highly educated, and his position as a Baptist minister would be appealing to a broad range of clergy, church members, and people in the community.

The Big Speech

When King arrived at Holt Street Baptist Church to speak at the mass meeting Monday night, it was packed to maximum capacity. One thousand occupied the inside, while 4,000 stood outside the church building. As he stood at the podium and began his speech, the crowd's enthusiasm made it clear to MIA leaders that the boycott would continue.

King's speech started out slow. It moved cautiously to a discussion of the vagueness of the bus segregation law that Rosa Parks was convicted of violating. As the momentum built, he spoke of the injustice of bus segregation. The remedy, according to King, was to seek change through protest that was not violent. Unlike the violence the Ku Klux Klan inflicted on its enemies, this protest would change the opponent with Christian love. As King spoke, the church filled with applause both from within and outside the building.

HE SAID...

" If we are wrong, the Supreme Court of this nation is wrong. If we are wrong, the Constitution of the United States is wrong. If we are wrong, God Almighty is wrong. If we are wrong, Jesus of Nazareth was merely a utopian dreamer that never came down to Earth. If we are wrong, justice is a lie. "

King moved on to the subject of God. God, he said, was on the side of justice, and justice would win. Thus, he stressed, God should be at the center of the protest. As King continued his speech, the audience, excited with passion, verbally responded in agreement. Lastly, he abruptly ended his speech with emphasis on the importance of uniting and having the courage to stand up for what was just.

Taking Charge of the Bus Boycott

After the mass meeting, the MIA sent the bus company a list of three demands. The first demand was that seating be implemented on a first-come basis, with blacks filling seats back to front and whites filling them front to back. The second simply required courteous treatment, and the last demanded the hiring of black bus drivers. To reiterate the MIA position, a meeting with city officials, the bus company, King, and other MIA representatives was held. However, the bus company refused to budge, claiming that the issue of bus segregation was a legal matter and they had no authority to change it.

> **FACT**
> Other southern cities, such as Mobile, Alabama, had implemented a first-come, first-served procedure of boarding buses. According to the 1947 state law, bus companies had the option of segregating seating, but were not required to do so; the decision was left to each city's discretion.

Without a compromise reached, the boycott continued. While the bus line was suffering financially, a different system of transportation had been working well for the boycotters. Taxis were shuttling boycotters around town for the cost of bus fare. After only a week of the boycott, the city threatened to enforce an ordinance that required taxis to charge riders a minimum fare of forty-five cents. It was more than the cost of riding the bus, so the fare would be unaffordable for most boycotters.

King got the idea to create a system of volunteer drivers after speaking to a friend who had participated in a bus boycott a few years earlier in Baton Rouge. That night at the mass meeting King explained the idea, and over 200 drivers volunteered. King had solved the first of many crises to come during the boycott.

While King faced criticism from whites in the community, by January he had clearly emerged as the leader of the boycott. MIA members were impressed with his leadership and reporters were surprised that a twenty-seven year old held such poise and maturity.

The First Arrest

With the taxi crisis solved, a new challenge arose. Police officers began harassing carpool drivers. It didn't help that on January 6, the Police Commissioner of Montgomery joined the Citizens Council, a white-supremacist group that used economic intimidation against blacks. With the commissioner's blessing, police officers began using such tactics as pulling over drivers, issuing bogus tickets, and dispersing groups waiting for rides.

King was also subject to police harassment. On January 26, he stopped at a carpool lot and picked up a few boycotters. A police car pulled behind him and began to follow them. He was careful to obey traffic rules, but was pulled over for driving 30 miles per hour in a 25-mile-per-hour zone. King was arrested, but was released when Abernathy paid his bail bond.

The Death Threats Begin

King's arrest energized the movement. King, however, was feeling the pressure of his leadership role. On January 27, while sitting at his kitchen table alone late at night, he received a threatening phone call. The caller warned him to leave town, or his home would be bombed. While it was not the first threat, King broke down. He became fearful and concerned for the safety of his family. Although he believed it would be cowardly, he contemplated leaving Montgomery.

THEY SAID...

" I believe that God has called Martin Luther King to lead a great movement here and in the South. But why does God lay such a burden on one so young, and so inexperienced, so good? King can be a Negro Gandhi, or he can be made into an unfortunate demagogue destined to swing from a lynch mob's tree."

—Reverend Glenn Smiley, as quoted in *Bearing the Cross*

As he often did in troubled times, King turned to prayer. He told God that although he was fighting for what was right, he felt weak and his courage was diminishing. According to King, he heard God speak to him. An inner voice told him to stand up for righteousness, justice, and truth. King was reassured that God would never leave him and he would never be alone. This was a defining moment in King's life, and it left him with the courage he needed to continue his leadership in the boycott, and later on as well.

King's faith in God's mission for him was quickly tested. Three days after the breakdown in his kitchen, the threats against him were finally carried out. While King was speaking at a mass meeting, Coretta and a friend were in the King home. A noise at the front of the home got their attention, and they proceeded to move to a back bedroom. Seconds later, a bomb exploded. No one was hurt, but the house was damaged.

King immediately came home from the meeting. As the police and hundreds of black onlookers surrounded the home, King took the opportunity to speak to the angry crowd. He emphasized that while violence was being used in an attempt to stop the boycott, to retaliate with violence was wrong. Drawing from Christian principles, he reminded them that they should love their enemies. Finally, he emphasized that even without his leadership, the movement would continue.

> **FACT**
> According to Coretta King, King's belief in the philosophy of nonviolent resistance really took root on that evening. Prior to the bombing, King had tried to obtain gun permits for his bodyguards, and in a February interview, he had stated that perhaps the federal government would intervene if whites shed some blood.

Bus Desegregation

The MIA, unmoved in its determination to change bus segregation, implemented a new plan of action. The group decided to attack bus segregation legally, by filing a lawsuit in federal court. The case, *Aurelia S. Browder et al. v. William A. Gayle*, included Claudette Colvin as one of the plaintiffs, as well as three other black women. As opposed to the previous demands for better treatment on buses, the suit sought to end bus segregation entirely.

The Indictments

While the case was moving forward, the city pursued legal action of its own. In an attempt to thwart the boycott, on February 21, the city indicted eighty-nine boycott leaders using a 1921 anti-boycott law. The next day, the indicted leaders, except for King, who was in Atlanta, posted bail bonds. King, accompanied by his father, turned himself in on February 23.

To the city's dismay, their legal strategy brought national attention to the boycott. At a mass meeting that week, King's speech with his message of continuing a campaign using Gandhi's passive resistance received nationwide news coverage. The *New York Times* featured the story on the front cover. With national coverage of the boycott, donations to the MIA increased beyond all expectations. In just two weeks, the organization received $12,000 from around the country.

Developing into a Leader

With the legal strategy underway, King still had a long way to go to hone his leadership skills. While the philosophy of nonviolent protest he had read about in college was taking shape in his movement toward nonviolent resistance, he lacked a complete understanding.

Interest in the Montgomery movement and its leader got the attention of longtime pacifists Bayard Rustin and the Reverend Glenn Smiley. Believing that the Montgomery protest could move throughout the South, Rustin, the former field secretary of the Fellowship of Reconciliation (FOR) and a former member of the Young Communist League in the 1930s, arrived in Montgomery from New York City on February 21. Smiley, a white Texan and the current FOR field secretary, arrived on February 27.

While King was skeptical of their interest at first, he soon warmed to both men. The men saw potential in King's leadership and charisma, and realized that he was not yet well-versed in the methods of Gandhi. King's familiarity with the method had never turned him into a convert, and this became especially evident to the shocked Rustin when he found a gun in King's home. So Rustin and Smiley set out to tutor King on Gandhi's nonviolent resistance and its application to the movement.

With the help of Rustin and Smiley, substantial progress was made in expanding King's knowledge of the method. King quickly absorbed the information and came to believe that the use of nonviolent resistance was a moral necessity. By combining the method with his Christian beliefs, he would later explain that the essence of passive resistance stemmed from the "teachings of Jesus."

However, Rustin, a homosexual who also had an arrest record, became a concern for civil-rights activist and New York colleague A. Philip Randolph. His sexual orientation, along with his former communist activity, could derail the first real steps made toward achieving success with nonviolent protest. If King's association with a former communist was uncovered, it could threaten the Montgomery movement and any future battles. Thus, Rustin hastily left for Birmingham. Despite his departure, he advised King privately and by mail. Rustin would continue to work closely with King during future civil-rights struggles.

THEY SAID...

" The glorious thing is that he came to a profoundly deep understanding of nonviolence through the struggle itself, and through reading and discussions which he had in the process. "

—Bayard Rustin, as quoted in *Martin Luther King, Jr.*

The Legal Battle

As the boycott in Montgomery continued, the legal battles moved ahead. On March 22, King, the first of the indicted leaders to be tried, was found guilty of conspiracy. He was sentenced to pay a $1,000 fine, $500 of which was for court costs, or he could spend 386 days in jail. Choosing neither, he appealed his conviction. His appeal was later rejected because of its late filing.

On June 5, 1956 the federal appeals court decided the *Browder* case. It ruled that bus segregation was unconstitutional, but it suspended its ruling while the case was appealed to the Supreme Court. Meanwhile, the city developed another legal strategy to stop the boycott. On Oct. 30, 1956, the city filed an injunction to bar carpools. It argued that carpools infringed upon the bus company's franchise. By this point, the MIA had purchased the automobiles used in the carpool, and a ruling in the city's favor threatened to end the boycott.

The MIA felt certain that the injunction would be granted. As they suspected, on November 13, the judge granted the injunction. However, good news surfaced as well. On the same day, the Supreme Court affirmed the appeals court ruling in *Browder* that segregation on buses was unconstitutional. The city, of course, petitioned for reconsideration, and in the meantime, the injunction stood. The boycott continued through volunteer carpools.

On December 17, the MIA won a victory. The Supreme Court rejected the city's appeal. Four days later, bus desegregation took effect. On the first morning of desegregation, King, Abernathy, Nixon, Parks, and Smiley all boarded the early morning bus that stopped in King's neighborhood. King got on first, and Smiley sat next to him. After 382 days, Montgomery's African American population could finally sit anywhere on the bus, including next to a white person.

HE SAID...

" Ultimately, victory in Montgomery came with the United States Supreme Court's decision; however, in a real sense, the victory had already come to the boycotters, who had proven to themselves, the community, and the world that Negroes could join in concert and sustain collective action against segregation, carrying it through until the desired objective was reached. *"*

With the Montgomery boycott behind him, King set out to expand the movement throughout the South. Little did he know that such a task would be so difficult. Now, as he approached his twenty-eighth birthday, he was a national figure who would experience the pressure of duplicating the Montgomery success throughout the South.

Chapter 7

THE CIVIL RIGHTS MOVEMENT ORGANIZED

KING ENJOYED THE AFTERMATH of Montgomery's success with the anticipation of achieving similar progress throughout the South. To carry out this mission, the Southern Christian Leadership Conference was formed to organize the movement. King was now in the national spotlight, and he increasingly found that fame failed to protect him from experiencing the extreme highs and lows of leadership. The lows of a bomb-shocked Montgomery and a faltering voter registration campaign were paired with the highs of the Prayer Pilgrimage to Washington and the fame that followed him.

The Montgomery Bombings

For two days, the integration of Montgomery buses went smoothly. However, the quiet throughout the city soon came to an end when angry segregationists lashed out. Their anger was first directed at King. During the early morning hours of December 23, 1956, a shotgun blasted through the front door of the King home. Nobody in the King family was hurt, and King decided not to report the incident to the police, but he did have a message for the attackers. At a mass meeting that evening, he announced that even if he were killed, the movement would continue. Bus desegregation, threatened King, was just the first of many gains that would be made in Montgomery. The attackers refused to accept desegregation, and struck back again. On December 28, shots were fired at two evening buses. One black passenger suffered minor injuries. The following day another bus was fired upon. In response, the city temporarily halted night buses.

Planning for the Expansion of the Movement

King was unaffected by the eruption of violence in Montgomery, and his mood was upbeat as the New Year approached. He was excited about the legal victory in Montgomery, and was ready to proceed with the next phase of the movement. Plans soon got underway. While traveling to Baltimore to speak at a fraternity convention, he met with his old friend Bayard Rustin at the airport. Rustin, excited to expand the success of Montgomery throughout the South, was convinced that King's leadership was needed to accomplish this goal. Rustin introduced him to his friend Stanley D. Levison, a white attorney from New York who was a member of the organization In Friendship.

Rustin and Levison discussed with King their ideas about expanding the movement. Other activists were interested in a united front, so they proposed that King hold a meeting with these Southern leaders. The Negro Leaders Conference on Nonviolent Integration was scheduled for January 10 and 11 at Ebenezer Church in Atlanta. Rustin formulated the agenda for the group. Bus desegregation was on the list, but Rustin wanted to expand the outlook. Voting rights was a main focus, since without this right blacks would remain politically powerless. Rustin also stressed that the involvement of citizens was key to a successful mass political-action campaign.

 What was the group In Friendship?

In Friendship was founded by Stanley Levison, Bayard Rustin, and Ella Baker in 1956 with the goal of raising money for desegregation movements throughout the South. The organization was instrumental in keeping the Montgomery boycott active with its substantial monetary donations to the Montgomery Improvement Association.

The Movement Faces a Temporary Interruption

On January 10, 1957 at 1:55 a.m., while King, Rustin, Abernathy, and Ella Baker were in Atlanta preparing for the meeting, anti-segregationists were still at work in Montgomery. Two bombs were detonated at the home of Rev. Robert Graetz. It destroyed the home, but the Graetz family emerged unharmed. Additional bombs were targeted at Abernathy. His home and church were bombed along with three other churches. King and Abernathy were immediately notified, and decided to return to Montgomery.

The following morning, the meeting continued without them. The gathering consisted of sixty Southern preachers, Rustin, Coretta Scott King, and Fred Shuttlesworth. King returned to Atlanta in time for the meeting the next day. The conference ended with the decision to meet again and to seek assistance from the federal government. They sent telegrams to President Dwight D. Eisenhower, Vice President Richard Nixon, and Attorney General Herbert Brownell. The telegram to Eisenhower urged him to vocalize his support for the *Brown v. Board of Education* decision, Nixon was extended an invitation to come to the South to learn more about violence against blacks, and Brownell's assistance was requested in the form of federal protection. The telegrams failed to elicit any response.

> **FACT**
>
> Despite the 1955 ruling in *Brown II* that desegregation should take effect with all deliberate speed, many school districts throughout the South resisted its implementation. It was common for schools to close rather than desegregate. In Prince Edward County, Virginia, for example, the schools were closed from 1959 to 1964 and only reopened when the Supreme Court ordered the implementation of integration.

Picking up the Pieces

In the meantime, the Montgomery City Commission ordered the discontinuance of all bus services. A $2,000 reward for information about the bombings was offered from the governor. King took the bombings hard. The violence, combined with the growing disunity in the MIA, had taken its toll. E.D. Nixon was jealous of King's fame and believed that he deserved more credit for the success of the bus boycott than he had received. King was not only exhausted, but he also felt guilty for the bombings. His feelings, in fact, were becoming overwhelming and uncontrollable—King had neither anticipated his involvement in the boycott nor was he completely prepared to become a national figure—and his emotion soon overtook him. A few days after the bombings, at a mass meeting as King led the prayer, he was overtaken with emotion as he prayed for his own death in order to spare other participants. He exclaimed that should someone die for the cause, despite his desire to live, he wanted to be the one. King, clearly shaken, was unable to continue the prayer and was assisted to a chair.

Weeks after his breakdown, King's prayer was almost fulfilled. One night while Coretta and Yolanda were in Atlanta, King awoke suddenly with the feeling that something was wrong. He woke up Bob Williams, who was on night watch, and told him that they should leave the parsonage. Within hours of their departure, a bomb placed near the home destroyed the front of the house and the black taxi stand nearby. Twelve sticks of dynamite found on the porch of the home were defused within an hour. King and Williams had escaped just in time.

A Surprising Defeat

What appeared to be good news arrived a few days later on January 31. Seven white men were arrested for all of the recent bombings. The black community's hope for justice, however, soon faded. Despite a confession from two of the bombers, a jury acquitted them on May 30. The charges against the remaining defendants were later dropped. At the same time, the prosecutor dropped the charges against the indicted Montgomery leaders.

HE SAID...

" Discouraged, and still revolted by the bombings, for some strange reason I began to feel a personal sense of guilt for everything that was happening. In this mood I went to the mass meeting on Monday night. There for the first time, I broke down in public. "

Another legal blow came when King's appeal of his earlier conviction for conspiracy was denied by the Supreme Court due to its late filing. He reluctantly paid the $500 fine. Regardless of these disappointing court rulings, the community quickly returned to normal with the restoration of the night buses on February 19.

Creating the Southern Christian Leadership Conference

The group of leaders reconvened on February 14. This time, ninety-seven participants met at the New Zion Baptist Church in New Orleans. They decided on the name the Southern Leadership Conference. King was elected president and Abernathy treasurer.

The group again sent a telegram to the president. It urged him to make a speech in support of civil rights. It also avowed that his failure to do so would lead to a Pilgrimage of Prayer to Washington. Yet again, Eisenhower was unresponsive.

King believed that if he met with Eisenhower, he could win him over. In addition to sending the telegram, at the urging of other leaders, King requested a personal meeting with the president. Once more, Eisenhower ignored King's request. While in favor of voting rights for blacks, other civil-rights issues such as school desegregation were the least of Eisenhower's concerns. Thus, a meeting with King was at the bottom of his list of priorities.

Dealing with Fame

By the time that the Montgomery bus boycott ended, King was famous. So famous, in fact, that he found it difficult to appear in public without being recognized. His speaking engagements were not only sought after, the events themselves were often filled beyond capacity. King quickly became well aware of the pitfalls of fame. He knew that if he allowed himself to become caught up in the praise of his leadership, an ego would quickly emerge. To counteract the effects of fame, he consciously made an effort to dispel any emerging beliefs of greatness. He constantly reminded himself that he was a symbol of the movement, that the boycott would have continued without him, and that there were thousands of participants who would never receive recognition for their contributions.

To the dismay of the leaders like E.D. Nixon who wanted credit for their part in the movement, King was featured on the front cover of *Time* magazine. King achieved a new level of prominence. His face and life story in this nationally published magazine held great prospects for him, especially with such a positive feature written about America's very own Gandhi. In preparation for the story, the magazine took great care in pursuing certain key aspects of King's life. The magazine featured King as a follower of Gandhi who had learned about him from extensive reading of his philosophy. The real truth, that King had only become familiar with Gandhi in college and was never an advocate of Gandhi's nonviolent resistance until after the Montgomery boycott began, failed to stop the magazine from stretching the truth.

HE SAID...

II When you are aware that you are a symbol, it causes you to search your soul constantly—to go through this job of self-analysis, to see if you live up to the high and noble principles that people surround you with, and to try at all times to keep the gulf between the public self and the private self at a minimum. *II*

In February, the *Time* issue was published with a portrait of King on the cover. The article explored King's role in the Montgomery boycott and profiled his life. This positive spin on King's acceptance of Gandhi's nonviolent resistance served to increase his public notoriety. Requests were made for his appearance on such television programs as "Meet the Press" and he was featured in the *New York Times Magazine*. While King was officially the face of the Civil Rights movement, his new status failed to influence President Eisenhower to meet with him. By the end of March, King decided not to press the issue, and instead began plans for the Prayer Pilgrimage.

Experiencing Freedom in Ghana

King's prominence had also reached international proportions by 1957. He was invited by Prime Minister Kwame Nkrumah to celebrate the independence of Ghana. King accepted the invitation, and left for Ghana a few days before the March 5 ceremony. Included in the journey were Coretta, A. Philip Randolph, Adam Clayton Powell Jr., and Mordecai Johnson. During their stay, King met with Nkrumah and attended various dinners and receptions. At one reception, he encountered Vice President Nixon. King, now politically savvy, quickly used it as an opportunity to urge Nixon to support the goals of the Civil Rights movement. King made headway with Nixon, who invited him to come to Washington for a meeting about civil rights.

> **THEY SAID...**
> *"* It was an immensely thrilling moment for Martin and me. We felt a strong sense of identity and kinship with those African people shouting 'Freedom!' in their different tongues. We were so proud of our African heritage, and saw in Ghana a symbol of the hopes and aspirations of all our people. *"*
>
> —Coretta Scott King, *My Life with Martin Luther King, Jr.*

King's visit to Africa cemented some ideas that he had about oppressed people. He observed that all oppressed people had to fight and struggle for their freedom; it is not easily given by the oppressor. Thus, Ghana was inspiring. If any nation exemplified suffering, it was certainly Ghana, King thought. Its struggle to achieve independence from European dominance was lengthy and hard fought. Persistence, in King's opinion, was the key to the success of any oppressed group. King left Ghana with the strengthened belief that civil rights would never come without a struggle or suffering. Ghana's story was one that inspired his commitment to the cause of equal rights.

Prayer Pilgrimage in Washington, D.C.

King returned to the United States to a special honor. He received the NAACP's Spingarn Medal for his achievements. The Prayer Pilgrimage was also on his mind. He met with Rustin and NAACP's Roy Wilkins to discuss the details of the Prayer Pilgrimage. The main focus of the demonstration was to obtain a response in support for the voting-rights bill from the Eisenhower administration. It was scheduled for May 17, 1957, the third anniversary of the Supreme Court decision on *Brown*.

Fifteen to thirty thousand people arrived for the Pilgrimage of Freedom at the Lincoln Memorial. Among the speakers, besides

King, were preachers like Reverend Fred Shuttlesworth and entertainers Sidney Poitier, Sammy Davis Jr., and Harry Belafonte. King took the podium last. This was his first national speech, so he had taken extreme care in planning it with valued input from Stanley Levison and Rustin. Both men had their own opinions as to what King should focus on, but King decided that in his speech he would emphasize the need for federal action in the protection of the right to vote in the South.

FACT

Stanley Levison was a long-time social activist supportive of civil-rights causes. He was a former communist, but by the time that he and King met, he had severed ties with the organization. Levison became one of King's closest advisors and friends. Without accepting any payment for his services, Levison offered his help with the preparation of King's taxes, speeches, and writings until King's death.

When King approached the podium, the crowd welcomed him with enthusiasm. King proceeded to chastise the federal government for its failure to protect the rights of black voters. It was his statement "Give us the ballot!" that received the most applause from the crowd. To Rustin's surprise, this simple declaration elicited a strong response. Just days before, Rustin had argued that blacks did not want to be given anything anymore. Instead, Rustin suggested that King say something to the effect of "We demand the ballot!" King remained convinced that his phrase was more effective. King was correct. All the years he spent at Crozer Theological Seminary developing his oratory skills became evident at that moment, as King's recitation of the phrase evoked a powerful response.

HE SAID...

" Give us the ballot and we will transform the salient misdeeds of the blood-thirsty mobs into the calculated good deeds of orderly citizens. Give us the ballot and we will fill our legislative halls with men of good will, and send to the sacred halls of Congress, men who will not sign a 'Southern Manifesto,' because of their devotion to the manifesto of justice. *"*

Not only were the participants at the march impressed, but the media was as well. *Ebony* magazine and the *Amsterdam News* wrote that he was one of the most influential black leaders of the time. King's speech at the Pilgrimage gave him national attention. His first national speech quickly expanded his leadership beyond Montgomery and into the national realm. Even the president and vice president were soon forced to acknowledge this.

Taking the Movement to the White House

With King's new role as a national black leader, he was able to take the movement into the federal realm. King was invited for a meeting on June 13, 1957 with Vice President Nixon. King, accompanied by Ralph Abernathy, arrived at Nixon's office. The meeting proceeded with King describing the violence directed toward blacks in the South. He asked Nixon to go south to speak against the violence. Nixon was reluctant to agree, but assured King and Abernathy that the voting-rights legislation was receiving strong support in the House, and could possibly pass in the Senate. The meeting ended without any immediate gains, but with an indication from Nixon that he would attempt to schedule a meeting with Eisenhower.

The federal wheels of justice kept turning as King worked on planning the next SCC campaign. The Senate was debating the civil-rights bill. Senate majority leader Lyndon Johnson, in favor of a version of the bill, worked toward its passage. Along with the vote of Senator John F. Kennedy, an amended civil-rights bill passed the Senate. The bill provided that those accused of violating a voting-rights law had the right to a jury trial. A jury trial of a white defendant in the South was almost certain to end in acquittal. The bill was a disappointment to King, civil-rights supporters, and even to Nixon.

> **FACT**
> Just before the passage of the civil-rights bill, Lyndon B. Johnson deleted an important provision that provided the government with power to sue to enforce school desegregation. John F. Kennedy voted in favor of the altered bill, which would later tarnish his reputation on civil-rights issues when he ran for president.

King kept up an intense travel schedule of speaking engagements around the country. He had little time to dedicate to the MIA, so it continued under the leadership of the secretaries. This, however, also meant that the MIA was inactive in the community. E.D. Nixon's jealousy also remained a problem. As treasurer, he made things difficult. He was concerned with how money was being spent, and resented the expense of King's phone calls and telegrams. Nixon wanted to resign as treasurer, but King convinced him to remain.

In addition to his minimal involvement with the MIA, King began to feel guilty about the lack of progress he made toward his goals at Dexter. When he had first started, he had established clear objectives for the ministry. Out of twelve months, he had only taught thirty sermons. He was being pulled in so many directions that it was difficult to keep up with every commitment. He was apologetic to the congregation, but with his busy schedule, little could change. In the midst of the chaos, the birth of his son Martin Luther King III came on October 23, 1957.

Crusade for Citizenship

King scheduled a third meeting for the Southern Leadership Conference for August 8 and 9. The group of one hundred met in Montgomery at Holt Street Church where the first order of action was to change the name of the organization. King felt that it was important to emphasize that the participants were from churches. Thus, the name was changed to the Southern Christian Leadership Conference (SCLC). Next on the agenda was King's proposal to concentrate on voter registration. The Crusade for Citizenship, as it was called, would bring awareness to the black masses about the importance of their right to vote. In addition, the program would tackle such issues as the collection of evidence of discriminatory voter practices to send to the federal government, distribution of educational materials to the black community, establishing voting clinics, and publicizing voter discrimination through the media outlets of radio, newspapers, and television.

On November 5, the SCLC met again. This time, it was decided that with a budget of $200,000, the Crusade would commence with rallies on January 20 in various southern cities. The lofty goal was to register 2.5 million black voters within a year. The SCLC was joined in their quest to register voters by the NAACP, who also had a program in the South. At the first meeting regarding the Crusade, some members had stated their concern about the program's competition with NAACP's effort. King assured them that it was not in direct competition, and even met with Roy Wilkins about the plan. According to King, an agreement was reached that the groups would later unify on the issue. However, King was naïve. It quickly became clear that the NAACP felt that the SCLC's plan was a threat to their registration goals. Just days after the SCLC November meeting, Wilkins announced to the press the NAACP's own plan to register 3 million new voters. The announcement came as a surprise to King, who had believed that unity was possible. Strife between the groups was slowly emerging.

Due to the inability to secure an organizer for the January Crusade rallies, they were postponed until Lincoln's birthday on February

12. Rustin was put in charge of organizing the rallies until someone could step into his place. Rustin's homosexuality again proved a barrier to his involvement in the South. In his place, In Friendship's executive secretary, Ella Baker, went south to organize. Baker arrived in Atlanta and began the planning. She found that the prospect of the rallies' success looked bleak, especially with the NAACP conspiring against the Crusade. The NAACP was actively using its ties within the SCLC to find out information about the progress of the organizing efforts. Through their allies, they thwarted Baker's effort to organize in Jackson, Mississippi where Medgar Evers served as the NAACP point of contact.

With the sabotage of the NAACP, the rallies appeared to be doomed even before they had begun. Even a press conference by King prior to the scheduled kick-off date failed to provide the momentum needed. Despite the lack of enthusiasm for the rallies, they got underway on February 12. King spoke at the rally in Miami. During the days that followed, little headway was made in the registration of new black voters. Although in some cities the Crusade had successfully increased registration, the gains throughout the campaign were minimal.

Meeting with President Eisenhower

As the SCLC effort to increase voter registrants continued, Eisenhower finally agreed to meet with King. King insisted that along with the inclusion of Randolph and the National Urban League's Lester Granger, that Roy Wilkins also take part in the meeting. On June 23, they met with Eisenhower at the White House for a thirty-minute meeting. Randolph led the meeting by reading a nine-point plan that the four men agreed upon ahead of time. Included in the plan was the suggestion for a provision of federal aid to assist in the integration of various communities, and a request that Eisenhower call for law and order in the South.

King followed up by urging Eisenhower to use his influence to provide moral leadership to the country. Eisenhower neither declined nor agreed to their recommendations, but he did agree to review them. The meeting ended after forty-five minutes. For King and the other leaders, it was disappointing that the meeting failed to elicit any promises from the president, while at the same time, the meeting was an indication of King's growing strength as a leader.

Chapter 8
LIFE-CHANGING
EXPERIENCES

LIFE CONTINUED TO BECOME more difficult for King. His constant traveling, combined with his full-time obligations at Dexter and the SCLC, made success at the national level increasingly elusive. His obligation to Coretta and his children was slowly slipping down toward the bottom of his list of priorities. For the next two years, King sorted through the good and bad of his complicated life. However, it was the bad that took prominence. A stabbing nearly ended his life, and his trial for tax evasion threatened his freedom.

King's Most Difficult Job

King's growing fame may have complicated his life at times, but it also provided him with important opportunities to promote the Civil Rights movement. Unlike his post-graduate search for a job, King was now bombarded with employment offers from universities and churches. One offer, however, caught his attention. It was the offer to write a book about the Montgomery bus boycott for Harper & Brothers. This was a good opportunity for King: A book about the success of the first nationally publicized nonviolent civil-rights campaign was a chance to earn money for the faltering SCLC and explain the tenets of nonviolent resistance.

Writing the book *Stride Toward Freedom* turned out to be one of the most difficult tasks that King had undertaken. With this new commitment, he found that his intensely busy schedule allowed little time to work on the book. On average, he had public-speaking engagements four times per week. While time consuming, it was a necessary occupation in order to sustain the SCLC. Furthermore, this was King's first book, and his inexperience only made the task more difficult. The situation became more challenging as the publisher imposed guidelines for style and content. Harper & Brothers wanted to appeal to a targeted audience, and specified that King's writing style should encompass both an intellectual and inspirational tone.

FACT

Harper & Brothers became so frustrated with King's slow progress on *Stride Toward Freedom* that they insisted he stop preaching. While he was unable to do so, he did agree to pay a Harper employee $2,000 of his $3,500 advance to serve as his advisor.

King, thoroughly overwhelmed, relied most heavily on Levison for assistance with the book. As he finished each chapter, he sent

Levison a copy. Levison's criticisms were harsh, but necessary. Levison said King's first drafts came extremely close to depicting his role in the boycott as central to the movement and cautioned King to remove any indicavtion of arrogance. Levison also criticized one chapter for lacking a good organizational structure and important information, and for including unimportant subjects. According to Levison, overall, the book needed a lot of work. King willingly made the suggested changes and finished the book in time for its publication in September 1958.

Unexpected Obstacle: The Stabbing

After King's book was published, he traveled to New York to promote it. He appeared on the live television show "Today" on September 17. On September 20, he signed books at Blumstein's department store in Harlem. As he sat behind a desk signing copies of the book, from among the crowd of around fifty people, a woman with sequined glasses appeared. She asked whether the man at the desk was Martin Luther King. King responded that he was, at which the woman pulled out a letter opener and stabbed the unsuspecting King in the left side of his chest. As the woman was restrained by onlookers, King maintained considerable restraint as he sat calmly in a chair with the letter opener still lodged in his chest until the ambulance arrived.

HE SAID...

II If I demonstrated unusual calm during the recent attempt on my life, it was certainly not due to any extraordinary powers that I possess. Rather, it was due to the power of God working through me. Throughout this struggle for racial justice I have constantly asked God to remove all bitterness from my heart and to give me the strength and courage to face any disaster that came my way. *II*

King was taken to Harlem Hospital. At the hospital, as surgeons prepared to operate on him, A. Philip Randolph, Roy Wilkins, and

New York Governor Averell Harriman waited impatiently for news about King's condition. It was at least an hour before surgery could begin. The placement of the blade impeded the ability of surgeons to operate immediately. While King lay on a gurney waiting for surgery, the assailant, forty-two-year-old Izola Ware Curry, was brought to the hospital for King's identification. King was able to identify her. Her bizarre identification of King indicated the severity of her mental condition, which was confirmed when she underwent a court-ordered psychological examination: She was diagnosed as schizophrenic. She was committed to Matteawan State Hospital.

Recovering from the Attack

Surgery finally began, and after four hours, surgeons successfully removed the letter opener. It was positioned between the heart and lung, and was dangerously close to the aorta. King was later told by doctors that just one sneeze could have resulted in the piercing of his aorta, killing him instantly. The surgery was a success, and his doctor anticipated that it would take two weeks for his recovery. With Coretta by his side, King enjoyed a relatively quiet time at the hospital. Along with the numerous get-well cards he received, the SCLC experienced a large increase in contributions, causing Ella Baker to create a SCLC office in the hospital.

Re-evaluating His Role in the Movement

While it wasn't the ideal situation, the stabbing provided an opportunity for King to reflect upon his beliefs. The experience did more than just confirm his belief in the power of nonviolence; it also enforced his perception that through suffering there was redemption. King believed that his current suffering was preparation for future violent attacks. The stabbing, however, affected King in another important way. According to Coretta, King's time for reflection stimulated intense feelings about the magnitude of his leadership position. He became severely concerned about making mistakes, a concern that would remain with King for the duration of his leadership role.

The intensity of his feelings subsided after he was released from the hospital on October 3. His recuperation continued for an additional few weeks at the home of a friend in Brooklyn. By the end of the month, he was back to work. Luckily for the SCLC, they financially benefited from King's injury, since his book, while receiving positive reviews, failed to earn the expected income.

Exploring India: Gandhi's Country

After King's complete recovery, he made plans for a long-anticipated trip to India. The idea emerged after the success of the Montgomery bus boycott. King's decision to embrace the concept of Gandhi's nonviolence led to the suggestion from Rustin and others that King take a trip to the country where the method of nonviolent resistance was born. King, enthused by the idea, had put off the trip on numerous occasions due to his busy schedule. The stabbing had slowed his pace, and he finally scheduled the trip with the financial help of an American foundation.

Meeting the People of India

King was accompanied by Coretta and Lawrence D. Reddick, the author of King's recently published biography and a MIA colleague. The trio arrived in Delhi on February 10, 1959 for a thirty-day tour guided by the Gandhi National Memorial Fund. The trip was a combination of speaking engagements, social functions with Prime Minister Nehru and Gandhi disciples, and a heavy travel schedule. For King, there were several highlights during the trip, but his visits to numerous notable sites sparked his interest: the tour of Patna, where they met with Gandhi-disciple Jayaprakash Narian; the visit to Ahmedabad, the place where the Salt March began; and a visit to the Taj Mahal were noteworthy.

103

HE SAID...

" The trip had a great impact upon me personally. It was wonderful to be in Gandhi's land, to talk with his son, his grandsons, his cousin, and other relatives; to share the reminiscences of his close comrades; to visit his ashram; to see the countless memorials for him; and, finally, to lay a wreath on his entombed ashes at Rajghat. *"*

Of all the things King encountered during his travels throughout India, it was the dire poverty he encountered that lingered in his memory. King discovered that it was common for a city like Bombay to have numerous homeless people who wore rags, begged for money and food, and slept on the street. King was immensely disturbed by the poverty, and found it difficult to withstand the urge to give help to the homeless. Although he was strongly cautioned not to help them, according to Coretta, in one encounter King reached into his pocket and gave needy beggars money.

Gaining a Deeper Understanding of Nonviolence

King also had a difficult time fighting the temptation to engage in political banter. He found willing participants in Gandhi disciples who also enjoyed a good debate. With one disciple, he explored the intriguing idea that since India gained its independence through nonviolence, it could set an example for the world by disarming itself. While an intriguing argument to King, at his last press conference on March 9, the press found it less than amusing. They questioned how King could believe this to be a wise decision, considering that Pakistan was a continuous threat. King, now fully converted to Gandhi's methodology, explained that a struggle was an essential part of the nonviolent method.

King's trip to India did more than just teach him about Gandhi; it gave him a new understanding and commitment to nonviolent resistance. He became fully convinced that it was the most powerful tool for oppressed people to gain freedom. Most impressive to King, however, was the outcome of the relationship between the oppressed and the oppressor. At a dinner he had with Prime Minister Nehru, he witnessed the civil and warm interaction between Nehru and the wife of the former viceroy of India. To King, this was a result of Gandhi's emphasis on love and nonviolence. King believed that it was only through nonviolence that this type of relationship could be achieved. It was the kind of reconciliation that King hoped for in America between white segregationists and blacks.

THEY SAID...

" Although unilateral disarmament was no less visionary a proposal than anarchy or anti-industrial communalism....It was the inspiration he had been seeking—how to extend the spirit of the Montgomery bus boycott as far as religion and politics would allow. He could advocate international nonviolence as a Negro and as a human being, as a Gandhian and as an American, as a minister and as a student of war.*"*

—Taylor Branch, *Parting the Waters*

King arrived back in Montgomery on March 21. Most Sundays were spent away from Dexter, so King viewed his presence as a good opportunity to share the details of his trip with the congregation. King reflected on the important revelations that he came to appreciate about Gandhi and the strength of his leadership. Gandhi's strength, stressed King, came from his commitment to evaluating his own faults, his release of material possessions, and his self-discipline in his private and public life. It was these traits, according to King, which contributed to Gandhi's success in freeing India from foreign rule.

Leaving Dexter Avenue Baptist Church

Upon King's return to Montgomery, progress in the Crusade remained stagnant. The voting-registration campaign was faltering, as little progress was achieved registering voters. In fact, in some situations voter registration had even gone backward. In Louisiana, for instance, ten thousand blacks were deleted from the rolls during a registration review. King attributed the failure of the registration drive to SCLC executive director John Tilley. King, with the support of the SCLC, fired Tilley. Ella Baker was temporarily appointed in his place while the search for a permanent director began.

In September, the SCLC met in Columbia, South Carolina. King, now concerned over the growth of the voter-registration drive, proposed some changes. First, he wanted to hire a publicist, namely Bayard Rustin. King assured the board that if criticism arose over him, Rustin would resign. Secondly, King needed to meet with Wilkins to resolve any hostility directed toward the SCLC because of their voter-registration campaign. Finally, King proposed that the SCLC consider moving beyond voter registration. The board, on the other hand, wanted King to allocate more of his time to the SCLC. They believed that King's full-time leadership was necessary in order to make gains in their work.

HE SAID...

" Unknowingly and unexpectedly, I was catapulted into the leadership of the Montgomery Movement....I, like everybody in Montgomery, was pulled into the mainstream by the rolling tides of historical necessity. As a result of my leadership in the Montgomery movement, my duties and activities tripled....So I ended up futilely attempting to be four or five men in one. *"*

King decided to take the recommendation of his board seriously. His guilt over his failure to pastor Dexter had become overwhelming. While complaints from the congregation had never been made, he felt that he was failing to fulfill his duty and obligation to the church. To work full time on SCLC efforts, King contemplated moving back to Atlanta. Daddy King welcomed the idea, and pressed him to copastor at Ebenezer. King reluctantly decided to resign from Dexter. On

November 29, he announced to the congregation that his resignation would take effect on the last Sunday of January 1960.

Moving the Family to Atlanta

Despite plans to move, King continued with his hectic schedule. He spoke to a crowd of nine hundred at the fourth anniversary of the Montgomery boycott. He also attempted to mend the relationship with the NAACP. He arranged for a meeting with Wilkins. The meeting in December produced a plan for a joint voter-registration effort. The goal, as they told reporters, was to increase black registration to 2.5 million by the November 1960 elections. On January 1, he arrived in Virginia to lead marchers to the state capitol, where he concluded the event with a speech. In the middle of January, King was one of the black leaders who met in Washington with Lyndon B. Johnson and other congressional members about civil-rights legislation.

King returned to Montgomery in time to say goodbye to the Dexter congregation. While he felt that it was time to move on, he was despondent about having to leave. He felt overwhelmed by all of his responsibilities in Montgomery, and knew that it was the right decision. Coinciding with his resignation at Dexter, on February 1, King stepped down as president of the MIA, and Abernathy took over the leadership. In Atlanta, the first days of February for the King family focused on settling into their home. The Kings rented a house in a humble neighborhood on the East Side near the church. King received a $6,000 yearly salary from Ebenezer. On February 7, King delivered his first sermon as copastor at Ebenezer, to a congregation of 1,200.

Trial for Falsifying Tax Returns

King's move to Atlanta gave him the time that he needed to concentrate on the goals of the SCLC. He formulated a plan that included the decision to continue work with the NAACP on voter registration and nonviolent workshops. King also found time to lend his support to the student lunch-counter sit-ins in North Carolina. The sit-in protests had begun on February 1, when four black college students from North Carolina A&T College refused to move from a Greensboro Woolworth lunch counter. Their actions had sparked a wave of sit-ins throughout the country. King received a call from a minister from Durham requesting his presence at a strategy meeting with sit-in participants from various cities. King agreed, and arrived on February 16 for the meeting. King used the opportunity to make some recommendations to the young protestors. From his own experiences, he suggested that they consider compromises, that they view the fight as between justice and injustice, that they serve jail time instead of paying the fines, and that they form a coordinating council. King also promised the support of the SCLC.

FACT

Ella Baker feared that an adult takeover of the student sit-ins was imminent, so on April 17, 1960, a group of students met at Shaw University to form the Student Nonviolent Coordinating Committee (SNCC). The group's headquarters was located in Atlanta, and King was given an advisory role.

When King returned to Atlanta the next day, his past tax problems finally caught up with him. A warrant from Alabama was issued for his arrest on felony charges of perjury. King was far from surprised; he had been aware of a grand jury proceeding on the matter, and had sought legal advice prior to his arrest. The charges stemmed from King's 1956 and 1958 tax returns. The IRS had noticed that his stated income was less than the money deposited into his bank account. King explained to the tax official that this was a result of accepting donations and paying the expenses of the MIA and the SCLC through his personal bank account. The auditor determined that donations to either group from King did not qualify as a tax-deductible donation.

Prior to leaving Montgomery, King paid the back taxes of $500, rather than contest the auditor's determination. Despite his payment, the Alabama government sought to enforce the law. This was an unusual course, especially since King paid the back taxes. Nonetheless, King's leadership in the Civil Rights movement served as an incentive to Alabama prosecutors. King, while confident in public, was upset. He feared that the public would believe the alleged charges were true.

THEY SAID...

" My husband's sense of morality was so offended by being accused of such a crime and attendant national publicity that he agonized to the point of feeling guilty. He realized that he could be vindicated only in the courts or in public debate and he felt that the public would be vulnerable to this attempt to destroy his image and to stop the Movement."

—Coretta Scott King, *My Life with Martin Luther King, Jr.*

Without the monetary means for his defense, some of King's friends created the Committee to Defend Martin Luther King in March 1960. The committee's executive director was Rustin. On March 29, the committee paid for a full-page ad in the *New York Times* entitled "Heed Their Rising Voices." The ad alleged that King's prosecution was part of a strategy of white segregationists to halt the movement. The ad, however, resulted in not only a lawsuit against the signers of the announcement, which included Abernathy, but in a significant response from the public in the form of donations to the fund.

On May 25, the trial began. King's lawyers included Fred Gray, Arthur Shores, and the lead attorneys Hubert Delaney and William Robert Ming. Of notable importance was the testimony of prosecution witness Lloyd Hale, the auditor. When cross-examined by King's defense team, his testimony was favorable. His responses to questions regarding his calculation of the back taxes and his comment that the state was unclear on King's actual income were desirable responses for the defense. Just three days later, on May 28, a jury of twelve whites acquitted King of all charges. The verdict came as a surprise to most, including King. He was ecstatic, and not just because incarceration in federal prison was no longer a threat; to King, his acquittal served as a reinforcement of his belief that white southerners could be moved by their moral conscience in favor of justice. King's faith in justice was renewed. During the next phase of his life, he set out to achieve this same kind of justice through appealing to the moral conscience of those in the federal government.

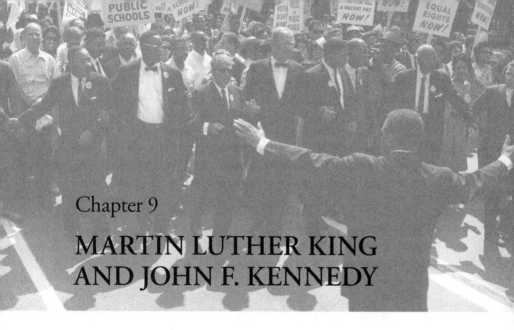

Chapter 9

MARTIN LUTHER KING AND JOHN F. KENNEDY

JOHN F. KENNEDY SHARED a unique relationship with King that was both defined and limited
by politics. King was disheartened when Kennedy
became president, because his support for the Civil
Rights movement failed to immediately reflect the
promises that he made as a candidate. President
Kennedy's early support of the movement encompassed little more than federal aid when violence
threatened to tarnish the nation's image. Thus, a
frustrated King came to believe that Kennedy's commitment to equality was nothing more than empty
promises.

The Meeting with Senator Kennedy

By June 1960, King still remained overwhelmed with work, despite his move to Atlanta. The slower pace he had anticipated failed to come. His mentorship continued with the SNCC, who shared the SCLC office; he still had a hectic travel schedule; and he was helping plan the picketing of the Democratic and Republican National Conventions. King's white friend, Harris Wofford, was brought into Senator John F. Kennedy's presidential campaign. Wofford, the first white person to graduate from Howard University School of Law and the coauthor of a book about Gandhi, was the civil-rights coordinator in the campaign. His close proximity to Senator Kennedy provided him with the opportunity to arrange a meeting between the Senator and King.

On June 23, the two met over breakfast at Kennedy's New York apartment. King entered the meeting with a skeptical view of Kennedy's stance on civil rights. His true colors, King believed, had emerged when he voted for a weakened version of the 1957 Civil Rights Act. At the meeting, King urged Kennedy to support such civil-rights issues as the right to vote and the eradication of discrimination in public housing. King also stressed the importance of strong leadership from the president. The meeting ended with Kennedy's affirmation of his support for King's civil-rights concerns. The right to vote, according to Kennedy, was at the top of his list.

THEY SAID...

" He agreed that there was a need for strong executive leadership and that this had not existed, and he felt if he received the nomination and was elected he could give this kind of leadership. He assured me also that he felt the whole question of the right to vote was a key and basic, and that this would be one of the immediate things that he would look into. *"*

—Coretta Scott King, *My Life with Martin Luther King, Jr.*

Three months later, in September, King and Kennedy met again in Georgetown. King was impressed that, within a short time span, Kennedy had come to grasp many civil-rights issues. This time, Kennedy openly told King that he sensed his 1957 vote on the civil-rights legislation hurt his ability to win over black voters. King agreed, and the meeting ended.

JFK on Civil Rights

To win the presidency, Kennedy quickly realized that his prior stance on civil rights had to change. First, he sought support from prominent blacks. Kennedy, however, was disappointed when baseball player Jackie Robinson endorsed Republican presidential candidate Richard Nixon. Without the endorsement of Robinson, that left Congressman Adam Clayton Powell Jr., who agreed to back Kennedy for $50,000. In return, Powell promised to make ten speeches in which he would give his support to Kennedy.

With Powell on board, Kennedy still hoped to secure a statement of support from King. Wofford headed up the communications with King regarding his endorsement. Because of his position as a civil-rights leader, King felt strongly that he could not endorse any political candidate. King, although committed to remaining nonpartisan, did agree to meet Kennedy publicly in the South. Afterward, he would issue a statement contending that as president, Kennedy would carry out the Democratic Party platform on civil-rights issues. King believed that if Kennedy met with him in the South, it would demonstrate his commitment to civil rights and his courage. After weeks of discussions between the parties about which southern state to meet in, it was decided to schedule the meeting in Miami. However, Kennedy swiftly called it off after King mentioned his plan to extend an invitation to Nixon.

Along with seeking support from black leaders, Kennedy increased his public endorsement of civil-rights issues. In speeches and interviews, Kennedy expressed the opinion that the office of president required a strong moral leader that would guide the country on the path to freedom for all of its citizens. Under such

113

leadership, according to Kennedy, the president should support the right to vote, the elimination of discriminatory hiring practices, equal opportunity, equality before the law, and the need for intervention in situations like the desegregation of Little Rock Central High.

FACT

Three years after the Supreme Court decision in *Brown v. Board of Education*, Little Rock, Arkansas volunteered to desegregate Little Rock Central High. White segregationists erupted in anger, and surrounded the school premises when the students attempted to enter the school. It was only after President Eisenhower sent the protection of a federalized National Guard that the students were able to attend Central High.

Despite his new vigor in support of civil rights, Kennedy found that he had to carefully avoid alienating white southerners. Kennedy's civil rights office, for instance, physically occupied a separate building from the national headquarters, and the phrase "civil rights" was purposely left out of the Kennedy-sponsored Democratic National Conference on Constitutional Rights. When Nixon's running mate promised that their administration would appoint a black cabinet member at a rally in Harlem, Kennedy seized the opportunity. Directing his comment to white voters, he publicly claimed that such a statement was racist, and that he would only appoint candidates who were qualified. To black voters, the claim of racism was a veiled comment that attempted to provide assurance to whites that under the Kennedy administration, a black cabinet member would not be appointed.

Arrested for Sit-In Protests

At the same time of King's communication with Senator Kennedy's staff, King was also pressured by SNCC students to participate in a sit-in planned for Rich's department store in Atlanta. The students argued that since Atlanta was where King grew up and he had frequented Rich's department store for years, he was obligated to participate. King was hesitant; Atlanta was his father's turf, and he had purposely refrained from challenging the city's discriminatory laws. While desegregation was moving at a slower pace than he preferred, he respected his father's leadership in the community.

THEY SAID...

*"*One of the most prized possessions in Atlanta was a Rich's charge plate, which the students were now urging Negroes to surrender in protest against the store's segregation. No, said the students, King never could be an intruder here. Rich's was a symbol of Atlanta, which was a symbol of the hopes of the South, and King was a symbol of the hopes of the Negro people. *"*

—Taylor Branch, *Parting the Waters*

Thus, the hometown of the nation's most prominent civil-rights leader remained largely segregated. The separate drinking fountains and the restrooms at the City Hall, as well as the segregated restaurants, theaters, and lunch counters, were constant reminders to the city's blacks that while the leader of the movement lived in Atlanta, they still lived by southern segregation rules. As King struggled with the decision, the students set out to convince him of the necessity of his participation. They appeared uninvited at his home, and even followed him to the airport, where they surrounded the helpless King in an attempt to elicit a favorable response. King barely survived the incident, but emerged with a growing sense of obligation.

Taking a Step Toward Gandhian Suffering

While King had clearly taken the stance that movement activists should suffer the consequences of arrest and incarceration as part of the nonviolent struggle, he had yet to personally employ his own advice. Just two years before, in September 1958, King had come close to spending time in jail after he was arrested in Montgomery during a trial involving a violent attack on Ralph Abernathy. Abernathy had been attacked by the husband of a woman that he allegedly had an affair with. When the case went to trail, King accompanied Abernathy to the courthouse. As soon as they arrived, they were prevented from entering the courtroom by two white police officers. When King attempted to get the attention of attorney Fred Gray, who was inside, the officers arrested him for loitering.

King was released on bond, and returned two days later for a hearing. He was found guilty of the new charge of refusing to obey an officer, and was fined $14 or fourteen days in jail. King was ready for the conviction. He had decided beforehand that he would refuse to pay the fine and serve the jail time in protest of the phony charges. By this time, the incident was national news, and Police Commissioner Sellers decided to quash the matter by paying the fine himself. A surprised and disappointed King was released from custody.

This was as close as King had come to implementing Gandhi's tactic of appealing to the moral conscience of the perpetrator through suffering. Now, King was again faced with the prospect of jail, and he was unsure whether he was willing to practice what he preached. Yet, King found the mounting pressure to participate unbearable. Initially, his previously scheduled meeting with Senator Kennedy for the same day had given him an excuse not to take part in the demonstration. However, now the meeting with Kennedy was called off. Finally, he agreed to join the students at the sit-in.

Suffering for the Movement

At eleven o'clock on October 19, 1960, King met a group of students outside of Rich's store. The group of thirty-six entered the department-store restaurant and refused to leave. They were arrested and taken to jail. When King was asked by the judge whether he would pay the bail or serve the time until trial, he responded that by staying in jail he hoped to raise the moral conscience of Americans about the injustice of the southern system of segregation.

116

HE SAID...

*"*Your Honor....I will choose jail rather than bail, even it means remaining in jail a year or even ten years. Maybe it will take this type of self-suffering on the part of numerous Negroes to finally expose the moral defense of our white brothers who happen to be misguided and thusly awaken the dozing conscience of our community. *"*

In the meantime, the days following King's arrest proceeded with more student sit-ins and more arrests. When Harris Wofford heard about King's arrest, he believed that it was a perfect opportunity for Senator Kennedy to exert his influence by obtaining King's release from jail. Unbeknownst to Kennedy, Wofford recruited Atlanta attorney Morris Abram to carry out the task. With the help of Mayor Hartsfield, a deal was made to drop the charges filed against all of the protestors in return for a thirty-day halt to demonstrations. This would be followed by negotiations with business owners to desegregate downtown. Mayor Hartsfield, believing that he was helping Senator Kennedy's campaign, announced to the press that Kennedy had intervened. A panic-stricken Wofford quickly notified the Kennedy staff of the situation, and after the shock had subsided, Kennedy issued a statement noting his inquiry into the circumstance.

Jail Time for King

On October 25, all of the protestors were released, except for King. A traffic ticket that he had received in May resulted in a twelve-month probationary period. King was unaware of his probation, and his continued incarceration came as a surprise. At the hearing to decide whether King's current arrest violated his probationary period, Judge Mitchell made a surprising decision. In spite of his attorney's contention that King's appeal of the September traffic-ticket conviction prevented his imprisonment until the judgment was upheld, the judge sentenced him to four months in state prison.

With the cry of a pregnant Coretta in the courtroom, King was hauled off to jail. The next morning at 3:30 a.m., King was quietly awoken and taken to a waiting police car. Within hours, a shackled King arrived at the prison in Reidsville. After putting on his prison uniform, King was placed in a cell, alone.

THEY SAID...

" Then I realized that Martin had been weakened by his days in jail, and was greatly depressed by this unexpected shock. He was relying on the deep reservoir of strength which I had always drawn from crisis situations, but I, too, was totally unprepared for the dreadful decision. *"*

—Coretta Scott King, *My Life with Martin Luther King, Jr.*

King found that incarceration was lonely, but quickly came to accept his sentence. An upbeat King requested that Coretta bring him books so that he could continue working on his book of sermons, entitled *Strength to Love,* and he asked her to visit him on the weekend during visitation hours. As he prayed continually for God to give him strength, he reassured Coretta that his suffering was a necessary part of the movement, and he encouraged her to have faith.

Support from President Kennedy

King's imprisonment created political confusion. A public statement for his release, or the lack of one, could be costly to a presidential candidate. President Eisenhower decided to remain quiet regarding King's incarceration. Presidential candidate Nixon decided to do the same, out of fear that support for King could hurt his campaign. Kennedy, on the other hand, decided just the opposite. On behalf of Harris Wofford, who had already spoken to the distraught Coretta King, Sargent Shriver, the head of the Civil Rights department, convinced Kennedy to call and offer her his support. When Kennedy spoke to Coretta, he expressed his concern. It was a risky move for his campaign, but it did win at least one additional vote. Daddy King, so touched that Kennedy had called Coretta, quickly changed his support from Nixon to Kennedy.

Release from Jail

In the meantime, Robert Kennedy, the brother and campaign manager of Senator Kennedy, boarded a plane headed for New York. He was unhappy with Wofford's interference, and believed it could hurt his brother's campaign. On the other hand, as an attorney, he was also shocked by the injustice against King. He knew that the judge's conviction was biased. When he reached New York, he called Judge Mitchell. He told Mitchell that the release of a defendant on bond was a right given to a defendant. The judge responded politely, and hung up.

FACT

In a 1964 interview with Robert Kennedy, he stated that he made the call after Atlanta Governor Vandiver suggested this course of action. Kennedy called Judge Mitchell from a New York pay phone. In the interview, he recalled that he told the judge that it would be helpful if he released King.

The next morning, on October 27, after hearing the legal precedent in favor of releasing King, Mitchell let King go on a $2,000 bond. King was flown back to Atlanta from Reidsville on a private jet. He was greeted by his family and a crowd of supporters.

On November 1, King took the opportunity to give a press statement thanking Kennedy for his concern. Although he decided that he would continue to remain nonpartisan, he came to believe that Senator Kennedy's support took moral courage. King, though, was realistic about Kennedy's dual motives. He understood that Kennedy's concern came from both humanitarian feelings toward him and political considerations. Despite this, King was impressed with his courage. His feelings about Nixon's lack of support were just the opposite. King had known Nixon longer and felt that they had a good relationship. He was surprised at Nixon's unwillingness to show his support. King felt that Nixon's inaction was a reflection of his lack of moral courage.

HE SAID...

" Senator Kennedy...was running for an office, and he needed to be elected, and I'm sure he felt the need for the Negro votes. So I think that he did something that expressed deep moral concern, but at the same time it was politically sound. It did take a little courage to do this; he didn't know it was politically sound. "

While Senator Kennedy's concern over King's incarceration failed to become a major story in the white press, it did garner substantial attention in black communities. To win the black vote, the Kennedy campaign, under the guidance of Wofford, took advantage of the situation. Flyers were distributed in black communities around the country with the headline "'No Comment' Nixon versus a Candidate with a Heart, Senator Kennedy: The Case of Martin Luther King." Just as Kennedy's actions had changed Daddy King's vote, it also proved rewarding when he won the presidency on November 7, 1960, with a slim victory of about 100,000 votes.

Supporting the Freedom Rides

King got right back to work after he was released from jail. His third child, Dexter, was born on January 30, 1961. Along with the changes in the federal government, progress came to Atlanta. By March 1961, an agreement had been reached between Atlanta's white leadership and the older black leaders. It was agreed that desegregation of stores and lunch counters throughout the city would take place in September, when desegregation occurred in the public schools. In return, the students would end their demonstrations.

At a mass meeting, the older black leaders were forced to defend their agreement against many outraged students. As Daddy King defended his position, he was subjected to angry outbursts by the crowd. King was hurt by the hostility toward his father, and made his way to the podium. He changed the mood of the crowd as he explained the difference between remarks in disagreement of the deal and remarks attacking a person's character. King was able to silence the anger. One month later, stores in Atlanta were desegregated.

Q: **Who was the group the Congress of Racial Equality?**
CORE, a product of the Fellowship of Reconciliation, was an interracial northern organization formed to effect change through the use of Gandhi's nonviolent resistance. Initially, its members were mostly white, but as the black-power movement took hold of the civil-rights climate, by 1966 it had become a mostly black organization.

King's support of Atlanta's older leaders led to criticism from the student activists. While King publicly showed his support for the older leaders, privately he agreed with the students. Despite this growing divide between King and the students, his support was sought from the students involved in the Freedom Rides, which were being organized by the Congress on Racial Equality (CORE). On May 4, 1961, thirteen riders, seven blacks and six whites, left the Washington bus terminal to travel throughout the South, with the final destination of New Orleans on May 17. The goal of the journey was to force the federal government to enforce the ruling in *Boynton v. Virginia*, which banned segregation in interstate travel.

The group of riders reached Atlanta on May 13. Thus far, the journey received little press coverage or trouble from white mobs. The next day, however, marked the beginning of violent attacks on the riders. On their way to Birmingham, just outside of Anniston, Alabama, the Klan was waiting for the first bus. When the bus stopped, Klan members boarded and began to beat the riders. As the bus was engulfed in flames, the riders escaped. The second bus in Anniston was also attacked. With Klan members on board, they proceeded to Birmingham. The riders were beaten, as the police were conveniently absent from the scene.

After a day of violence, the riders were unable to find a willing bus driver. They made the decision to fly to New Orleans in time for the May 17 rally. A group of ten riders were unsatisfied with the shortened Freedom Ride. They decided to continue on from Nashville to Birmingham. When they reached Birmingham, Police Commissioner Bull Conner arrested them, claiming that it was for their protection. Initially three riders were released, and that night the other riders were dropped off near the Alabama-Tennessee state line. The riders were determined to continue, and returned to the Birmingham station. Again, they faced the problem of securing the services of a bus driver. By this time, the rides had become national news. The Justice Department interceded on their behalf by working with the state of Alabama.

The next day, on May 20, the riders began their journey to Montgomery, with the protection of state troopers. When they arrived in Montgomery, the protection of the riders reverted to the city police. As they got off the bus, they were attacked by a mob. Abernathy and MIA representatives were able to safely escort the riders from the scene. It was later determined that the police commissioner had purposely given the mob time to attack the riders by delaying the arrival of the police.

King arrived on May 21 to speak at a rally at Abernathy's First Baptist Church that evening. King spoke to a crowd of 1,000 people about the importance of nonviolent resistance in the defeat of segregation. King also stressed the significance of the involvement of the federal government as the violence against the riders increased. As the rally continued, unbeknownst to the participants, a white mob surrounded the church. Their presence was announced when they began to break the windows with rocks. Federal marshals managed to keep them out of the church by using tear gas. King was upset and fearful. He went to the basement, where he called Attorney General Robert Kennedy. Kennedy reassured King that the National Guard would soon arrive to help the marshals. By early morning, guardsmen arrived at the church. Those inside the church remained inside until the mob dispersed. They were finally able to leave at 5:00 A.M.

Despite this new setback, the riders were still determined to continue their journey. Furthermore, their latest plan involved King—they wanted him to join them. King was hesitant, and explained that another arrest while he was on probation could result in further criminal penalty. The students were dismayed with his response, and again, doubts of King's leadership arose. It was decided that the riders would continue to Jackson, Mississippi. On May 24, the ride began without King. The two buses arrived without incident in Jackson, but the riders were arrested for trespassing when they entered the white waiting room.

Robert Kennedy responded to the latest problem by contacting King with the recommendation for a temporary halt while he worked out the release of the riders. King explained that the riders were determined to stay in jail, since it was part of the philosophical method of nonviolent resistance. Kennedy perceived King's statement as hostile, and was angered. The conversation ended with King reiterating that federal intervention was unnecessary, since the riders were determined to stay in jail. King announced to the press that the rides would continue on May 29 or 30.

King's long-term goal to awaken the moral conscience of the nation was finally realized as a result of the Freedom Rides. On May 29, Robert Kennedy announced the submission of a petition to the Interstate Commerce Commission. If passed, it would enact regulations against segregated interstate travel facilities. The regulations were scheduled to take effect on November 1, 1961. King was ecstatic with the result of the Freedom Rides; however, the students came away with a deepened resentment toward King, the nation's civil-rights leader they increasingly referred to as "De Lawd."

Meeting with President Kennedy

Now that President Kennedy was in office, King had expected the support of the administration on the civil-rights issues discussed prior to the election. Concerned over the lack of progress, King attempted to arrange a meeting with the president. According to Kennedy, the Bay of Pigs invasion made a meeting inopportune. However, time was made for King to meet secretly with Robert Kennedy and other staff from the Justice Department and the White House. They met for lunch at the Mayflower Hotel, where it was explained to King that the federal government had very little power outside of the realm of voting rights. After the lunch, King returned to the White House with Wofford for a tour. When President Kennedy heard of King's presence, he came out of his office to greet him. It was a brief conversation, in which the president promised his support for King's efforts in voter registration. King, true to his word, kept the lunch meeting with Robert Kennedy and the brief encounter with President Kennedy a secret.

Although he had the support of Kennedy for voting rights, the issue of discrimination in housing received little if any attention from the Kennedy administration, as had been promised prior to the election. King began to question his former confidence in Kennedy's moral leadership. Harris Wofford tried for months to arrange a meeting between King and President Kennedy. Kennedy finally agreed, and the two met at the White House on October 16, 1961. King asked the president hard questions about why civil-rights initiatives had received only slight attention. King also urged Kennedy to declare all segregation illegal through the issuance of a "Second Emancipation." Kennedy explained that his lack of progress on civil-rights issues, besides the ICC desegregation regulation on interstate travel, was a result of the lack of support from Congress. Overall, King was dismayed with the president's failure to support civil rights.

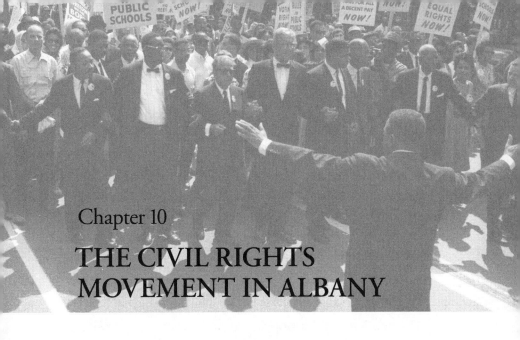

Chapter 10

THE CIVIL RIGHTS
MOVEMENT IN ALBANY

IN THE ALBANY MOVEMENT, just like in the Montgomery bus boycott, King was thrust into an unexpected campaign. This time, however, not only was his leadership in the crusade unanticipated, his presence was greeted with hostility. The lack of unity within the Albany Movement, Chief Pritchett's use of nonviolent tactics against the campaign, and the unsuccessful decision to seek redress with the political structure resulted in a nationally publicized failure.

ulSegregation In Albany

In 1961, the city of Albany, Georgia had reached a population of 56,000. Nearly one-half of its citizens were black. Despite the large African American population and the existence of a local chapter of the NAACP, significant gains had failed to emerge. Jim Crow laws enforced segregation in bus and train stations, parks, hospitals, and in city jobs, and even segregated polling places had sprouted up. Discrimination was especially evident in a black residential section of the city where residents had neither sewer lines nor paved streets.

The SNCC Arrives in Albany

Albany's large black population and the city's large size drew SNCC representatives. Charles Sherrod, a SNCC field secretary, arrived in Albany during the late summer of 1961 to determine the city's viability for a voter-registration drive. Upon Sherrod's return from Albany, as King looked on at a SNCC meeting, an intense debate ensued over the merits of a voter-registration drive as the next campaign. It was decided that the SNCC would pursue both voter registration and a direct-action campaign.

Testing the Desegregation of Travel Facilities

Sherrod returned to Albany in the fall with colleague Cordell Reagon. Their goal was to prepare the city for a voter-registration drive. Sherrod and Reagon's youth, however, worked against them. Albany's older black leaders were fearful of the kind of chaos the group would bring to the city. While the SNCC hoped for their cooperation, Albany's older blacks only wished for their speedy departure. Sherrod and Reagon, sensing the hostility, moved their focus from voter registration to training and recruiting students from the all-black Albany State College. The goal was to have them properly trained in preparation to test the ICC ruling, which was scheduled to take effect on November 1, 1961.

The test got off to a rocky start. On November 1, Sherrod and Reagon rode the bus from Atlanta to Albany. When they arrived at the Albany terminal, their entrance to the white waiting room was blocked by police officers. Determined to test the regulations, that afternoon they organized a group of nine volunteers, who entered the white waiting room. The group was ordered to either leave or face arrest. They left the station, then notified the federal government of Albany's noncompliance with the ICC regulation.

FACT

Albany State College, now Albany State University, was originally founded to provide religious and industrial training for African Americans. Within fifteen years of its creation, in 1917, it became a state-supported two-year college with the expanded focus on agriculture and teacher training. In 1943, after numerous name changes, it became a four-year institution. The university is now considered a historically black college.

Creating the Albany Movement

The SNCC's testing of ICC regulations only increased the hostility of Albany's black leadership. On November 17, they planned a meeting to discuss what current measures could be taken to change segregation. Unexpectedly, they were joined by SNCC representatives and Albany students. The meeting ended with a joint partnership. It was agreed by all of the attendees, except for a NAACP representative, that the organization, the Albany Movement, would serve the role of communicating their demands to the city.

As it turned out, just as the NAACP was threatened by the voter-registration efforts of the SCLC, they were hostile toward the growing prominence of the SNCC. In an effort to take the lead in Albany, they decided to test the ICC regulations. On November 22, the NAACP Youth Council sent three students into the bus station, where they took a seat in the white waiting area. They were arrested, and promptly released on bail. The act garnered a substantial response from students at Albany

State. Hundreds of students converged on the bus station, whereupon two students who refused to leave were arrested. On Monday, November 27, the trial of all five defendants began, and quickly ended. They were fined $100 and sentenced to fifteen days probation.

Community Upheaval

As the NAACP tried to convince the leadership of the Albany Movement to lessen their involvement and allow the NAACP to take the lead, the SNCC had plans of its own. They planned to attack the segregation in Albany by scheduling a Freedom Ride from Atlanta to Albany by train on December 10. When the eight riders arrived in Albany, they were greeted by Police Chief Laurie Pritchett, his officers, a white mob, and a crowd of black supporters. As they stepped off the train, they entered the white waiting room. Pritchett ordered their evacuation of the room, and they obeyed. As they waited outside to be picked up, Pritchett ordered their arrest for the obstruction of traffic and disorderly conduct.

All refused bail, and their trial began the next day. Albany State's young black students were inspired by this latest act of injustice. A group of 267 marched to City Hall, where they were all arrested. The next morning, a group of less than 100 marched to City Hall and were also arrested. Two more groups of demonstrators converged upon City Hall, where they too were arrested. The day ended with the arrest of nearly 500 protestors.

Inviting Martin Luther King to Albany

The arrests of the protestors made national news. Sensing that the Albany Movement was unable to financially and legally sustain a lengthy battle, the leadership, despite the disapproval of the SNCC, decided to extend an invitation to Abernathy and King to come to Albany. King, Abernathy, and Wyatt Walker, the executive director of the SCLC, arrived in Albany on Friday, December 15. The group arrived in time for a mass rally at Shiloh Baptist Church that evening. As they entered the church, the crowd, unlike the SNCC, was excited about their arrival and burst into a rendition of the song "Freedom." After speeches from King and Abernathy, the rally ended with a plea from Albany Movement leader Dr. William Anderson for the black community's participation in the demonstration the following day.

Jailed for Parading Without a Permit

The following morning began with a scurried attempt by Anderson to come to an agreement with Albany's white leadership over desegregation. After hours of negotiation, an agreement fell through. The march, announced Anderson to the Albany community, would proceed at 4:00 P.M. King received an unexpected invitation to join the demonstration, and feeling the pressure to stay and offer his support, agreed.

THEY SAID...

" King and his SCLC colleagues had been in town just twenty-four hours and had a far from complete understanding of the issues and internal tensions that had predominated during the preceding six weeks. Still, King knew that he could not desert this movement at its most pressing moment. *"*

—David J. Garrow, *Bearing the Cross*

With King, Abernathy, and Anderson at the front, the marchers made their way toward City Hall. All the while, Chief Pritchett and his officers followed their procession. When the marchers reached an intersection that divided the black side of town from the white, their procession was blocked by police officers. Despite a warning from Pritchett to halt or face arrest for parading without a permit, the marchers refused to budge.

They were all arrested. King, Abernathy, and Anderson were taken to Sumter County jail in nearby Americus. Meanwhile, the media converged on the city. King and Anderson decided to stay in jail, while

Abernathy posted bond and returned to Atlanta to garner support. He urged protestors in Atlanta to join the movement in Albany.

The Truce and Its Failing

In the meantime, with King and Anderson incarcerated, SCLC's Wyatt Walker, along with Albany Movement's Marion Page, headed the effort to seek negotiation with Albany's white leadership. With the presence of King, the SCLC was thrown into the forefront of the movement by the media. Albany leaders, such as Marion Page, were unhappy that what had started out as a locally controlled movement was becoming one where credit was given to the SCLC.

Negotiating an Agreement

On December 18, King and Anderson remained in jail, as their trial was postponed while negotiations began between the city's black and white leadership. At the negotiations were Page, movement attorneys C.B. King and Donald Hollowell, Mayor Kelley, and Chief Pritchett. A tentative agreement was made that the protestors would be released on cash bonds that could later be exchanged for security bonds, and in return the demonstrations would cease for sixty days. Furthermore, it was agreed by all parties that the establishment of a biracial committee would commence between thirty and sixty days, and that the desegregation of bus and train stations would take effect.

Page and the attorneys consulted with King, Anderson, Ella Baker, and other leaders in the movement about whether to accept the deal. King offered the opinion that Page should make sure that the agreement was put in writing. Page, however, was not yet a shrewd tactician, and was unable to secure a written agreement from Pritchett and Kelley. Page, motivated to obtain the release of the demonstrators, assured King that the word of both men was enough to act upon the verbal agreement. So, despite the urging to get the agreement in writing, Page accepted the deal.

Later that afternoon, King and Anderson paid their bonds and were released on bail. Page announced to the press that an agreement had been reached. One day later, however, Pritchett and Kelley told the reporters just the opposite. Pritchett stated that a formal agreement had never been made, and that the charges against the demonstrators remained. Furthermore, he stated, desegregation of Albany's travel facilities was a mute point since the ICC desegregation ruling had already taken effect.

FACT

Marion Page was angry over press statements that the SCLC was in charge of the movement. An irritated Page maintained to the press that the Albany Movement had been started locally and was led by local leadership, and he unwaveringly maintained that there was no desire for Albany to become a national movement.

The SNCC's Whispering Campaign

Reporters quickly told their readers that the Albany Movement was a failure. The press also had a firsthand account of the fallout between the various civil-rights organizations. While the rivalry between the NAACP and the SNCC had remained steadfast for several years, the press was preoccupied with another rivalry. News stories focused on the enmity between the SNCC and the SCLC. Many SNCC members were still upset with King for refusing to join them on the Freedom Rides. They viewed his lack of participation in the rides as a reflection of what they deemed a double standard of King's leadership. His encouragement to serve the jail time rather than post bond was increasingly interpreted by the SNCC as a standard applied to them and not to King.

Egging on these news stories were SNCC's Charles Jones and Ella Baker. Baker had left the SCLC when Wyatt Walker was appointed executive director, and now served in an advisory role to the students. In off-the-record declarations, she told reporters of how she believed that the SCLC took money allocated to the SNCC. Baker also indicated to reporters that the failure of the agreement was the result of the local black leadership's desire to settle quickly in order to get King and the SCLC out of town.

Why did Ella Baker spread disparaging remarks to the press about the SCLC?
The Civil Rights movement was essentially led by men. Ella Baker, while an experienced organizer, felt the effects of this hard reality. Her position as executive director of the SCLC was only temporary, until a man was found as a replacement. Her leadership of the SCLC was unrecognized by Wyatt Walker and others who claimed that John Tilley directly preceded Walker.

As Baker and Jones spread rumors to the press, King left Albany. When he agreed to come, he had failed to anticipate that he would become an active participant in the movement. Now, with his stature as a civil-rights leader, his name was attached to the emerging failure of the movement. Sensing the hostility to his presence in Albany, King went back to Atlanta.

The Economic Boycott

Although King left Albany, the movement continued to go forward. Local black leaders, along with help from the NAACP, were preparing a list of requests in preparation for the January 23 city commission meeting. In the meantime, protests in Albany continued. A bus boycott ensued when a black rider refused to move to the back of the bus; Charles Sherrod was arrested for his refusal to move from the segregated lunch counter at the bus station; and businesses that refused to hire black employees were subjected to boycotts. On January 23, Page and Anderson requested that the board agree to the terms of the December 18 settlement. Kelley concluded the meeting without discussing the request.

By the end of January, the bus company and the white business owners began to feel the effects of the economic boycott. The bus company finally balked under the pressure, and was ready to end the segregated seating arrangement, unless the city could subsidize the bus company. The commission declined the subsidy idea. In preparation of desegregation, the company sought assurance from the city commission that the enforcement of bus segregation laws by the city would end. The commission, with the exception of Kelley, refused to agree to such a progressive step. The local businesses, however, were strongly in favor of ending segregation. They supported the bus company's request, and sought to submit to the terms of the Albany Movement. The bus company made one last request to the commission hoping that the support from the business owners would influence them. Again, their request was denied. Due to the loss of profit, the bus company was forced to cease services temporarily.

Martin Luther King's Trial

For months, Albany's black residents continued their boycotts of the buses and local businesses. The city commission still refused to budge. In the meantime, King made headway with SCLC's new programs. He traveled throughout the south on the People-to-People tour making speeches and appearances in an effort to recruit participants for the SCLC Freedom Corps. The goal of the Freedom Corps was to promote voter registration. King also formed the Gandhi Society of Human Rights, an organization to handle the larger donations to the SCLC.

King interrupted his travels to appear at his Albany trial on February 27, 1962. Pritchett testified for the prosecution. The trial lasted for about two hours, and finished when the judge declared that his ruling would take place within sixty days. King resumed his tour of the South, and returned to Albany with Abernathy for sentencing on July 10. King and Abernathy were found guilty and sentenced to forty-five days in jail or the payment of $178 in fines.

King had returned to Albany with a renewed sense of his obligation to the movement. Diane Nash, a SNCC activist, had sent out a memo that spring relaying the reason she decided to serve a jail sentence in Mississippi. In the memo, she reiterated the importance of serving jail time for an unjust sentence in order to appeal to the moral sense of Americans. She further noted that the movement leaders needed to subject themselves to the same conditions. King took the criticism in stride. This time, the decision for Abernathy and King was easy—they would serve the time in jail.

THEY SAID...

" Dr. Anderson brought us up to date on the temper of the Negro community....He mentioned that several people had made it palpably clear that they would go to jail again and stay indefinitely. From all of these words we gradually concluded that we had no alternative but to serve the time if we were sentenced. **"**

—David J. Garrow, *Bearing the Cross*

News of King's incarceration spread throughout the Albany community, and the Albany Movement organized a rally at Shiloh Baptist Church. The next day, students joined for a demonstration downtown. They were promptly arrested. Hope for negotiations with the commission resumed when Pritchett made an appearance at the church and Mayor Kelley agreed to present requests to the commission; however, a potential snag developed. To the dismay of King and Abernathy, two days after their incarceration they were released. Pritchett claimed that an unknown black man paid their fines. Despite King's protestation that he had never agreed to the posting of his bond, Pritchett released them. It was later discovered that no such black man existed. Mayor Kelley had been fearful of protests and that activists would converge on the city if King and Abernathy remained in jail. He had determined that the only solution was to release them.

Protest in Albany Resumed

This unauthorized release angered King and served as an incentive for him to stay. Later that day, King, Abernathy, Anderson, and C.B. King resumed negotiations with Pritchett. At first, a resolution seemed promising, but with each day of negotiation, Pritchett increasingly wavered on his previous promises. It was soon clear that an agreement wouldn't be reached, so the movement tried another approach. They requested a face-to-face meeting with the commission. Negotiations with law breakers, declared the commission, would not take place. Shortly thereafter, Pritchett announced that negotiations with King and Abernathy wouldn't continue. In response, the Albany Movement launched a new round of protests at lunch counters and other segregated facilities.

The Legal Battle

A July 10 march on City Hall was planned. At the same time, Mayor Kelley was part of a trip to Atlanta, where Albany's white leadership successfully secured a July 10 temporary restraining order from U.S. District Court Judge J. Robert Elliot. To the dismay of Albany's blacks, the injunction banned protest marches. The order specified that the named leaders, which included King, would face federal contempt charges for disobeying the order. King was outraged by this latest maneuver, but decided not to march. He contacted the Justice Department seeking Robert Kennedy's intervention. He was told that they lacked the power to intervene in the legal order, and King was advised to seek its reversal.

While attorneys worked on obtaining an order to reverse Judge Elliot's judgment, King and Albany Movement leaders came up with a new plan. They realized that while the leaders were specifically named in the order, others who remained unnamed could march. One hundred volunteers marched to City Hall and were arrested. Three days later, the Albany legal team won a victory. They secured a promise from Chief Appellate Court Judge Tuttle that he would overturn the order the following day. Just as he promised, the order was vacated and protest marches were free to resume.

> ## THEY SAID...
> **"** Although King was willing to obey the injunction, the SNCC staff argued vociferously that the movement should defy the unjust decree. King's passive acceptance of the situation, they contended, was just one more example of his excessive moderation and was dampening the enthusiasm the black community had generated over the preceding week. **"**
>
> —David J. Garrow, *Bearing the Cross*

A Day of Penance

That same day, forty marchers proceeded from Mount Zion Baptist Church toward City Hall. Before they could reach it, they were arrested. In response, some of the hundreds of black onlookers that had followed the procession began throwing rocks and bottles at the police. There were no major injuries, but negative publicity resulted. King announced that in order to prevent any further violent outbursts, a "day of penance" would take effect. During this time, all marches would cease. The SNCC was unhappy with King's decision. Not only had he refused to march, but now he was calling for a halt to the movement. Like Albany's white leadership, they had increasingly resented King's presence because they felt that he'd taken over leadership from the Albany Movement.

Ending the Albany Movement

Despite the increasing dislike of King's presence, he remained in Albany. Days later, King, Abernathy, Anderson, and a few other Albany black residents tried a new approach. They walked down to the City Hall, where they requested a meeting with the city commission. Pritchett denied their request, and instead threatened to arrest them if they stayed. Undeterred, they refused to leave. They prayed and then were arrested. This time, King's incarceration failed to spark the public outrage it had just two weeks earlier. Over the following days, only a few protests ensued.

The situation in Albany gained the attention of President Kennedy. In a press statement, President Kennedy stressed his inability to understand why the city officials refused to meet with Albany's black leadership. He said he believed that they were being unreasonable. Robert Kennedy followed up on the President's concern. He met with CORE, SCLC, and NAACP representatives to discuss a resolution for Albany. It was agreed to offer King's departure from Albany in exchange for a meeting. On August 8, the federal government further imposed itself into the situation. As the trial regarding the request for an injunction against protestors was underway, the Justice Department filed a brief in opposition to the city's injunction.

On August 10, King and Abernathy's trial for their most recent arrest began. After a swift hearing, they were pronounced guilty and sentenced to suspended sixty-day sentences and $200 fines. They were released from jail, and returned to Atlanta for a few days. While King was away, progress was stagnant. He returned only to find that when Marion Page requested clarification on the city's position at a city commission meeting held on August 14, his request failed to elicit any response. Sensing the end of the protest movement, Anderson made a difficult decision. Protest would cease as concentration was shifted to voter registration.

Failure in Albany

By all accounts, even among Albany's black community and leadership, the city commissioners had won. Chief Pritchett's likeability and sophisticated composure impressed the media. In addition, he had outsmarted the Albany Movement by using its own tactic of nonviolence against them. He had been able to successfully contain the movement by reacting without violence. Accordingly, the lack of police violence was a strategic move that limited the public outcry for justice.

HE SAID...

" There were weaknesses in Albany, and a share of the responsibility belongs to each of us who participated. There is no tactical theory so neat that a revolutionary struggle for a share of power can be won merely by pressing a row of buttons. Human beings with all their faults and strengths constitute the mechanism of a social movement. "

In a *New York Times* article, the reasons for failure in Albany were summed up. First, Chief Pritchett was smart, and he had enough jail space to house all of the protestors by sending them to nearby jails. Second, Pritchett took advantage of the rivalry between the SCLC, the NAACP, and the SNCC. In addition, he received help from local blacks who were opposed to the movement and was able to gain information about the future plans of the movement from these blacks. Third, the black leadership had made tactical errors by failing to provide adequate leadership when King was in jail, and by increasing their demands when King arrived in December. Last, the *Times* article stated, Pritchett's ability to maintain order without violence prevented federal intervention.

King, however, believed that President Kennedy's failure to lend his moral support to the movement was the major factor that led to failure. King realized that as long as violence wasn't perpetrated against protestors, President Kennedy had little interest in intervening. Thus, according to King, it was the president's desire for law and order rather than justice that led to his actions and inactions. Ultimately, though, King perceived that his unplanned participation was the biggest error. King vowed that in the next campaign, he would learn from the mistakes of Albany.

Chapter 11

SUCCESS IN BIRMINGHAM

KING FELT THAT HE had learned from the Albany Movement. In Albany, he had made many mistakes, and he was determined not to repeat them. He approached the Birmingham campaign with a renewed vigor. He knew that the city's police commissioner, Bull Connor, could be either an ally or an enemy, depending on how he reacted to the protestors. King decided to take a chance on Birmingham; he desperately needed a win.

Segregation in Birmingham

After King's departure, Albany continued its protests, but the greatest success came with the registration of 1,200 voters by the end of September 1962. Registration of black voters resulted in enough votes to force a run-off election for a city commission seat between a black businessman and a white candidate. Within a year, segregation laws in Albany had been repealed. Nevertheless, while Albany experienced a hard-won victory, the greatest gain for King was learning from his failure there.

The Lessons of Albany

It was in January 1963 that King finally had a chance to reflect upon the failures of Albany. It was a series of tactical errors, he concluded. The Albany Movement had failed to focus on one form of segregation. By doing so, a win would have been more achievable and would have uplifted the community. Furthermore, King believed that the focus on negotiating with the commissioners was misplaced, especially since Albany blacks had limited political power. Instead, negotiations should have focused on the business owners who were already suffering economically from the boycott.

HE SAID...

*"*The mistake I made there was to protest against segregation generally rather than against a single and distinct facet of it. Our protest was so vague that we got nothing, and the people were left very depressed and in despair. It would have been much better to have concentrated upon integrating the buses or the lunch counters. One victory of this kind would have been symbolic, would have galvanized support and boosted morale. *"*

It was with these lessons that King considered the idea of going to Birmingham, Alabama. Fred Shuttlesworth, the leader of the

Alabama Christian Movement for Human Rights (ACMHR), had urged King to come. Shuttlesworth, while at the time no longer living in the city, remained preoccupied with the desegregation of Birmingham. His move from the city had been a hesitant one; he was influenced by the violence directed toward him and his family. His church, Bethel Baptist, was bombed three times from 1956 to 1963, and in September 1957 his family was attacked by a mob when he attempted to enroll his children at an all-white school.

The Strength and Weakness of Bull Connor

The leaders of the city supported the violence directed toward Shuttlesworth and other blacks in the community. One such supporter was Police Commissioner Eugene Connor, also known as Bull Connor. In May 1961, it was Connor who allowed the beating of the Freedom Riders when they were in Birmingham. Connor was so opposed to integration that when the desegregation of parks was ordered in January 1962, Connor and the other commissioners responded by closing them. Both whites and blacks feared him. He suppressed the slightest movement of any white toward desegregation and used violence against blacks who stepped out of line.

FACT

Bull Connor's Birmingham had earned a national reputation for its violent flare-ups against blacks. His allowance of the violence against the Freedom Riders contributed to the city's reputation as one of the south's biggest holdouts of deseg-regation. The city was often called Bombingham, or as one article labeled it, A City in Fear.

The SCLC was well aware that Birmingham's unwavering commitment to segregation could pose a threat to winning a victory. Bull Conner ruled the city with a heavy fist on the side of segregation. He had even successfully managed to keep the powerful labor unions from occupying the city, a clear testament to his strength and control. On the other hand, the SCLC determined that Bull Connor could be an asset to the campaign. Unlike Albany's Chief Pritchett, who used nonviolence as a tactic against them, Connor could easily be provoked to anger. If Connor reacted to nonviolent protest with violence, King anticipated that it would force President Kennedy to step in as he had done when violence erupted during the Freedom Rides. According to King, if a southern segregation stronghold like Birmingham could be broken, so could any southern city. This time, King was prepared for success, failure, or even death.

Project C: The Protest Campaign

King anticipated that this time the presence of the SCLC would go unchallenged. They already had the support of Shuttlesworth, the head of the ACMHR, and anticipated little interference from the SNCC, CORE, or the NAACP, who weren't conducting campaigns in Birmingham. The SCLC decided they would begin the campaign on March 14, following local elections on March 5.

Birmingham was controlled by three city commissioners and a mayor, but the election threatened to change this with the selection of a new mayor and the dissolution of the commission. Bull Connor dominated the current power structure, and was threatened with loss of power. Connor, along with more moderate candidates Tom King and Albert Boutwell, was running for mayor.

As campaign plans got underway, many of Birmingham's black and white leaders were anxious to end Connor's reign. They hoped that with the election of the favorite, Boutwell, discussions of desegregation could begin. Business owners were especially anxious, as they were suffering financially due to the boycott of their stores. They realized that with Connor in power, compromise in the form of desegregation would never be allowed. There had been a brief halt to the boycotts months before when King came to town for the SCLC annual convention. Prior to the convention, store owners and black leaders came to the agreement that if segregation signs were discarded and an agreement was made to engage in discussion, the protest would stop. After the end of the convention and the departure of King, Connor pressured the store owners into putting the signs back up. The boycott resumed.

Planning the Campaign

Meanwhile, the SCLC began laying out its plan. The SCLC and the ACHMR agreed to work together, and all decisions throughout the campaign would be made jointly. SCLC's goals for Birmingham were simple: They would focus on the desegregation of stores and the employment of black sales associates. From their experience in Albany, they learned that an important part of any agreement would encompass the dismissal of the charges against the protestors. Furthermore, they would seek the establishment of a biracial committee to negotiate desegregation. Finally, the city itself would need to make changes. Their demands to the city would encompass the reopening of recreational facilities and opportunities for black employment in city-government positions.

FACT

Fred Shuttlesworth organized the Alabama Christian Movement for Human Rights in 1956. The purpose of the organization was to promote direct action in Birmingham in an effort to end segregation.

The Birmingham campaign got off to a late start. The mayoral election ended in a run-off between Boutwell and Connor, and the final outcome was postponed until April 2. The SCLC decided to begin the campaign on April 3. This gave King more time to focus on other issues. His fourth child, Bernice Albertine, was born on March 27, and the always-pressing issue of securing capital for SCLC projects was intensified by the upcoming campaign. On March 31, King arrived at the New York apartment of black entertainer and active civil-rights supporter Harry Belafonte. Belafonte had arranged for King to address northern supporters regarding the Birmingham campaign. The evening was a success: King raised $475,000.

Beginning the Campaign

The April 2 election resulted in a victory for Boutwell. King arrived in Birmingham that evening. He spoke at a mass rally about the campaign, and seventy-five people volunteered to participate in the demonstration planned for the following day. On April 3, the demonstrators converged on downtown stores, and only a few were arrested. The campaign was off to a slow start. King, however, continued his effort at mass rallies to recruit demonstrators. For the following day's demonstration, even fewer volunteered. This time fifty protestors participated and ten were arrested. For the April 5 demonstration, Shuttlesworth only managed to rally thirty people to join him in the march to City Hall. The marchers were stopped before they reached their destination and were arrested.

Facing Resentment from the Community

With the support of Shuttlesworth and the ACHMR, King had anticipated the support of the black community. The turnout was disappointing and surprising. A combination of barriers worked against the campaign. First, Shuttlesworth's reputation in the black community was that he was an autocrat; he made all of the decisions without input from others. While his confidence was admired by the younger and less well-off blacks, middle-class blacks could hardly tolerate him. His courage was respected by all, but his inability to get along with others was a large part of the reason for the lack of support.

Shuttlesworth's style of leadership was not the only barrier. Some of Birmingham's more-conservative blacks viewed the election of Boutwell as promising. They believed that under the leadership of Boutwell, retail businesses would desegregate voluntarily. King doubted this, as Boutwell had voiced his plan to support the continuation of segregation during his campaign. Another glitch in the plan, in King's view, was the fact that Boutwell's mayoral term would begin after the Alabama Supreme Court resolved the issue of when Connor and the two other commissioners were required to step down. Connor vowed to remain in his powerful position until the court rendered a verdict. Thus, because of the lack of support for Shuttlesworth and the failure to gain substantial support from local blacks, success in Birmingham looked bleak.

THEY SAID...

" By that time it was clear to King that he had made several miscalculations about Birmingham. Despite public statements to the contrary, SCLC was finding it difficult to recruit the large number of potential demonstrators it had anticipated. The problem was rooted in Fred Shuttlesworth's controversial stature among Birmingham blacks.... "

—David J. Garrow, *Bearing the Cross*

MLK and Fifty Protestors Arrested

Despite the difficulty garnering community support, King remained determined in the effort. The rallies continued nightly, and King announced that he would soon subject himself to arrest. King believed that with the likelihood that Connor would eventually react to the protests with violence, headway could finally be made. King finally got what he hoped for when his brother, A.D. King, led a march on the fourth day of the campaign. Connor could withstand the temptation no longer. He arrested the protestors, which numbered less than thirty, as a group of onlookers observed. When a bystander provoked a police dog, the dog attacked the man. The press finally had a story.

The Movement Gains Momentum

Press coverage of the violence created excitement in the SCLC ranks—the movement appeared to be making gains. In addition to rallies, King held meetings with black pastors and business leaders with the intent of gaining their support. The prospect of success appeared to increase with the recent violent eruption, and King's meeting produced support from businessman A.G. Gatson, as well as the Baptist Ministers Conference.

King decided that he and Abernathy would march on April 12, Good Friday. A stumbling block, however, threatened to end the plan. A state circuit-court judge issued a temporary injunction barring protests. King was determined not to make the same mistake he had made in Albany, and decided to march in defiance of the order. His decision became more uncertain as he learned that almost all of SCLC's funds set aside for Birmingham were gone. Without money, the protestors, who had been promised that they would be bailed out within a week, would remain in jail.

An Act of Faith

On Friday morning at the Gatson Motel, King considered whether to march as planned or to leave in order to solicit more donations. Either way, the movement might come to an end. Without funds for bail, protestors would remain incarcerated, but leaving could halt the movement. King turned to movement insiders for help with the decision. After debating the best course of action, King turned to prayer. Within thirty minutes, he made a decision. In an act of faith, he decided to disobey the injunction.

King recruited his good friend Abernathy to lead the march with him. The two leaders, along with fifty others, began the march on the afternoon of Good Friday. Just blocks into the protest to City Hall, Connor and the police awaited their arrival. They were quickly arrested, an event caught on film by the press. King was separated from Abernathy and placed in solitary confinement.

Spending Time Behind Bars

The police were intent on thwarting any effort at communicating with King. When a request was made by King's attorney to see him Friday night, he was told that he could only visit King with a guard present. By Saturday, King was permitted to meet with attorneys, but it was unclear what further access was allowed. The SCLC's Wyatt Walker urged Coretta to speak to the president about the issue. A hesitant Coretta finally agreed, and spoke to the president's press secretary. Robert Kennedy responded to Coretta's call with the assurance that he would investigate the matter. Monday, Coretta received a call from President Kennedy informing her that King was fine, and that he had arranged for her to speak with him. When King called Coretta, he was pleased to hear that Kennedy had responded.

Letter from Birmingham Jail

The protest in Birmingham had come under increasingly negative scrutiny from white ministers. Together, they issued a letter in the April 12 edition of the *Birmingham News* criticizing the movement. King's old friend, Billy Graham, had even joined in the criticism when, during his Easter Sunday service, he urged the protestors to stop their campaign. While King was in jail, he decided to respond to the criticism. On a daily basis, his handwritten response was smuggled out by his attorney and given to Walker. The letter, however, was not published until mid-May, near the end of the Birmingham campaign.

King's letter set out to explain to the local white ministers why the movement in Birmingham was necessary. According to King, it was not a hasty move, but rather a well-planned direct-action movement that used economic pressure on store owners who fell back on their promises to remove segregation signs. Furthermore, negotiation was the desired result; however, since the other parties wouldn't agree to negotiate, nonviolent direct action served as a means of creating tension, thereby eliciting a response that would eventually lead to negotiation.

To the ministers' assertion that the movement was untimely, King responded that a privileged group never willingly gave up their privileged position. In his experience, those who have not suffered can easily insist on patience. On the other hand, the violence against blacks and the despair suffered by the children who feel inferior create an urgency that can't be avoided. King continued with a stinging indictment about moderate whites, such as the ministers. In his view, these moderates impeded progress more than the KKK. Their devotion to order rather than justice was a reflection of their preference for a false peace.

HE SAID...

" Actually, we who engage in nonviolent direct action are not the creators of tension....We bring it out in the open, where it can be seen and dealt with. Like a boil that can never be cured as long as it is covered up but must be opened with all its ugliness to the natural medicines of air and light, injustice must be exposed.... "

King called for understanding of the oppressed blacks' desire to seek justice through demonstrations, prayer pilgrimages, sit-ins, and Freedom Rides. It was the pent-up frustrations and desire for freedom that created the urgency in blacks to respond, he argued. While a growing movement of blacks encouraged violent response to injustice, King reiterated his support of nonviolent action. However, in his opinion, he was unfairly called an extremist. Nevertheless, he embraced this categorization as one that put him in the company of Abraham Lincoln, Paul, Martin Luther, and John Bunyan. Most important was that he be viewed an extremist for justice rather than an extremist for injustice.

Finally, King expressed his disappointment with the white church. He was dumbfounded that white churches failed to stand behind the cause of justice. Instead, alleged King, they stood quietly on the sideline as injustice was inflicted on blacks. It was baffling and disappointing that white religious leaders were content with accepting the status quo. Even more disconcerting was their praise of the Birmingham police's handling of the demonstrations. King's letter, written before the police violence against demonstrators, acknowledged the lack of violence, but made it clear that behind closed doors blacks were treated inhumanely in jail. Most shocking to King, however, was the white ministers' support of the use of non-violence in order to preserve the immoral goal of segregation. King concluded that while the participants in the Civil Rights movement may remain unrecognized now, America would eventually recognize the real heroes.

Police Violence

As King sat in jail, protests continued. King's brother, A.D. King, led a group of twenty-nine marchers from the Sixteenth Street Baptist Church to the jail. They were stopped before they could reach the jail, and arrested. As the arrests were being made, a group of onlookers began throwing rocks at the police. The police response to the aggression of the bystanders was to begin hitting them with clubs. The violent incident between bystanders and police was captured by the media, and the pictures were publicized throughout the nation.

Release from Jail

Luckily for A.D. and the other arrested protestors, Belafonte had managed to raise more money for bail. With this news, King decided that he would pay his bail on April 20. Two days later, King's trial began. On April 26, he was found guilty of violating the restraining order. He was sentenced to five days in jail and a $50 fine. While King appealed, the sentence was deferred.

A Controversial Decision

King's conviction did little to inspire the black community. The nightly rallies were slowly declining in participants. Without protestors, King knew that the movement in Birmingham would come to an unsuccessful end. Two eager young civil-rights activists had come

149

to Birmingham to assist. The SCLC's James Bevel and CORE's Isaac Reynolds believed that there was an obvious remedy to the situation. Most of their time had focused on training black high school students in the method of nonviolent resistance. The response had been substantial, and they proposed to King that protestors could be drawn from this group.

THEY SAID...

" Having submitted his prestige and his body to jail, and having hurled his innermost passions against the aloof respectability of white American clergymen, all without noticeable effect, King committed his cause to the witness of schoolchildren. *"*

—Taylor Branch, *Parting the Waters*

King was skeptical about the idea, but at the same time, he was concerned with the dwindling press coverage. He had always maintained that change would only come if the moral conscience of Americans was ignited. To do this, the press was needed to capture any violent outbursts by the police. King, while under pressure from older blacks in the community to leave the high school students out of the campaign, decided to extend an invitation to the students for the gathering on May 2 at the Sixteenth Street Baptist Church.

The Demonstrations Make Headlines

By noon on May 2, the church was full of anxious high school students. As Bevel had predicted, the turnout was impressive. Bevel and Wyatt Walker took command of the demonstration, sending a group of students toward City Hall. As they emerged from the church singing and clapping, they were quickly arrested. Two more groups were sent out of the church, and they too were arrested. By 4:00 p.m., 600 students had been arrested.

FACT
Leaflets instructing the students to meet at the Sixteenth Street Baptist Church at noon had been distributed throughout Birmingham's high schools. Bull Connor was aware of the planned walkout by the students, and he instructed the school superintendent to expel all students who participated.

Not even the mass demonstration by the teenagers could elicit negotiations with Birmingham's white leadership. The following day, another mass of students demonstrated. This time, 1,000 emerged from the Sixteenth Street Baptist Church. Connor was intent on impeding their progress. He set up a blockade that included buses, police cars, K-9 units, and fire engines. With black onlookers watching the event from the nearby Kelly Ingram Park, Connor gave a warning to the students. When they refused to obey, fire hoses equipped with fogging nuzzles sprayed them. They continued marching, and were sprayed with high-pressured water hoses. As demonstrators were arrested, Connor released the K-9 units. Three teenagers were bitten by the dogs, their injuries requiring hospital treatment. Within an hour, protestors had dispersed.

The Associated Press caught the grizzly scene of fire-hosed students and dog attacks on camera. One notable shot was of a man trying to fight off a dog as it attempted to bite him in the stomach, while a police officer looked on. The photos appeared on the front page of newspapers around the world. The images were so disturbing that President Kennedy, as King had predicted, was ready to intervene. He sent Burke Marshall to Birmingham along with Joseph Dolan, the Assistant Deputy Attorney General.

King announced that the following day, Saturday, May 4, more demonstrations would begin. Connor, determined not to repeat the previous day's violence, immediately trapped Saturday's protestors inside the church. Connor's attention then moved from the church to the black onlookers in Kelly Ingram Park who openly goaded the police. Unable to control his temper, the response, like the day before, was to quiet them with fire hoses. As many fled the park, Bevel was able to restrain the angry crowd, but not before the press photographed the violent images. Again, the nation received a photographic report on the violent tactics of the Birmingham police.

Winning Birmingham

By the time of the Saturday demonstrations, Marshall and Dolan had reached Birmingham and quickly entered into talks with the white business owners. After a brief discussion, they convened until Sunday. Meanwhile, King was back in Atlanta for the day, and the white business owners began to feel pressured to end the violence in the city. They agreed to meet with the black leadership that evening. The demands, which remained the same, were presented to the business owners. They asserted that some store owners had made progress toward promoting black employees and removing segregation signs, but refused to consider the creation of a biracial committee or the dismissal of the charges against the demonstrators, claiming they had no power over those matters.

When King returned on Monday, he was informed of the discussions by Marshall. King was disappointed, and announced that another demonstration would take place. That afternoon, as Connor and his officers looked on without using the hoses, 1,000 protestors marched toward Kelly Ingram Park where they were arrested. The jails were full by this time, so they were put in an uncovered outdoor space.

Monday night, the two sides met again. Whites agreed to promote some black employees to sales positions, but wavered over desegregating lunch counters. Without a resolution, a Tuesday march was planned. This time, Tuesday's protestors marched in various groups. Six hundred demonstrators marched toward downtown. None were arrested, and they successfully made it to the downtown business district. Later that afternoon, other demonstrators were not so lucky. Bystanders began throwing bricks and rocks at the police, which led to the use of fire hoses on the demonstrators. Fred Shuttlesworth was part of the demonstration and was hit by the strong current of a water hose. He was taken to the hospital as a result.

Disunity Within the Campaign

As Shuttlesworth recovered in the hospital, intense negotiations continued late into the night. Progress was made on the agreement to desegregate stores when Boutwell became mayor, the employment of blacks, and the establishment of a biracial committee. The issue at large was the dismissal of the charges against the protestors. Wednesday morning, King proposed that the demonstrations be temporarily halted, due to the positive results of the negotiation. When Shuttlesworth was released from the hospital and heard about the suspension, he erupted in anger when he met with King. According to Shuttlesworth, King's failure to confer with him was evidence that King had disregarded his opinion, and that he clearly thought that he was "mister big." King tried, with no success, to settle Shuttlesworth down.

Hours later, King was in for another surprise. A judge had ruled that King and Abernathy needed to pay $2,500 in appeal bonds or go to jail. They refused to pay, and were taken to jail. Shuttlesworth, having heard this latest news, decided to lead a demonstration. But before he could begin the protest, he was convinced to speak to Robert Kennedy. Kennedy assured him that an agreement was imminent, and that he should postpone the protest. King and Abernathy were quickly released from jail when A.G. Gatson paid their bonds.

The Birmingham Truce Agreement

King and Shuttlesworth mended their relationship. At a press conference that night, King announced that protests would resume upon the failure to reach an agreement by 11:00 a.m. May 9. By 11:00 a.m. the next morning negotiations continued without a final agreement. King announced that demonstrations would remain halted as long as negotiations continued. The issue holding up a settlement was the need for bail money for the protestors who remained in jail. The white business leaders refused to pay the bail. Gatson was willing to pay some, but more money was needed. Marshall, however, found a way to secure the necessary funds—several labor organizations agreed to fund the bail.

THEY SAID...

" I remember an all-night session in which there was disagreement...between Martin King and Fred Shuttlesworth about whether or not to accept the propositions that were then on the table from the white businessmen. It was a moment of difficulty and drama, but in the end, Dr. King exhibited enormous patience and enormous prudence... *"*

—Burke Marshall, *Voices of Freedom*

On May 10, the agreement was announced to the press by Shuttlesworth, with King, Abernathy, and Walker standing by. The terms of the agreement stated that within thirty days of the implementation of Boutwell's administration, restrooms and drinking fountains would be desegregated, within sixty days lunch counter desegregation would occur, and within fifteen days from the termination of demonstrations a biracial committee would be established.

Community Upheaval

One day after the successful agreement was announced, the home of A.D. King was bombed just before midnight. Neither A.D. nor his family was injured. Shortly thereafter, another bomb detonated near the window of King's room at the Gatson Motel. Luckily, King had already left for Atlanta. Suspiciously, the Alabama state troopers assigned to guard the motel had mysteriously disappeared prior to the bombing, returning after it detonated. An angry group of black bystanders responded with violence. They threw bricks at the officers and set a car on fire. The officers attempted to control the crowd by hitting them with their clubs. News of the violent riot had reached newsstands by early morning.

King returned to Birmingham. As he worked his way throughout the black community seeking their resolve to end the violence, President Kennedy federalized the Alabama National Guard, just in case their services were needed. Within a day, the violence quieted and King left. Weeks later, King's return was necessary. He returned on May 20 to discuss the latest crisis involving 1,100 high school students who were expelled for missing school due to their participation in the demonstrations. Local leaders were ready to boycott all white businesses, but King recommended that they pursue a legal strategy instead. After calling off the boycott, they filed a motion with the Fifth Circuit Court of Appeals seeking an order to reinstate the students. With Judge Tuttle presiding, the order was granted less than two days later.

Despite the initial glitches during the Birmingham campaign, the mistakes made in Albany hadn't been repeated, and King had launched his first successful campaign since Montgomery. While he enjoyed the victory, he remained disappointed at Kennedy's continued failure to provide the country with moral leadership. King, now more than ever, was determined that the next campaign should focus on increasing the pressure on Kennedy to publicly support civil-rights issues.

Chapter 12

THE MARCH ON WASHINGTON

TODAY, MARTIN LUTHER KING'S "I Have a Dream" speech still resonates in the American memory. It was at the 1963 March on Washington that King's poetic discourse stirred the conscience of Americans. The speech, which was nearly perfect in tone and substance, was televised to the nation by the major networks. The nation not only heard King's call for equality, they saw that among the marchers, whites had also gathered to support the cause of equality. With civil-rights legislation pending, it was only a matter of time before gains were recognized throughout the nation.

A Protest for Jobs and Freedom

The success of the Birmingham campaign was inspiring for King—he had achieved a difficult victory. Birmingham had renewed nationwide interest in the civil-rights campaign. This was especially evident in the increase of donations to the SCLC. King felt quite certain that with national attention on civil-rights issues, Kennedy would feel the pressure to act. King believed his victory moved him one step closer to winning the president's support for the ban on all segregation. On May 30, he sent a telegram to President Kennedy with a request for a meeting. To King's dismay, he was informed that Kennedy was unavailable.

Kennedy's interest would have to be sparked through a dramatic demonstration, concluded King. The idea of a March on Washington was discussed among SCLC staff, and the plan for a two-day demonstration in Washington had also been circulating in A. Philip Randolph's inner circle. Randolph's idea had actually come twenty years earlier, when he threatened President Franklin D. Roosevelt with a march on Washington if he failed to address the issue of federal employment discrimination in the defense industry. Roosevelt responded with the creation of the Fair Employment Practice Committee, thereby halting Randolph's march.

The goal of Randolph's demonstration was to bring attention to the economic inequality plaguing blacks. Randolph had laid out his idea to the NAACP and the SCLC during the Birmingham campaign, but received little response. The NAACP was unconvinced of the potential accomplishments such a march could garner, and King and the SCLC were busy in Birmingham. Now that the Birmingham campaign was over, King was ready. An excited Randolph quickly began planning the march.

King went to work informing the press of the plans. In early June, King told the *New York Times* that if the President failed to publicly support desegregation, then an interracial mass march on Washington would take place. This announcement, though it should have come as a surprise to the Kennedy administration, did not. King's friendship with former communist Stanley Levison had sparked the interest of the government. Fearful that America's civil-rights leader was consorting with the wrong people, the FBI placed a wiretap on Levison's phone. Shortly after King's May 30 telegram to the President, the FBI recorded a call between King and Levison discussing whether to support Randolph's idea of a Washington march. The President was quickly informed of the plan.

FACT
A. Philip Randolph had committed his life to uplifting the black working class. Since blacks were barred from most labor unions, in 1925, Randolph founded the Brotherhood of Sleeping Car Porters and was eventually able to successfully secure a railroad contract with the Pullman Company.

Kennedy soon began to feel the pressure to create civil-rights legislation. On June 1, Robert Kennedy met with advisors to discuss ways to attack segregation laws. Robert Kennedy advised the president to support the desegregation of all public facilities, and the president agreed. On June 11, the President's newfound dedication to equality was publicly proclaimed as he spoke after the day's troubling events in Alabama. When two black students attempted to register at the University of Alabama, Governor Wallace blocked their entrance to the building. The President was forced to order the Alabama National Guard to escort the students to the administration building. That night, the President made a shocking endorsement: He announced his support for the end of segregation and racism. An immensely satisfied King suggested that now that they had the president's support, the demonstration should focus its attention on gaining the support of Congress.

Organizing the March

With the SCLC, CORE, and SNCC all supporting the march, planning began. The NAACP wasn't yet on board with the plan, but Roy Wilkins did attend the planning meeting in late June. The meeting went over important issues such as financing the march and the potential date, and it was decided that each organization would have one representative directly involved in making the decisions.

Accusations of Communists Within the SCLC

Meanwhile, the President submitted a civil-rights bill to Congress. He was hopeful of its passage; his mood changed, however, when he heard a press statement regarding the planned March on Washington. Dismayed by the news, President Kennedy immediately scheduled a meeting with King and other black leaders. The meeting began with Kennedy's strong caution to abandon their plans. He asserted that this move could jeopardize the passage of his civil-rights bill, and pleaded with them to wait. King explained the necessity of the march; that it was important for the American people to understand the civil-rights issues that plagued the black community. The meeting ended with both sides refusing to budge on the issue.

President Kennedy had another issue he wanted to discuss with King privately. He took King aside and made one more request of him, a personal one. Kennedy urged King to fire Jack O'Dell, the head of the SCLC office in New York. He also strongly suggested that he sever his ties with Stanley Levison. Kennedy stressed that they were both known communists by the FBI and that King's association with them could hurt the movement and even the passage of the civil-rights bill. King asked for proof of these allegations, but Kennedy declined to provide any.

By this time, King and Levison had developed a close relationship, and the idea of terminating the friendship was less than appealing. King decided to ignore the president's warning, and plans for the march proceeded. NAACP's Wilkins finally gave his support to the march. The group discussed the purpose of the march as a tool to petition Congress to pass Kennedy's civil-rights bill, but the focus would also include bringing attention to the growing problem of black unemployment. The African American unemployment rate had skyrocketed to twice that of white unemployment. Also on the list were the demands for a $2 per hour minimum wage, an end to employment discrimination, a federal works program, and the ongoing fight for the desegregation of schools. With the demands decided on, August 28 was chosen for the March on Washington for Jobs and Freedom.

THEY SAID...

" King was concerned that the administration took the problem so seriously as to have the president convey a personal warning, but he was no more moved to sever his ties with Levison or O'Dell by Kennedy's admonition than he had been by the half-dozen cautionary notes sounded by Robert Kennedy, Burke Marshall, Harris Wofford, and John Seigenthaler. *"*

—David J. Garrow, *Bearing the Cross*

In the meantime, pressure was mounting on King to address the issue of O'Dell and Levison. On June 30, the *Birmingham News*, based on leaks from the FBI, published a story claiming that the SCLC's O'Dell was a communist. King reluctantly asked O'Dell to resign, due to the unfounded, but potentially damaging, effects of the allegations to the SCLC. The movement, according to King, was foremost. Levison sensed that an attack on him by the FBI was next. He urged King to sever ties with him as well. King was adamantly opposed to the idea, but Levison finally convinced King that they should end all direct contact, but continue to communicate secretly through a trusted intermediary. King, although unhappy, agreed to the arrangement.

Opposition to the March

With the threat to the movement eliminated, the planning for the March on Washington proceeded. Randolph was selected as director and Rustin served as his deputy. A budget of $65,000 was established and King, Randolph, John Lewis of the SNCC, James Farmer of CORE, Roy Wilkins, and the Urban League's Whitney Young all served as cochairmen. By late July, the board came under the leadership of a biracial committee. The addition to the board included UAW President Walter Reuther, Protestant Reverend Eugene Carson Blake, Rabbi Joachim Prinz, and Mathew Ahmann, a Catholic.

Martin Luther King and Mathew Ahmann in a crowd.

At first, the planned March on Washington produced some skepticism. It came from black leaders such as J.H. Jackson of the National Baptist Convention and James Meredith. While this was disheartening, it was not crippling to the march. A vote against the march by the president would lessen the strength of their appeal to Congress. The board had another issue to tackle. The D.C. police and the Kennedy administration had become increasingly concerned that violence was a likely prospect at the march. In response to that concern, the city began to prepare for the possibility. The sale of liquor was prohibited, store owners prepared for the worst by removing merchandise from their stores, hospitals were put on notice to have staff available, and 4,000 troops stood ready to intervene.

FACT
This was the first time in three years that Rustin and King had worked together. Their relationship ended after Adam Clayton Powell threatened to release a story that King and Rustin were lovers if King failed to remove Rustin from the SCLC's New York office. Randolph encouraged King to remain strong under the pressure, especially since it was untrue. Rustin, however, knew that King was worried, so he resigned.

King gave the Kennedy administration assurance that it was a peaceful march to the Lincoln Memorial, not involving any form of civil disobedience. King emphasized the goals of the march. It was a march in support of the civil-rights bill, was meant to bring attention to the economic concerns affecting blacks, and King stressed that he hoped the result of the march would lead to a heightened moral conscience among Americans. On July 17, the president finally publicly announced his support for the march.

Rustin had concerns of his own. His fear, however, stemmed from concern about the potential attacks on marchers. The Civil Rights movement thus far had often led to violent altercations with white segregationists when blacks demonstrated. Two thousand buses were scheduled to bring marchers to Washington, and he was fearful that like the attacks on the Freedom Riders in 1961, the demonstrators on the buses could face violent hostility. Beyond safety issues, he had practical concerns as well. There was food to prepare, toilets to bring in, temporary drinking fountains to install, and first-aid facilities to equip. Organizing the speakers and performers was also a large task, and in the end he decided that each speaker would receive seven minutes.

Significance of the Lincoln Memorial
In 1922, the Lincoln Memorial was erected as a monument to honor President Abraham Lincoln. Though it was a monument to the

president who gave freedom to slaves, thus far it had represented little more than the continuing dream of equality for blacks. Even at the dedication ceremony, the inequity of blacks was evident by the segregated seating for blacks in the audience. One concession was made: African American leader Robert Russa Moton was the featured speaker.

One of the first events symbolizing protest at the Lincoln Memorial was the performance of singer Marian Anderson in 1939. Anderson was a well-known opera singer at the time, and had traveled the world performing. When Howard University requested the rental of Constitution Hall for Anderson's performance, their request was rebuffed. The denial attracted the attention of Secretary of the Interior Harold Ickes, who proceeded to plan Anderson's performance at the Memorial instead. On April 9, in front of an audience of 75,000, Anderson, with the statue of Abraham Lincoln behind her, performed on the steps of the Memorial.

FACT

Singer Marian Anderson had never intended her gift as a singer to affect anything other than the music industry. In fact, she was reluctant to become involved in racial issues. After her performance at the Lincoln Memorial, she again unwittingly furthered the cause of racial equality when, in 1955, she became the first black to perform at the Metropolitan Opera in New York.

Before long, marches and demonstrations at the Memorial became commonplace. In 1954, a celebration of the 91st anniversary of the Emancipation Proclamation was attended by 1,000 participants. Martin Luther King had even taken part in a demonstration at the Memorial. In May 1957 at the Prayer Pilgrimage for Freedom, in front of thousands, King gave his first national speech. One year later, 10,000 students demonstrated in the Youth March for Freedom. Now,

King again planned to use the Memorial's symbolism of freedom to draw attention to the continued denial of rights of the nation's black citizens.

The Participants

The day of the march, August 28, 1963, finally arrived. Busloads and trains full of people, white and black, arrived by the thousands at Union Station and the Baltimore tunnel. It was a unique arrival, one that was accompanied by the singing of freedom songs such as "We Shall Overcome." As the participants proceeded to the Washington Monument that morning, they were entertained by a variety of singers. Among the performers were singers Joan Baez, Odetta, Bob Dylan, the SNCC Freedom Singers, and Peter, Paul and Mary.

HE SAID...

" They came from almost every state in the union; they came in every form of transportation; they gave up from one to three days' financial sacrifice. They were good-humored and relaxed, yet disciplined and thoughtful. They applauded their leaders generously, but the leaders, in their hearts, applauded their audience. *"*

There were a few glitches along the way. First, it was originally planned for the leaders of the March to lead the procession of marchers to the Lincoln Memorial from Pennsylvania Avenue. By noon, however, thousands of marchers made their way toward the Memorial without the leaders. To proceed as planned, King and the leaders were forced to squeeze into the procession as photographs were taken of this historic march. More pressing, though, was the controversial text of the SNCC's John Lewis. Robert Kennedy and Archbishop Patrick O'Boyle, who was scheduled to give the opening invocation, had read the speech the day before and found its tone disheartening. It used controversial language about a revolution, a scorched earth, cheap political leaders, and racist judges. O'Boyle, upon reading the speech, threatened to walk out and take the other white religious leaders with him.

The leaders of the March on Washington marching from the Washington Monument to the Lincoln Memorial.

Just minutes before the commencement of the program, King, Rustin, Randolph, Lewis and Eisenhower's pastor, and civil-rights supporter Rev. Eugene Carson Blake, gathered in a small temporary room behind the statue and urged Lewis to accept the changes made to his speech. After a lengthy discussion, Lewis agreed, and a potential disaster was halted. The marchers sat surrounding the reflecting pool as the commotion over Lewis's speech was being ironed out. The three-hour rally began with O'Boyle's opening invocation, and included an unscheduled speech from Fred Shuttlesworth. Among the speakers were Lewis, who delivered his revised speech, Randolph, performances by Marian Anderson and Mahalia Jackson, and a speech from Rabbi Joachim Prinz. King, last to speak, was introduced by Randolph.

The Speech: "I Have a Dream"

While Lewis's speech caused grumbling over its content, King's, on the other hand, hadn't even been written before his late night arrival to Washington, D.C. on August 27. King, like the other speakers, was supposed to have his speech ready the day before the march so that the press could receive copies. Just like he had done many times before, King sat down that night and hammered out an outline, and then handwrote the speech late into the night. The speech was typed and given to the press the next morning.

By the time King took the podium, it was evident that there were a significant number of whites dispersed among the black majority. Among the crowd of 250,000, 25 percent were white. This was a pleasing vision to King, especially since the goal of the march was to appeal to the moral sense of white America. What better way to do this, then to show the nation that white supporters of civil rights had grown substantially in the past few years. In addition, this event, unlike many other black events, received press coverage. CBS had provided live coverage of the event, and when King began his speech, NBC and ABC interrupted their regular programming to cover the event.

King began his historic speech. Emancipation, according to King, had given blacks freedom, but after 100 years, discrimination and segregation prevented blacks from enjoying America's prosperity. King proceeded to direct his comments to white America. He reminded them of the Constitution's assertion that all men were entitled to life, liberty, and the pursuit of happiness. The time for change was now, he asserted. He stressed that the nation should take the demands for equality seriously. The Civil Rights movement was not a passing fad, but a battle that would endure until equality was achieved.

King then turned his attention to the blacks. He strongly urged that the crusade should remain pure and dignified. The emerging movement toward black militancy and violence were destructive means that would fail to produce the desired result. Not all whites, King emphasized, were untrustworthy. Many, especially the white participants at the march, were evidence of this fact. Suddenly, King decided to put his prepared text aside. He remembered a speech that he had given in Detroit, Michigan and many other times, and he decided to use it.

Martin Luther King delivering his famous "I Have a Dream" speech.

He proceeded to encourage blacks to remain steadfast in their fight until desegregation throughout the nation had occurred. Continuing his extemporaneous speech, King finally came to what is now the most recognized part. "I have a dream," he proclaimed. His dream included brotherhood, the hope that Mississippi would become a place where there was freedom and justice, that his own children would be judged by their character and not by their skin color, that in Alabama black and white boys and girls would no longer let racial segregation come between them, and that justice and equality would take place throughout the nation.

King ended the speech with the phrase "Let Freedom Ring." Just twenty-four years earlier, from the steps of the Lincoln Memorial, Marian Anderson recited that same phrase when she sang the song "My Country, 'Tis O Thee." Now King, after reciting the words to the song, used this phrase to dramatize the effects that freedom could have. For America to be great, proclaimed King, freedom was necessary. The powerful conclusion came with King's recitation of the phrase "Let Freedom ring…." Each time he recited this phrase, King named a state where freedom would come. His speech ended with the recitation of his belief that one day whites and blacks could come together and sing the Negro spiritual, "Free at last, free at last, thank God Almighty, we are free at last."

HE SAID...

" I have a dream that one day, even the state of Mississippi, a state sweltering with the heat of injustice, sweltering with the heat of oppression, will be transformed into an oasis of freedom and justice. I have a dream that my four little children will one day live in a nation where they will not be judged by the color of their skin but by the content of their character. I have a dream today. "

An aerial view of the crowd, the reflecting pool, and the Washington Monument.

The Nation Was Watching

After King's speech, Rustin announced the goals of the march, and the crowd verbally assented. Benjamin Mays ended the march with a benediction. The six black leaders, along with the four white leaders of the march, went to the White House to meet with President Kennedy. Kennedy was elated with the tone of the march, and was especially impressed with King's speech. The group of leaders ate and discussed with Kennedy the prospects of legislation addressing employment discrimination, since his current legislation failed to attack this issue. Kennedy, hopeful that his current bill would pass

169

Congress, stressed the importance of focusing on the present bill and of remaining optimistic about the bill's passage. After press photos, the group headed off to a television interview, where they reiterated the goals of the march.

The leaders of the March on Washington and President Kennedy meet after the demonstration. From left to right: Secretary of Labor Willard Wirtz, Mathew Ahmann, Martin Luther King Jr., John Lewis, Rabbi Joachim Prinz, Rev. Eugene Carson Blake, A. Philip Randolph, President Kennedy, Vice President Johnson, Walter Ruether, Whitney Young, Floyd McKissick.

The first mass African American event had been a success. Violence was nonexistent, the speeches were moderate, and the marchers had traveled from around the nation to participate. Rustin had successfully worked out every detail, including the clean-up crew that swept through the Monument grounds, leaving it just as it had been prior to the March. It was King's speech, however, that pushed him to the forefront of the movement. According to FBI Assistant Director William Sullivan, King was now "the most dangerous and effective Negro leader in the country."

Chapter 13
POLITICS

AS MARTIN LUTHER KING enjoyed the afterglow
of his speech at the March on Washington, he was
suddenly reminded of the reality of discrimination
when a bomb in Birmingham killed four girls. King
got back into action, and this time it was all about
politics. The civil-rights legislation still hadn't been
approved by Congress, President John F. Kennedy
was assassinated, and the presidential nomination
of Barry Goldwater seriously threatened to halt the
gains made toward equality.

Sixteenth Street Baptist Church Bombing

The elation over the success of the March on Washington suddenly came to an end when segregationists bombed the Sixteenth Street Baptist Church in Birmingham, Alabama on September 15, 1963. Four young girls were killed, and twenty people were injured. The Birmingham campaign had been a triumph until this point. It had been nearly four months since the Birmingham movement had concluded, and desegregation had begun. In mid-July, the negotiated changes finally came. A biracial committee was formed and met on July 16. Shortly thereafter, segregation laws were repealed.

THEY SAID...

*"*I was shocked by the bombing. It happened right after the March on Washington, which was such a great experience. It was a great moment of fulfillment, when Martin gave his 'I Have a Dream' speech, and we really felt the sense of progress, that people came together, black and white, even though the South was totally segregated. We felt that a sense of oneness.*"*

—Coretta Scott King, *Voices of Freedom*

Birmingham's black community was angered by the reversal of progress. Violence broke out: Police were assaulted with rocks and other debris; a black teenager was shot and killed; and scores of other people were injured. King returned to Birmingham the day of the church bombing. He found that the despair in the black community and the violent reaction was beyond his repair. Alabama's Governor Wallace failed to act. King determined that the only option was for the federal government to take control of the city. The following morning, King asked for a meeting with the president.

Requesting Support from the Federal Government

King delivered the eulogy for three of the slain girls on September 18. The following day, King, Abernathy, Shuttlesworth, A. G. Gatson, and other Birmingham leaders met with President Kennedy. King explained that Birmingham's black community was unstable and needed the protection of the federal government. King recommended that Kennedy send federal troops to protect blacks from state troopers. Kennedy responded warmly, but denied the request. Instead, he promised to send representatives to Birmingham as mediators. Further, he explained that he hoped to gain the support of the white Birmingham leadership during his meeting with them.

FACT

By 1968, the FBI discovered the identity of the men responsible for the bombing, but closed the case. It was reopened in 1971, 1988, and 1997, which eventually led to the prosecution of the suspects. By 2002, Robert Chambliss, Bobby Frank Cherry, and Thomas Blanton Jr. had all been sentenced to life in prison. Herman Frank Cash died before a case could be established against him.

Returning to Birmingham

King left the meeting hopeful, but was soon dismayed by the president's lack of action. By the end of September, King was certain that Birmingham required direct action. At the SCLC convention, he proposed that aggressive steps be taken to force the city government to address the chaos in the city. He decided that he would return for mass demonstrations and launch an economic boycott. King's plan was quickly put to a halt. Birmingham's local black leadership expressed their disfavor with the idea. According to A. G. Gatson and Arthur Shores, King's presence in Birmingham and all the press coverage that would follow was the last thing they wanted. Thus, help from King was no longer welcome.

King, however, was unprepared to give up Birmingham. He felt an obligation to see the negotiation to fruition. King hoped that the threat of protests would effect change. On October 7, to the dismay of local black leaders and the white community, King returned to Birmingham. His first demands were for the city to hire twenty-five black police officers and for a meeting between local black and white leadership to resolve the issue of current hiring practices. If the city failed to meet the demands, they would again face demonstrations. King's threat failed to move Mayor Boutwell or the city council to action.

The local white leadership was not alone in their lack of motivation to act. King tried to rally the community, and while he gained some approval for his plan, he failed to convince local black leaders to stand by him. Without their support, a dejected King left the city. By early November, King finally gave up on Birmingham. Danville, Virginia became King's next target.

The Assassination of John F. Kennedy

King arrived in Danville on November 15, only to find that a campaign needed to be planned elsewhere. Word of the proposed SCLC demonstration in Danville influenced the city's white leadership to negotiate with the black community. In a written agreement, city officials promised to enter into biracial talks and to invoke a nondiscriminatory hiring policy. As King contemplated a potential new campaign, while at home in Atlanta on November 22, he heard the news that President Kennedy had been assassinated.

King was saddened by the news of Kennedy's death. Kennedy, in his opinion, had come a long way in his stance on civil rights. Though for much of Kennedy's first few years in office he had done little for the movement, King felt that the president's civil-rights legislation, although lacking on some important issues, was finally a step closer to supporting the movement. King was also impressed with Kennedy's nationwide speech on June 11, 1963, in which he called for the end of racism and segregation. King believed that Kennedy was finally changing his position on civil rights.

HE SAID...

" Uniting his flair for leadership with a program of social progress, he was at his death undergoing a transformation from a hesitant leader with unsure goals to a strong figure with deeply appealing objectives. *"*

President Lyndon B. Johnson and Civil Rights

Vice President Lyndon B. Johnson stepped in as president after Kennedy was assassinated. Johnson had been a senator when the 1957 civil-rights bill was passed. He was instrumental in not only its passage, but also in the weakening of the bill. Although Johnson did vote for the bill, reassuringly for King, he refused to support the 1956 Southern Manifesto, which condemned the Supreme Court school desegregation decision. Nevertheless, King was still unsure of Johnson's standpoint on civil rights. His record as a senator failed to show his support for civil-rights issues and his advocacy of civil rights was nonexistent.

Martin Luther King Jr. pictured with President Lyndon Johnson, Whitney Young, and James Farmer at a meeting on January 18, 1964.

King and President
Johnson at a
later meeting on
March 18, 1966.

King also had other concerns. He continued to communicate
with Levison through an intermediary, and on one occasion met with
him personally in New York. The FBI had expanded the phone taps
to include Bayard Rustin and King's home and office. A news article
relayed that the new president might soon disclose information about
a black leader who was associated with an individual with ties to
the communists. King's concern regarding President Johnson's opinion on civil rights, and his continued communication with Levison,
was quickly put to rest. On November 27, Johnson announced that
in honor of President Kennedy, Congress should speedily pass the
civil-rights bill. A relieved King got back to work on planning the
1964 voter-registration drive. Within days, he was interrupted for a
December 3 meeting with Johnson. To King's relief, his contact with
Levison was not mentioned, and he emerged from the meeting with
a sense of contentment upon hearing that Johnson was committed
to the civil-rights legislation and supported voter registration.

Influencing the Passage of the Civil Rights Act

The meeting with President Johnson had a positive affect on King's
mood. He had an enjoyable Christmas at home with his family. After

the holiday, his busy schedule returned to normal. He was named *Time* magazine's "Man of the Year" for 1963; on January 18 he met with the president, whereupon he learned of his planned war on poverty; and his latest and third book, *Why We Can't Wait*, about the Birmingham campaign, continued to cause problems. Pressure was mounting from the publisher for the book's completion. The ghost writers had finished everything except the last chapter; King quickly dispensed with this problem by offering guidance on its completion.

He finally received some much-needed rest in February. He vacationed in Puerto Rico, and days later flew to Honolulu. February also produced results for the civil-rights legislation, which passed the house on February 10, 1964. This was not a surprise; the real test came when it made it to the Senate. King was quite aware that a filibuster could halt its passage.

Taking Protest to St. Augustine, Florida

With a filibuster looming, King determined that public pressure should be mounted on Congress to pass the bill. Associate James Bevel suggested going back to Birmingham, but the other members of the SCLC considered it unwise. Other places, such as Montgomery, Mobile, and Selma were also ruled out. St. Augustine, Florida, the town known as the "Nation's Oldest City," eventually received the attention of the SCLC. One good thing about St. Augustine was that it was familiar with and prepared for protest. The black community took up protest in the 1950s, and a rejuvenated attack on segregation was started when the city proclaimed that if granted, it planned to spend federal financial aid on its 1965 quadricentennial celebration.

Q: **What is a filibuster?**
A filibuster is a deliberate attempt by a legislator to delay the passage of legislation by giving a very long speech.

St. Augustine had a population of 25,000, out of which 25 percent were black. The city was also home to a strong local KKK group. St. Augustine had garnered some press coverage when a wave of violence erupted against demonstrators involved in protests during the summer of 1963. Three local blacks were beaten, a car and a home were set on fire, and a shotgun blast exploded through the front door of a home. Despite the chaos engulfing the community, the federal government declined to step in. Another rash of protests began in late March when demonstrators from the North arrived to support St. Augustine's black community. The demonstrators were arrested and released within a week. Community members, overwhelmed by the chaos, contacted the SCLC for help.

Meanwhile, King was plotting how he would respond to the likely filibuster of the civil-rights bill in the Senate. Upon the urging of SCLC's Wyatt Walker, King contemplated the idea of a fast, the same tactic that Gandhi used to effect change in India. News of the situation in St. Augustine reached King in early May. The fast was put on hold, and King determined that St. Augustine was the perfect place to launch the next campaign. The momentum of the March on Washington was declining, and a new civil-rights campaign was a good way to remind the public of the continuing inequality.

King Organizes the St. Augustine Campaign

King arrived in St. Augustine on May 18 for a mass meeting. He left, and returned in time to witness a successful evening march and rally on May 26. At the behest of Wyatt Walker, who joined King in St. Augustine, King initiated the new tactic of night marches. On May 27 and 28, as he traveled throughout the nation earning desperately needed funds for the SCLC, night marches began. When 200 marchers reached the old slave market downtown, they encountered a white mob of 250. Luckily, they received the protection of the police and the protestors remained safe. King's rented house, on the other hand, was shot full of bullets. In order to provide protection for the marchers, King requested federal intervention, but it was rebuffed.

On June 3, the marches were temporarily put on hold after the movement filed a petition seeking an order of protection and an investigation into police conduct. It was alleged and later confirmed that Sheriff L.O. Davis and the local Klan leader were close friends. As the judge reviewed the evidence, King set off again for speaking engagements. On June 9, the judge ruled that the police were required to protect the protestors.

Arrested in St. Augustine

King returned in time for the June 10 demonstration, only to find remnants of his house; it had been burned down. In obedience to the judge's order, that night, 200 officers protected the 400 marchers against the white mob of 600. The next day, King determined that despite the positive support the civil-rights bill was receiving in the Senate, it was time to draw more attention to the St. Augustine protests. King, now joined by Ralph Abernathy and several other associates, requested service at the segregated restaurant in the Monson Motor Lodge. The group remained in the Lodge until the police came and arrested them.

THEY SAID...

" Martin and I decided to take on the burden of the campaign ourselves by seeking arrest. It was easy enough in St. Augustine. All we had to do was go over to the Monson Motor Lodge, stroll into the dining room, and ask to be served. The proprietor told us blacks could not be served in his establishment and asked us to leave. We refused and he called the police. *"*

—Ralph Abernathy, *And the Walls Came Tumbling Down*

While in custody, King gave secret grand-jury testimony regarding the St. Augustine situation. On June 13, after King posted bond, he left for a new round of speaking engagements. In the meantime, the protests and arrests continued as the grand jury proceeded with its hearing. King was hopeful that the grand jury would recommend the establishment of a biracial committee. Hope was dashed by the unexpected act of seven protestors on June 18. Monson Motor Lodge was again the target of desegregation. A group of whites and blacks jumped into the outdoor segregated pool, and were arrested for trespassing. Prior to the incident, the grand jury was about to announce their recommendations. However, they reconvened and held hearings on the latest occurrence. Shortly thereafter, the grand jury emerged with their report. They recommended that King and the SCLC leave St. Augustine. After thirty days without protest, the grand jury would form a biracial committee.

King was disappointed with the thirty-day term of the report. He was even further dismayed when his offer to end marches for a week in return for the immediate formation of a biracial committee was rejected. Protests continued when a group of demonstrators entered a segregated beach and were attacked by an angry group of Klan members. That night, the Klan became even more active, when they staged their own event downtown, just in time to welcome 200 civil-rights demonstrators. It was a brutal meeting that resulted in a battle between highway patrolmen and the Klan. Most marchers were able to retreat safely, with injuries sustained by only nineteen.

King Leaves St. Augustine

The violence renewed the effort for the white and black leadership to come to a conclusion. The federal government still held off on sending help as King had previously requested. As King maintained hope of progress in St. Augustine, on June 20, the Senate passed the Civil Rights Act of 1964. Ten days later, Governor Bryant announced that a four-man biracial committee had been formed. As it would turn out, the committee never existed. It did, however, provide King with the exit he needed.

The crisis in St. Augustine ended just in time. King arrived in Washington for the July 2 signing of the bill into law by President Johnson. The bill prohibited segregation in public places, gave the federal government power to enforce school desegregation, and established a Commission on Equal Employment Opportunity. Although St. Augustine had ended badly, King's goal to influence the passage of the civil-rights legislation had been a success.

HE SAID...

" The Civil Rights Act of 1964 is important even beyond its far-reaching provisions. It is historic because its enhancement was generated by a massive coalition of white and Negro forces. Congress was aroused from a century of slumber to a legislative achievement of rare quality. *"*

Opposition to the Presidential Candidate Barry Goldwater

The civil-rights bill and the end to St. Augustine had coincided perfectly. Politics was still on King's mind and with the presidential election nearing, Barry Goldwater was quickly emerging as the front-runner for the Republican Party. When Kennedy ran for office nearly four years before, King had rejected the idea of giving his endorsement to a candidate. This time, he was having second thoughts on his policy of remaining nonpartisan. The election of Goldwater threatened to redact the recent momentous gains in civil-rights legislation. Goldwater, in King's opinion, was dangerous because he was one of the few Republican Senators to vote against the Civil Rights Act.

King decided to voice his opinion. At the Republican National Convention held in San Francisco on July 7, King spoke to the platform committee about his opposition to the nomination of Goldwater. He stressed that even with the recent passage of legislation, civil rights was an ongoing issue. He made several proposals that were of little interest to the Republicans, who nominated Goldwater as their presidential candidate on July 15.

Testimony Before the Democratic Convention

King had failed to make headway with the Republicans regarding his opposition to Goldwater, so he turned his attention and support to the Mississippi Freedom Democratic Party (MFDP). With the passage of the Civil Rights Act, desegregation was proceeding throughout Alabama; thus, a SCLC campaign was no longer urgent. Members of the MFDP and King set out for Mississippi on July 21. Threats on King's life reached a new height, and the FBI was sent to protect him. King, undeterred by the threats, took the MFDP's plan to seat its black delegation at the Democratic Convention on a door-to-door campaign.

FACT
The MFDP was organized in 1964 with the help of the SNCC. It was comprised mainly of black Mississippians. The goal of the organization was to challenge the seating of Mississippi's white delegation at the Democratic National Convention. For years, blacks had been excluded, thus their goal was to unseat the white delegates.

King was optimistic about gaining the support of the president for the MFDP's delegates. The president, however, had his own concerns. The election was nearing, and he feared that further demonstrations would move the election in favor of Goldwater. After he signed the Civil Rights Act into law, he requested that the black leaders impose a moratorium on demonstrations until after the election. Johnson, therefore, had little interest in supporting the seating of the black delegates. Such a move, he anticipated, could result in his loss of the presidency.

Without Johnson's support, the group carried on with their campaign. On August 22, King received the chance to speak to the Democratic National Convention on behalf of the MFDP in Atlantic City. King urged the credentials committee to seat the black delegates.

It was Fannie Lou Hamer, cofounder of the MFDP, who delivered the most powerful oration to the committee that day. At the nationally televised meeting, Hamer spoke of her own experience in the South working to register voters. In her chilling testimony, she recounted the brutality that she faced regularly working as a civil-rights activist.

Hamer's and King's testimonies led to a proposed deal, which was supported by Johnson. Two predetermined members of the MFDP, one black and one white, could cast votes as delegates, and the remainder of the group could attend the convention as guests.

The deal was less than what the MFDP had hoped for, but it was a step toward desegregating the democratic delegation. As the group weighed the pros and cons of accepting the deal, King remained quiet until his opinion was requested. He stated that he, too, wavered on a decision. On one hand, the deal would benefit his voter-registration efforts; on the other hand, if he were a black Mississippian, he would vote against the deal. King decided that he leaned more toward accepting the offer. Nevertheless, the MFDP voted against accepting the deal.

THEY SAID...

" Both King and Rustin preached practical politics. They talked about the 'big picture,' they explained that it was time now for the movement to begin shifting beyond protest and demonstration and climb into the arena of politics. And everyone needed to understand, they said, that there is no dishonor in compromise. *"*

—John Lewis, *Walking with the Wind: A Memoir of the Movement*

Winning the Nobel Peace Prize

With the finality of the MFDP's decision, King, Coretta, and Abernathy headed off to Europe in September. They traveled to Berlin, Rome, where he met with Pope Paul VI, to Madrid, and

London. He returned to his usual busy schedule in Atlanta. On October 13, the pressure of his leadership role finally caught up with him. He checked into an Atlanta hospital, where it was determined that he was suffering from a viral infection and was overweight. As King settled into the comfort of rest and relaxation at the hospital, Coretta called him the following day with the news that he had won the 1964 Nobel Peace Prize.

Martin Luther King and Coretta Scott King in 1964.

It was not a complete shock to King. Months before, requests were made for copies of his books and speeches. The news provided King with the fortitude he needed to continue his leadership. The combination of bad health and the stress of the movement had depleted his spirit; the news was perfect timing. King felt renewed in his commitment to the Civil Rights movement. Now with the international community behind him, the award served as a confirmation that he was doing the right thing in his fight for equality. King humbly proclaimed that the award was not for him; instead, he would accept it on behalf of the Civil Rights movement. More than just recognition, there was also a financial perk to winning the Nobel Peace prize. He was to receive $54,000, which he decided was for the movement.

HE SAID...

" But then I realized that this was no mere recognition of the contribution of one man on the state of history. It was a testimony to the magnificent drama of the Civil Rights movement and the thousands of actors who had played their roles extremely well. In truth, it is these 'noble' people who had won this Nobel Prize. *"*

Martin Luther King at a press conference on November 6, 1964.

On December 4, King flew to London prior to the December 10 award ceremony at Oslo University in Norway. What should have been an exciting time for King turned out to be a time of intense anxiety. In November, FBI director J. Edgar Hoover publicly called King the "most notorious liar in America." The FBI had continued its wire surveillance on King. Not only did the taps reveal that King still communicated with Stanley Levison, even more damaging information now threatened to end King's moral leadership of the movement. King's extramarital affairs had been captured by the FBI listening devices placed in his motel rooms, and Hoover was quick to spread the rumors to the press. By the time King left for Oslo, he was so overwhelmed by the potential publication of Hoover's allegations that he found it difficult to enjoy his accomplishment.

King put all of his worries aside. He had learned long ago to disguise his internal feelings. As he made the rounds, giving speeches and meeting people, he successfully masked his worry. By the time that he made his speech in Oslo, his nerves had quieted. He accepted the prize on behalf of the Civil Rights movement. The award moved King's concern beyond equality and into the realm of peace. During his acceptance speech, he spoke about the use of nonviolent resistance beyond the Civil Rights movement, and shared his long-term vision of world peace.

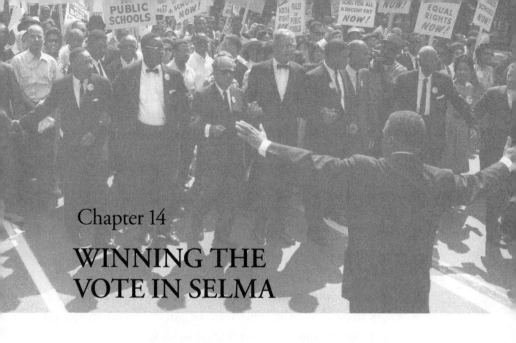

Chapter 14

WINNING THE VOTE IN SELMA

WINNING THE NOBEL PEACE Prize signified the emergence of King's opposition to all violence, including America's participation in the Vietnam War. For now, King continued to focus on the Civil Rights movement. World peace was a lingering thought, but more important to King was the continued threat of the disclosure of his extramarital affairs. In the New Year, despite his anxiety, his leadership would have to continue. This time, he would tackle the right to vote in Selma, Alabama.

Disenfranchisement of Selma's Blacks

The passage of the Civil Rights Act of 1964 was a victory for the movement. Nevertheless, it failed to incorporate strong protection for the right to vote. Discriminatory registration tactics continued against blacks throughout the South. Such methods included the use of literacy tests and poll taxes. It was common for whites who could barely read to pass the test, while educated blacks failed. Selma, Alabama was a southern city that excluded the majority of black residents from registering. Among the 29,000 residents in the city, 99 percent of its white population was registered to vote. The SNCC had been aware of the discrepancy in registered white and black voters in Selma, so in 1963 they began a campaign to end voter discrimination and to desegregate downtown.

HE SAID...

" When the Civil Rights Act of 1964 was passed, many decent Americans were lulled into complacency because they thought the day of difficult struggle was over. But apart from voting rights, merely to be a person in Selma was not easy. When reporters asked Sheriff Clark if a woman defendant was married, he replied, 'She's a nigger woman and she hasn't got a Miss or a Mrs. in front of her name.' "

King returned to the United States with voting rights on his mind. President Johnson, who had won the election, invited King to the White House. At their meeting, King immediately stressed the importance of a voting-rights bill. Johnson agreed, but explained that with the recent passage of the Civil Rights Act, it was too soon for more progressive legislation. King was undeterred by Johnson's response. A campaign in Alabama had been put on hold as a result of the movement in St. Augustine. Selma, determined King, would be the SCLC's next campaign. Just as he had used St. Augustine to provide momentum and pressure for the passage of the Civil Rights Act, Selma would place pressure on Johnson to sign voter protection into law. Despite the SNCC's presence, the SCLC would move ahead with its campaign in Selma, since the black community was both united and ready to challenge the status quo.

King's Personal Weakness Threatens the Movement

The SNCC, surprisingly, welcomed the help from their rival. The joint campaign was named "Project for Alabama—Political Freedom Movement." The first day of the project commenced on January 2, 1965 with a mass meeting. King left Selma with an optimistic outlook that success was possible. In addition, it appeared that the uniting of the two civil-rights organizations would give the campaign the strength it needed to effect change. To an innocent observer, it appeared that the SNCC and the SCLC had put their rivalry aside for the cause.

While Selma thus far was proceeding as planned, the threat of public exposure still loomed large in King's mind. Matters were made worse when Coretta notified him that she had received a suspicious tape and a letter. For over a month, it had sat at the SCLC office and she had just received the anonymous package. Believing that it was a copy of one of King's speeches, she opened it. After King listened to the tape and read the letter with associates, he knew that the sender was J. Edgar Hoover. The tape, while it failed to worry Coretta about her husband's faithfulness, contained explicit recordings of sexual activity. The letter, in addition to calling King a fraud, threatened to expose King and urged him to commit suicide.

King was now more on edge than ever. His worry turned into depression. King and his close associates were unsure how to proceed. At an early December 1964 meeting, King, Abernathy, Young, and Walter Fauntroy had ended the meeting with Hoover without a mutual agreement as to FBI surveillance. King and his associates had urged Hoover to stop his campaign against him, because it could result in harm to the Civil Rights movement. Hoover was undeterred by their arguments. Nevertheless, while another meeting seemed fruitless, Abernathy and Andrew Young met in Washington with FBI agent Cartha "Deke" DeLoach. They assured him that King was not a communist and spoke to him about the surveillance of King's private life. DeLoach denied the surveillance and said little. The meeting came to a disappointing end without an agreement with the FBI to discontinue their campaign against King.

THEY SAID...
" King was extremely vulnerable, and his heightened status as the moral symbol of the American civil rights struggle could vanish over night, Nobel Prize or not, if the FBI succeeded in getting its tawdry leaks into the press. *"*

—David J. Garrow, *Bearing the Cross*

Gaining Momentum in Selma
In spite of his depression, King's obligations to the movement were far more important. He returned to Selma on January 14. Four days later, Selma's demonstrations finally began. King and SNCC's John Lewis led a procession of 400 marchers to the courthouse to register voters. Sheriff James Clark instructed the applicants to wait in the alley for their turn to take the literacy test. As King waited with the marchers, American Nazi party members made their way through the crowded ally toward King. King, in search of publicity, hoped to elicit some type of response. He entered into a discussion with them, and extended an invitation for them to speak at the mass meeting that night.

King, Lewis, and the applicants left the courthouse without a single registrant. Next on the agenda was to test the desegregation of the Albert Hotel. King and a few of his staff entered the hotel and waited at the check-in desk. As he stood at the counter, he was completely unaware that James Robinson, one of the Nazi's he encountered at the courthouse, was lurking nearby. Robinson stepped forward and punched King two times in the face. Robinson was restrained by

John Lewis and arrested by the police. King revoked the invitation to the Nazi party to speak at the mass meeting.

FACT

John Lewis began his work with the SNCC during the Freedom Rides of 1961. In 1963, he became chairman of the organization. After the Civil Rights movement, Lewis went on to become an Atlanta City Council Member, and in 1981 he was elected to Congress.

Nationalizing the Movement

King, now a veteran at organizing campaigns, knew that to draw national attention to Selma and the voter rights issue, something drastic needed to occur. He was hopeful that like Birmingham's Bull Connor, Sheriff Clark would lose his temper. The following day, January 19, the marchers again arrived at the courthouse for registration. This time, Sheriff Clark erupted in anger when they failed to move into the alley quickly enough. Unable to control his temper, he grabbed Amelia Boyton and roughly pushed her to a police car. As King stood across the street observing, the press captured the scene. The day resulted in the arrest of sixty demonstrators. With the successful start, King left Selma for a round of speeches.

On January 20, while King was out of town, the registrants were sent to the courthouse in three groups. The first group, led by John Lewis, were greeted by Sheriff Clark when they arrived at the courthouse. He pointed to a door and instructed them to enter from that entrance. Lewis responded that they preferred to enter from the front door. Clark immediately arrested the marchers. The second batch of demonstrators also insisted on using the front door, and they too were arrested. When the third group arrived, Clark was clearly agitated. When they refused to move from the sidewalk, he arrested them also. By the end of the day, 226 protestors had been arrested.

King's return on January 22 was accompanied by two supportive events. First, more than 100 black teachers followed the lead of the demonstrators the days before when they marched to the court-house in protest of the unfair implementation of voter registration. The second positive reinforcement to the campaign occurred when U.S. District Judge Thomas granted the movement's request for a temporary restraining order barring the police from interfering with the registration of applicants.

The order did little to deter Sheriff Clark. On January 25, as King again stood across the street from the courthouse, he witnessed Sheriff Clark's violent response to the arrival of the marchers. After Clark pushed several marchers, fifty-three-year-old Annie Lee Cooper took matters into her own hands. As the media caught the latest scuf-fle, Cooper punched Clark in the head and was quickly restrained by officers. The press was ready when Clark approached the restrained Cooper and hit her on the head with his police club. The media atten-tion put Selma on the front page of newspapers around the nation.

King's Arrest

King left Selma, then returned in time for his leadership of the February 1 demonstration. King, Abernathy, and 260 marchers left the Brown Chapel for the courthouse. As was anticipated, they were swiftly arrested for the violation of parading without a permit. From jail, King continued to direct the movement. Among his lengthy list of instructions was a legal strategy. He instructed the SCLC leader-ship to seek an injunction against the continuing arrests and for more-relaxed voter-registration requirements. On February 4, Judge Thomas did just as King requested: His order instructed the regis-trars to loosen their standards on the test. Thomas ordered that the registrar was required to process at least 100 applications per day, that minor mistakes on the application should be ignored, and that demonstrators who peacefully provided support for applicants should not be arrested.

HE SAID...

// This was the U.S.A. in 1965. We were in jail simply because we could not tolerate these conditions for ourselves or our nation. There was a clear and urgent need for new and improved federal legislation and for expanded law enforcement measures to finally eliminate all barriers to the right to vote. //

With news of the judge's order, King was bailed out of jail the following day. It wasn't before he heard the pleasing news of President Johnson's support of voting rights. Just after Judge Thomas's order, Johnson publicly announced his support for the campaign in Selma. Coinciding with King's release was the publication in the *New York Times* of his "Letter from Martin Luther King Jr. from Selma, Alabama Jail." In the letter, King discussed the injustice experienced by Selma's blacks. He asked for the support of Americans and requested financial help.

Meeting with Vice President Humphrey

Johnson's support of the Selma campaign pleased King. He wanted to meet with him to discuss voting rights. A meeting was scheduled to take place with Vice President Humphrey and Attorney General Nicholas Katzenbach first, and then King would meet with the president for an unpublicized meeting. King left Selma February 9 for his afternoon meeting in Washington. At the White House, King expressed his dismay at the harassment and intimidation that many southern voters encountered when they attempted to vote or register to vote. He encouraged the drafting of cohesive legislation that would eliminate all of the tactics at preventing blacks from securing the right to vote. In King's secret meeting with the president, Johnson assured him that he was in favor of securing voting rights and that Congress would soon receive a proposal.

Bloody Sunday

While the support of the president lay with the movement, King knew that pressure for civil-rights legislation needed to continue. He returned to Selma, where things had only gotten worse. First, James Bevel was involved in an altercation with Sheriff Clark in which he was hit repeatedly by Clark when he refused to leave the courthouse. The second wave of violence occurred when Clark doled-out punishment to a group of 165 marchers.

King continued to split his time between the Selma campaign and his other obligations. He was overworked, and soon felt the consequences of his actions when his health began to seriously decline. His exhaustion was furthered by the emerging dissatisfaction the SNCC expressed about the SCLC's leadership. King maintained a schedule that incorporated rest along with his leadership of marches. In between bouts of recuperation, he led marches in Selma, as well as in the nearby towns of Perry and Camden. Sheriff Clark also struggled with exhaustion, but he recuperated in time for the march that would later become known as Bloody Sunday.

Planning the March to Montgomery

A 54-mile march from Selma to Montgomery was planned for March 7. King, although dejected and increasingly concerned about his safety, planned to lead the march. Malcolm X had been assassinated on February 21, and King had just been told by the attorney general of a failed assassination attempt that was planned for when he was in Marion, Alabama. The exhaustion, the constant traveling, and the steadily increasing threats on his life made the Selma march less-than-appealing. Nevertheless, with the good news of President Johnson's voting-rights bill, King knew that it was important to keep pressure on the passage of the bill.

As the SCLC planned the details of the march, the SNCC debated internally about whether they would endorse it officially. By now, their resentment of King's leadership role had reached a boiling point. It was decided that despite their animosity toward him, the group would not support the march, but members were free to participate as individuals. With the SNCC's issue solved, a new glitch in the plan emerged. The SCLC learned that in addition to Governor Wallace's order to stop the marchers before they reached Montgomery, he also ordered troopers to stop the procession by any means necessary. James Bevel and Hosea Williams immediately became concerned about King's safety, especially in the wake of the recent assassination plot. Upon Bevel's urging, King agreed to remain in Atlanta, where he could rally support for the cause.

THEY SAID...

" Martin had been receiving an excessive number of death threats as the result of the Selma campaign, perhaps more than at any other time in his career; and with negotiations in progress between our leader and the president of the United States, no one wanted to risk losing him. *"*

—Ralph Abernathy, *And the Walls Came Tumbling Down*

The Bloody March

When Sunday morning arrived, King was safe in Atlanta leading services at Ebenezer. Bevel and Williams were keenly aware of the dangers that lay ahead. They had scouted the area and found that Clark's officers waited along the path to the Edmund Pettus Bridge. On and across the bridge was another hurdle—state troopers awaited their arrival. As the more-than-500 demonstrators gathered for the march at Brown Chapel, doubts as to the wisdom of this increasingly dangerous march emerged. Williams and Bevel debated whether to go forward, and decided to seek King's advise. Through Abernathy, the details of the dilemma and the desire to continue were conveyed to King. King, although hesitant, agreed that the march should proceed as planned.

More than 500 marchers, with SNCC's John Lewis and SCLC's Hosea Williams in the lead, emerged from the chapel. They proceeded unimpeded toward the bridge. When the bridge was in sight, they could clearly see the armed white onlookers in front of the *Selma-Times Journal* building and the news media safely out of the way, but ready to capture the day's events. When they reached the crest of the bridge, they saw the Alabama state troopers, along with Sheriff Clark's officers, on foot and horseback extended across the bridge to Highway 80. Their procession was interrupted by the voice of Major John Cloud, who ordered them to leave the bridge. The marchers stood motionless. Within minutes, Cloud directed his men to remove the marchers by force. As the white onlookers cheered, the troopers and officers on horseback attacked the demonstrators with nightsticks and tear gas. The marchers, many of whom were injured, quickly scurried back to Brown Chapel with Clark's officers close behind, beating anyone within their reach. Seventy-eight demonstrators were injured.

FACT

According to Lewis, when they reached the crest of the bridge, he and Williams jokingly suggested that they jump into the river. They decided that they could neither turn back nor move forward, so they stopped. Within minutes, Lewis remembers being hit on the head and falling to the ground. As he struggled to stand, the tear gas caused him to choke as he attempted to breath.

Despite the cloud of tear gas, the media got the story. That evening, Sunday's afternoon massacre was televised throughout the nation. King also saw the televised reports. After communicating with the march leaders, he set out to garner support from around the country for a Tuesday march, while movement attorneys sought a court order prohibiting interference in the march. The news reports helped garner the support of Congress. As King had projected, voting rights for blacks suddenly became an urgent matter.

Leading the March to Edmund Pettus Bridge

The expected ruling from Federal District Judge Frank Johnson hadn't come by the time King reached Selma. To the dismay of King, Judge Johnson agreed to issue a ruling only after a complete hearing. Johnson threatened that if the Tuesday march proceeded as planned, he would issue an order prohibiting it. The SNCC wanted to march regardless of Judge Johnson's order. King was hesitant to call off the march, but he was also reluctant to disobey a federal court order. By the time of the mass meeting on Monday night, while he spoke to the crowd about Tuesday's march, he had tentatively decided to cancel it. Throughout the night, he was tormented by his decision, and by morning, he changed his mind.

Accepting a Controversial Alternative

President Johnson scrambled to get a handle on the situation before the violence of Bloody Sunday was repeated. He sent federal Community Relations Service Director LeRoy Collins to mediate the situation. Collins approached King with an idea. He proposed that if King would agree to only lead the marchers across the bridge to the troopers, and then lead them back to the chapel, he would approach Sheriff Clark with the arrangement. King agreed to consider it. When Collins told Sheriff Clark of the idea, he was hesitant at first, but then agreed that if the predetermined route he specified were followed, the officers and troopers would allow the procession to march onto the bridge, as long as they turned around and retreated.

 Q: Why was King hesitant to violate the court order when he had done so on previous occasions?

King made a clear distinction between federal courts and state courts. State-court judges were often biased on the side of segregationists. He stressed the importance of respecting federal courts because they had become an ally to the Civil Rights movement.

At 2:30 P.M., King led the group of 2,000 marchers, white and black, from Brown Chapel en route to Edmund Pettus Bridge. Collins caught up with him just in time. He gave King the hand-drawn map from Clark, and informed him that the marchers could proceed peacefully across the bridge as long as they followed the route and turned around when reaching the troopers. King promised nothing, but agreed to try. The procession of marchers walked the same path they had two days before. King led them across the bridge to within fifty feet of the troopers. He prayed first, and other preachers stepped forward and delivered their own prayers. The prayers ended with the singing of "We Shall Overcome." Then, King turned and led the marchers back across the bridge to Brown Chapel.

Collins and President Johnson were relieved. Back at the chapel, however, an angry group of SNCC members and Selma teenagers were unhappy with the shortened march. They were angry that King had led them across the bridge only to retreat. King explained that their retreat was necessary, since breaking through the troopers was impossible. King declined to tell them the real reason for the turnaround. However, the SNCC's suspicion that King had arranged a secret deal was confirmed by King's own testimony at Judge Johnson's March 11 hearing. Even more outraged at what they termed King's betrayal of the movement, they announced that they were moving their Atlanta SNCC headquarters to Montgomery.

President Johnson's Support of the Movement

President Johnson was motivated more than ever for the passage of voting-rights legislation. He invited Alabama's Governor Wallace to the White House, where he reprimanded him for his lack of understanding that blacks were being denied the fundamental right to vote. To speed up the process, Johnson met with Senate Majority and Minority leaders for a confirmation of their support for the bill. Finally, Johnson gave his public support to the right to vote. On March 15, he spoke to a televised joint session of Congress. He condemned the violence in Selma, the denial of voting rights to blacks, and emphasized that the willingness of blacks to risk their lives for equality had awakened the moral conscience of Americans. King was deeply moved by Johnson's speech, and was unable to stop the flow of tears.

THEY SAID...

" Then, Lyndon Johnson uttered the movement's slogan, vowing that 'we shall overcome....' Listening to the president's repeated invocation of that hallowed phrase as he watched in the Jacksons' living room, Martin King was overcome by emotion. His colleagues and friends had never seen him cry before. *"*

—David J. Garrow, *Bearing the Cross*

The Victorious March to Montgomery

On March 17, two days after President Johnson's speech, King experienced another victory. Judge Johnson ruled that the SCLC's march from Selma to Montgomery could proceed. The plan was for a procession of demonstrators to begin a five-day march to Montgomery on March 21. Despite President Johnson's recent scolding of Governor Wallace's actions in Selma, Wallace still resisted fulfilling his obligation to protect the marchers. He refused to give them the protection of the Alabama National Guard, claiming that the state could not financially afford the expense of the guardsmen. Johnson took matters into his own hands, and federalized 1,800 Alabama National Guards.

When the day for the march arrived, King led 3,000 marchers from Brown Chapel, across Edmund Pettus Bridge, and onto Highway 80, until they reached their campsite 7 miles from Selma. Three hundred marchers stayed at the campsite, while the rest returned to Selma. While receiving protection from guardsmen, they ate and slept in the tents. The second and third day, with a tired King in the lead, they traveled an additional 27 miles. On the fourth day, King left the march for a fundraising rally in Ohio.

HE SAID...

" Once more the method of nonviolent resistance was unsheathed from its scabbard and once again an entire community was mobilized to confront the adversary. And again the brutality of a dying order shrieks across the land. Yet, Selma, Alabama, became a shining moment in the conscience of man. *"*

He returned the following day to lead the procession. Twenty-five thousand protestors marched through Montgomery to the state capitol. From a platform on the steps of the state-capitol building, King spoke to the marchers about his growing concern for taking the movement beyond voting rights to segregation in housing and schools and to the war on poverty. For the emerging black militants, King had another message. He encouraged them to refrain from using violence or from protesting in a way that would humiliate whites. Instead, he stressed the need to win the friendship of white Americans.

Passage of the Voting Rights Act

On August 6, 1965, President Johnson signed the Voting Rights Act into law. The act prohibited the discriminatory practice of literacy tests nationwide. The prohibition of poll taxes was not included in the bill, but shortly after its passage, the federal government successfully challenged the use of them in *Harper v. Virginia State Board of Elections*. In addition, the legislation provided that in areas of the country where the tendency was toward discriminatory voting practices, all changes to voting requirements first had to receive the approval of the Attorney General.

Chapter 15

TAKING NONVIOLENT RESISTANCE TO CHICAGO

WITH THE PASSAGE OF the Voting Rights Act, King emerged from Selma with another victory. Now, his growing concern over the plight of poverty and discrimination of northern blacks would take center stage in his quest for equality. King returned to Atlanta tired, but motivated to move the fight beyond southern inequality. The ghetto of Chicago would be his testing ground for an attack on discrimination against blacks in the North.

Northern Ghettos

It was the segregation in the South and the availability of jobs in the North that influenced the influx of blacks migrating to northern cities. From 1940 to 1960, the northern black population increased from 4 million to 9 million. Yet, while Jim Crow laws were absent in the North, blacks experienced a new kind of segregation; they lived in segregated neighborhoods and in high-rent rundown tenements. The opportunity to live outside of black neighborhoods was virtually nonexistent. Those attempting to make the bold move into a white neighborhood often faced a violent response. Whites held firmly to their segregated residential communities, fearful that black residents would lower property values.

FACT

African American playwright Lorraine Hansberry grew up in Chicago during the migration of blacks to the city. She later recalled the memorable experience of her father moving her family into a white neighborhood when she was a small child. Although it later resulted in a legal victory, the family was subjected to violence and vandalism.

Blacks also experienced the disparaging economic conditions of being black in the North. Loans were not only difficult to obtain, but there were stricter guidelines for blacks. Employment opportunities were slim, and blacks, often lacking the latest in technical training, experienced an unemployment rate twice that of whites by the 1950s. Schools offered blacks even less, and overcrowding in black schools was rampant. To counteract the congestion, places like Boston and Chicago provided night schools for the black students who had been squeezed out of daytime classes. As was often the case, white schools could easily educate the excess black students, but prejudice and fear of disease and black delinquency motivated their inaction. The situation reached a heightened intensity when, in

1963 and 1964, boycotts of schools in the northern cities of Boston, New York, and Chicago were on the rise.

Choosing Chicago

King's interest in black poverty in the North motivated him to take nonviolent resistance north. With the passage of the Voting Rights Act, the problems in the South had finally received the federal attention that King had fought long and hard for. Now King sought equality for northern blacks who lived in slums, experienced economic inequality, and had little opportunity to raise their plight beyond the depth of poverty.

HE SAID...

" Selma, Alabama, had been our pilot city for the Voting Rights Bill of 1965, and I had faith that Chicago, considered one of the most segregated cities in the nation, could well become the metropolis where a meaningful nonviolent movement could arouse the conscience of this nation to deal realistically with the Northern ghetto. *"*

King turned his attention to several northern cities. He considered New York, but Congressman Adam Clayton Powell Jr. would likely resist the effort. Philadelphia also wasn't an option, since the SCLC rival, the NAACP, would certainly resent their presence. Chicago was also a consideration. King was familiar with Chicago due to his numerous fundraising trips there, and he had even led a Coordinating Council of Community Organizations–sponsored march there on July 26, 1965.

King had learned from Albany not to discount the power of support from the community, and Chicago appeared to be the ideal place to start the campaign to eliminate northern racial inequity. Chicago already had a well-established organization in the city which could work jointly with the SCLC. Because of the Coordinating

Council of Community Organizations's (CCCO) experience in lodging a campaign using nonviolent resistance, and King's belief that Mayor Richard Daley was a supporter of civil rights, King concluded that Chicago encompassed all that was needed for the SCLC's first northern campaign.

FACT

The CCCO was formed in 1963, when the Chicago community lodged a campaign against the unfair education system. It resulted in an October boycott by 225,000 black students who refused to attend school.

To launch a campaign, however, money was needed. The SCLC's funds had declined substantially from their spring project, Summer Community Organization and Political Education (SCOPE). The purpose of SCOPE was to recruit northern volunteers to come south for voter-registration drives. Donations resulting from Selma had provided $1.5 million, but little was left for Chicago. With the passage of the Voting Rights Act, Americans clearly felt less inclined to contribute, as the Civil Rights movement appeared to have ended.

Opposition to the Vietnam War

Furthermore, King, the SCLC's biggest fundraiser, did little to help their financial situation when he spoke out publicly against the Vietnam War. Initially, King's early opposition to the war went no further than discussions with his close associates. J. Edgar Hoover still held the tantalizing information that threatened to bring the movement to an end over King's head. Although King was concerned about the public exposure, after promptings from Bayard Rustin and Stanley Levison, he began to express his disagreement with the war more and more. In a July 2 speech, King bravely expressed his unpopular opinion about the war. He told the audience that a settlement should be negotiated to end the war.

King went even further with his comments about the war. In August 1965, he announced to the press that he intended to send letters to President Johnson, the governments of North and South Vietnam, the USSR, and China in an attempt to force negotiations. Johnson, a former ally, became increasingly frustrated with King's newfound passion. He sent an intermediary to persuade King to stay out of the war issue. King, however, remained unconvinced. That is, until he was informed that his letter-writing campaign could be construed as the criminal offense of attempting to influence U.S. foreign policy through negotiations with foreign powers. King reluctantly dropped the matter.

THEY SAID...

" He also felt that LBJ was fundamentally a decent president who really did want to use the power of the office and the federal government to address the serious social and economic problems of poor Americans. He felt, in this, the president was a potential ally who could be even better than FDR, except for his tragic weakness on the war. *"*

—Stokely Carmichael, *Ready for Revolution: The Life and Struggles of Stokely Carmichael*

Although King, like many antiwar advocates of the time, did feel the pressure to remain silent, he took a risk by furthering his campaign against the war. While he declined a full-fledged leadership role, the war did concern him when it led to budget cuts that affected poverty programs. King took the issue to the SCLC board members, who finally agreed to issue a statement against the war in April 1966. On prior occasions, the board had been opposed to a SCLC statement denouncing the war. Now, they stated in a declaration that U.S. involvement was immoral on two fronts. First, they opposed the government's assistance of the South Vietnamese military. Second, on the home front, resources needed to combat poverty were being siphoned away from poor Americans to the war effort. When the press received the resolution, the *New York Times* noted the unpopularity of this opinion. According to a recent opinion poll, they found that 41 percent of the respondents resolved that the more blacks spoke out against the war, the less they wanted to support the cause of civil rights. King was treading on thin ice when it came to public opinion about the war. Nevertheless, he was undeterred.

Organizing the Campaign

King announced the SCLC's Chicago campaign on September 1, 1965. Chicago was perfect for three reasons, King asserted. First, it was the second-largest northern city, and if it could be broken, then any northern city could be broken. The second reason was that Mayor Daley held the power, as opposed to cities like Albany, where commissions controlled the city. Third, he anticipated that the religious community was behind the movement. King, however, would soon find out that a win in Chicago was not as easy as it appeared.

Mobilizing the Community

The focus of the campaign in Chicago was narrowed down to the issues of integrating schools, employment, housing, poverty, and welfare. Just like in the South, King told reporters that the goals would be won through nonviolent action. He emphasized that since unjust laws in the North were less prevalent, the method of nonviolent resistance would be different. The goal was to bring the issues to the forefront, to bring awareness of the black ghetto, and to elicit a response. While the CCCO was well versed in nonviolent resistance, King's SCLC associates were unsure whether the black community understood the method. Despite this misgiving, they concluded the community would learn the technique.

Defining the Goals of the Campaign

As King traveled throughout the nation, financial concerns continued to plague the SCLC. A check for $190,000 was stolen by a field staffer, and Abernathy's relaxed style of controlling the budget had led the SCLC to spend more each day then it took in. While King worried about the finances, the organization of the project was placed on the shoulders of Reverend James Bevel. Bevel worked tirelessly on narrowing down the reasons the black ghetto continued to exist, and he began to mobilize the community. The organizers worked out of the Warren Avenue Congregational Church. They held community workshops on the method of nonviolent resistance, recruited gang members, and Jesse Jackson, a divinity student, led the effort to recruit black ministers.

FACT

James Bevel, a former SNCC member, was recruited by the SCLC to work as a field secretary during the Albany campaign. Bevel's out-of-the-ordinary attire of a Jewish yarmulke, and his equally peculiar habits, often clashed with SCLC's Executive Director, Wyatt Walker. Nevertheless, King found that he was an asset to the organization.

The Chicago project was planned to begin on January 6 and 7, 1966. King arrived in Chicago a day before the scheduled kickoff. The plans for the campaign were defined by Bevel in a thirteen-page text. The largest problem facing Chicago's blacks, wrote Bevel, was economic exploitation. Unlike the campaigns in Birmingham and Selma, where specific goals were formulated prior to the project, Chicago's goals were broad. When King was asked by reporters to define the objectives, his vague answers were an indication of the lack of direction. King also made the announcement that he planned to experience the ghetto firsthand by living in a rented west-side apartment with his family. His planned stay in the ghetto was intended to draw attention to the uninhabitable conditions of the slum, and as a result, energize rent strikes. He planned to live there for the three days out of the week he would be in Chicago.

Moving the Family to Chicago

King left Chicago for other obligations, as the CCCO and the SCLC struggled to establish the goals of the movement. King's departure left the task of renting the apartment to SCLC staff. A four-room apartment for $90 per month was secured for King's family. Located in the Lawndale ghetto, his apartment sat on the third floor of an old building. When the manager became aware of the intended occupant, the apartment was quickly made habitable.

HE SAID...

" During 1966 I lived and worked in Chicago. The Civil Rights movement had too often been middle-class oriented and had not moved to the grassroots levels of our communities. So I thought the great challenge facing the Civil Rights movement was to move into these areas to organize and gain identity with ghetto dwellers and young people in the ghetto. *"*

On January 26, King and Coretta returned to Chicago and moved into their Lawndale apartment. The children joined them a few months later. While the building manager may have perceived the apartment and building as fit for human habitation, Coretta disagreed. She was shocked by the condition of the building. She described the common dirt-floor hallways as harboring the stench of urine due to the homeless who regularly used the building as a toilet. Beyond the condition of the building, when the children arrived, they had little to do but play outside in an ally. Even King noticed that the heat and the small space which they all occupied increased the tension between family members.

The Chicago Freedom Movement

The lack of finances was a never-ending problem for the SCLC. The northern movement, and the ongoing small movements in the South, garnered less-than-adequate donations. King announced that a fundraising effort entitled the "Chicago Freedom Festival" was scheduled for March 12. Coinciding with this announcement, Mayor Daley had his own proclamation. On February 9, in an attempt to lessen the impact of King's Chicago campaign, Daley declared that he was on a mission to eliminate the city's slums by the end of 1967.

Gaining the Support of the Community

The Chicago project was moving at a slow pace. One program that was working, however, was Operation Breadbasket. Jesse Jackson, a participant in the Selma campaign, had used the program to market and gain the support of black ministers who were otherwise disinclined to support the movement. Operation Breadbasket, created by the SCLC four years earlier, used the threat of consumer boycotts to initiate the negotiation of jobs for blacks. With King's blessing, Jackson had organized the project in Chicago. On February 11, the program was officially launched, as King spoke to a crowd of more than 200 ministers. The motivated ministers established committees to study employment discrimination throughout the city.

King successfully won the support of black ministers, but within the movement, disunity between the CCCO and the SCLC staff emerged. The campaign still struggled to outline its goals. This was a problem for the CCCO, who felt that the disorganization, along with Bevel's unorganized style, was producing only modest results. Bevel and other staff members had begun to mobilize East Garfield Park, but their door-to-door approach produced almost no response.

Meanwhile, the rally resulted in a net of $80,000. However, community support for the Chicago campaign continued to plague the movement. Chicago's black conservatives, who had the political ties and money, preferred legal tactics as opposed to civil disobedience. In addition, blacks on Daley's staff remained opposed to the movement. Support from the labor unions also proved to be surprisingly tricky. While some unions supported the effort, the powerful ones like the Chicago Federation of Labor and the Industrial Union Council refused to give their backing.

THEY SAID...

" Daley had blacks on his staff and black officials and some black ministers who marched with Dr. King in the South...but on Daley's plantation, they had press conferences and urged Dr. King to leave Chicago, saying there is no place for you here. It really broke his hear.... *"*

—Jesse Jackson, *Voices of Freedom*

A Question of Morality

What appeared to be a victory, or at least progress toward one, occurred in February. King took over the South Homan apartment building with the intention of making repairs with the rent money that the Freedom Movement intended to collect from the occupants. This was a bold move for King, who explained to the press that the morality of the situation overrode the legal issue. Not everyone agreed with him. The press and black U.S. District Judge James Parsons condemned the act as theft. King's actions did draw the attention of the welfare department, who cited the owner with twenty-three code violations, but declined to give the Freedom Movement the rent money for the repairs.

Nonviolent Resistance under Attack

As the movement rolled into May, King announced plans for a June 26 mass rally of 100,000 to take place at Chicago's Soldier Field. The plans came to a halt when James Meredith was shot while leading the Mississippi March against Fear on June 6. King flew out to Mississippi to lead the march with SNCC's Stokely Carmichael and CORE's Floyd McKissick. The Civil Rights movement took on a new twist when the term "Black Power" was used by Carmichael at a rally. King feared the misinterpretation of the term as promoting black separatism would lead to the flight of white supporters. He quickly countered the term with his own stance on nonviolent resistance, and the importance of having pride in one's heritage.

The Chicago Riot

The Chicago rally was rescheduled for July 10 due to King's trip to Mississippi. The rally also took on a new goal: It would focus on ending unfair housing by establishing an Open City. The poorly planned rally received a low turnout of just 30,000. The rally ended with a march led by King to City Hall, where like his namesake, Martin Luther, he posted a list of demands on the city's door. The demands included the call for immediate school desegregation, fair employment guarantees, and the termination of housing discrimination. The next day, King and associates met with Mayor Daley about their demands. The meeting began with a civil tone, but ended in anger on both sides.

One day after the meeting with Daley, on July 12, a riot broke out when the police shut off a fire hydrant that had been opened by a group of youths. It was a hot day, and the neighborhood children were using the hydrant to cool down. When the police arrived and began to shut it off, six youths who intervened were arrested. Violent protest over the arrests spread throughout the community. Upon hearing of the chaos, King immediately went to the police station to seek the release of the youths. King obtained their release, and went to Shiloah Church, where he urged the crowd to refrain from any more violence. His request was ignored by most as they left the church.

The next morning, King canvassed the city seeking understanding on both sides. He met with the police commander, residents, gang members, and even the aggrieved youths who were arrested. His actions failed to make progress in relieving the tension in the black community. That evening, violence erupted throughout the community again. Store windows were broken, gunfire was heard, and Molotov cocktails were thrown. The following night, July 14, King continued his quest to end the violence. This time, he visited each neighborhood by car. He pleaded with residents to stop the violence. By 4:00 A.M., the community was quiet.

HE SAID...

" Riots grow out of intolerable conditions. Violent revolts are generated by revolting conditions and there is nothing more dangerous than to build a society with a large segment of people who feel they have no stake in it, who feel they have nothing to lose. "

King decided to take his pleas to the gangs. Late into the night on July 15, he met with the leaders of three Chicago gangs in his apartment. King patiently listened to their complaints over the lack of employment and their living conditions. He, in turn, suggested that they approach their grievances from a nonviolent stance. After hours of explaining alternatives to violence, by morning, King had convinced them to stop their members from participating in the violence.

The riot had done little to help the Chicago campaign. First, Daley blamed King for the rioting. Second, since the emergence of the term "Black Power," the media was quick to define the violence in Chicago as an indication that not only was the Civil Rights movement over, but that King's leadership in Chicago lacked direction. The use of nonviolent resistance in the South had proven effective for King, but now he faced a much different situation in the North, and he was unsure of how the northern situation could be solved. He did make one important decision: he quickly disassociated himself with the term "Black Power." He told the media that the term was dangerous to the movement and was used out of desperation.

The Summit Agreement

Just as he had done in the South, King decided to elicit change through mass demonstrations. On July 29, fifty demonstrators converged upon Gage Park, where the office of a discriminatory real-estate business was located. They planned to stay overnight, but quickly retreated when a crowd of 1,000 angry whites made it clear that their safety was in jeopardy. The next day, 500 demonstrators returned to Gage Park, where they were attacked by white bystanders with rocks and bottles as the police looked on. On July 31, the marchers returned by car, and again were hit with bottles and rocks as the police stood by. As the protestors retreated toward New Friendship Church, their cars, which were parked nearby at Marquette Park, were overturned and set on fire.

On August 5, King and 500 demonstrators returned to Marquette Park, where they parked their cars before proceeding to the real-estate office in Gage Park. One thousand police officers were stationed for their protection from the white mob of 4,000. As King emerged from his car, he was hit by a rock on the right side of his head. As photographers captured the incident, a stunned King fell to one knee as he was surrounded by his staff. King, undeterred, got up and led the crowd on the march as the white mob threw rocks and bottles.

The Summit Meeting

Mayor Daley began to feel pressured to negotiate a settlement. A meeting between the civil-rights leaders and the city officials took place August 17. At the meeting, the Freedom Movement read its nine demands. Included in their demands was a call for the enforcement of anti-discriminatory housing ordinances, the termination of discriminatory lending practices, the realtor association's discontinuance of support for the legal challenge to housing ordinances and to the state open-housing bill in the legislature, and the end to building only public-housing high rises in slums. Mayor Daley, the Chicago Housing Authority, and the Chicago Mortgage Bankers Association agreed to the demands, and proposed that the marches stop. The meeting bogged down when the Chicago Real Estate Board (CREB) refused to require their members to discontinue the practice of housing discrimination.

> **Q:** **Why was the CREB opposed to discontinuing housing discrimination?**
> The CREB argued that it was not their organization that was the problem. Instead, they asserted that the practice of housing discrimination was a reflection of their clients' wishes.

The one unanimous decision they did come to was the agreement to form a subcommittee. A committee of twelve, out of which five were Freedom Movement members, was given the assignment to submit their terms to the committee in nine days. To the dismay of Daley, there would be no moratorium on marches. King explained to the group that marching was the only power that blacks had, and to give this up would leave them powerless. Meanwhile, on August 19, Daley received a state-court injunction requiring that police receive twenty-four-hour notification prior to a march, restricted marches to one per day, and limited the number of participants to 500. The SCLC, with their faltering funds, could hardly afford to pay the fines if protestors were jailed for an unlawful march. The conclusion, King decided, was to march in the outlying areas not included in the injunction, like in the Cicero area. The Cicero area, a hotbed of white hostility, was the targeted area for an August 25 march.

Progress was made by the subcommittee, so the Cicero march was canceled indefinitely. When the members of the summit meeting reconvened, the CREB agreed to all of the demands, including the withdrawal of the opposition to the state legislation, the enforcement of nondiscriminatory practices of real-estate agents, and the termination of discriminatory lending by financial institutions. In exchange, the marches would cease unless discrimination in housing continued. In addition, Daley agreed to modify the injunction. King and the movement agreed to accept the terms. The marches would cease as long as the demands were implemented. The meeting ended with words of hope for the successful implementation of the agreement and praise for the consensus from King.

THEY SAID...

" When Dr. King and Daley signed that accord, it was a great day. It was a great feeling because we understood the hardship that Dr. King went through to get that done. . . . But one thing that we learned that Dr. King always said so very cleverly is that you cooperate to operate. *"*

—Nancy Jefferson, *Voices of Freedom*

The Aftermath of the Summit Agreement

At the time, the Chicago-summit agreement appeared to be a victory. However, even if discrimination were not present, most blacks could hardly afford to buy a home in a white neighborhood. Further negativity threatened the agreement. At the rally where King disclosed the terms of the agreement to the crowd, calls for Black Power were heard. A SNCC flyer at the rally read "WAKE UP, BROTHER! WE GOT TO GET US SOME BLACK POWER—SO THE BLACK MAN CAN SPEAK FOR HIMSELF!"

CORE was also dissatisfied with the agreement. The gains, asserted CORE's Robert Lucas, were too modest. Although he did not blame King, he did claim that through more effective negotiations, substantial gains could have been made. The Cicero march into the hostile white neighborhood, which had been planned by King a month before, was now a renewed effort by Lucas. King urged him to reconsider, but Lucas, determined to make a statement against the faltering Chicago-summit agreement, led a march of 250 in Cicero on September 4, 1966. This time when things were thrown at the demonstrators, they retaliated by throwing them back.

When King left Chicago, he believed that he had won some gains for the community. Little did he know that implementation, just like

215

in the South, would be slow to come. With Chicago behind him, he was anxious to expand into other northern cities.

However, while King focused on the northern ghettos, he could not forget that the emergence of the Black Power slogan was quickly splintering the movement.

Chapter 16

BLACK POWER
AND THE MISSISSIPPI
MARCH

AS KING STRUGGLED TO move SCLC efforts to the
North, he encountered a disheartening challenge
to his new campaign. While participating in James
Meredith's Mississippi March against Fear during
the Chicago campaign, the Black Power slogan
made its way into public discourse. King, while
hesitant to publicly condemn the slogan, believed
that even though it had a positive effect on promoting black pride, the negativity of the motto could
cause an irreparable division within the Civil Rights
movement.

James Meredith Shot

On June 6, 1966, while King was working on the Chicago campaign, civil-rights activist James Meredith began his 220-mile March Against Fear from Memphis, Tennessee to Jackson, Mississippi. The march was intended to encourage voter registration, while at the same time serving as an example of how to stand up to white authority. Thirty miles into the march, near Hernando, Mississippi, Meredith fell to the ground upon seeing a man aiming a shotgun at him. However, it was too late; he was shot in the back and the legs. The shooter, forty-one-year-old Aubrey James Norvell, was arrested, and later sentenced to five years in prison. Meredith was taken to the hospital by ambulance, and while his prognosis initially seemed serious, it was later determined that his injuries were minor.

FACT

James Meredith, a longtime activist, had won a legal battle to attend the University of Mississippi years earlier. In 1961, when he applied to the university, he was denied admission because of his race. In 1962, Meredith became the first black to attend the University of Mississippi.

Continuing the March

When King heard of the assault on Meredith, he immediately decided to continue the march. His plans for the Chicago campaign were put on hold. King, CORE, and the SNCC agreed that if Meredith approved, they would unite in the effort. While King wanted to draw attention to the continued assault on blacks in the South through nonviolent means, SNCC and CORE had other ideas. The march, they determined, was a perfect opportunity to bring national attention to Black Power.

The SNCC had begun to move toward Black Nationalism and separatism, which had been promoted by Malcolm X prior to his death. Malcolm X had emerged in the early 1960s as the Nation of Islam's black crusader. While King taught that integration, redemptive suffering, reconciliation, and a beloved community could be achieved through nonviolent resistance, Malcolm X appealed to blacks, especially those in the northern ghettos, with his more-militant view on race relations and his rejection of the use of nonviolence. He sought redemption through racial separation and his rhetoric was antiwhite. Integration with "blue-eyed devils," according to Malcolm X, was undesirable. It was under this context of divergent views that the March Against Fear would take place.

On June 7, King, CORE's Director Floyd McKissick, and SNCC's Chairman Stokely Carmichael arrived at the Memphis hospital to speak with Meredith about continuing the march on his behalf. The group was happy to hear that Meredith supported their plan. They came to the consensus to expand the purpose of the march to include stricter enforcement of the Voting Rights Act.

HE SAID...

*"*When order was finally restored, our executive staff immediately agreed that the march must continue. After all, we reasoned, Meredith began his lonely journey as a pilgrimage against fear. Wouldn't failure to continue only intensify the fears of the oppressed and deprived Negroes of Mississippi? Would this not be a setback for the whole Civil Rights movement and a blow to nonviolent discipline? *"*

After receiving Meredith's assent, a group of twenty-one began the march near Hernando, where Meredith had left off. They immediately encountered resistance from highway patrolmen, who ordered them to move to the shoulder of the road. After a verbal exchange between King and an officer, a scuffle ensued when the officers began pushing the marchers to the side of the road. Carmichael, agitated by the exchange, attempted to charge the officer, but was restrained by King. Sensing the situation could soon get out of control, King convinced the others that the wise choice was to continue the march from the shoulder of the road.

Ideological Division Within the Movement

After traveling 6 miles and speaking at a rally that evening, King, Carmichael, and McKissick met with the NAACP's Roy Wilkins and the National Urban League's Whitney Young to discuss their planned endorsement of the march. The discussion quickly turned sour when the proposed goals of the march were discussed. Unlike Young and Wilkins's desire to focus on marching in support of President Johnson's proposed civil-rights legislation, Carmichael preferred to focus on marching against fear, and endorsed inviting the armed Deacons for Defense to participate. Carmichael further strained the negotiations when he asserted that if any focus on legislation was part of the march, it should be on the need for improvements to the legislation. King sat silently as Carmichael vigorously debated with Wilkins and Young. By the end of the meeting, Wilkins and Young had withdrawn their support of the march.

FACT

Bogalusa, Louisiana's Deacons for Defense was an armed self-defense group. Their purpose was to protect the black community from violent attacks by such groups as the Ku Klux Klan. It was agreed to include them in the march to provide protection for the marchers.

Deciding upon the Objectives

The following morning, the March Against Fear objectives were announced to the press by King and McKissick. Contrary to Carmichael's previous refusal to support the legislation, the leaders announced that in addition to the support of the civil-rights legislation, they were also calling for a revised and strengthened bill. Furthermore, they sought the implementation of the voting-rights bill and the creation of anti-poverty programs. A few days later, the additional goal of voter registration was added, and it was decided that the marches into various cities would include voter canvassing.

Black Power Takes Root

Over the next few days, as the march covered more miles, participants numbered from 200 to 400. King's presence was sporadic due to his leadership of the Chicago campaign and his SCLC responsibilities. The one continuous theme that King tried to combat was Carmichael's insistence that white participants remain absent from the march. King stressed the importance of appearing unified, and Carmichael agreed. King, however, still feared that during his absence, Carmichael's inclination to diverge from nonviolent resistance and his discouragement of white participants could lead to dire consequences. He hoped to keep the growing ideological division out of the press.

King's fear would come to the forefront on June 16, when the marchers arrived in Greenwood. It began with the city's denial of permission for the marchers to set up their tents at Stone Street Negro Elementary School. A face off began between the Public Safety Commissioner and Carmichael and two SNCC associates. When they refused to leave the school, they were arrested.

After Carmichael's release that evening, he returned to find that the marchers had received permission to camp at the Broad Street Park. Carmichael was irritated by this new development. At the rally that evening, his emotion overflowed. An angry Carmichael told the crowd that they should burn down all courthouses in Mississippi. He next claimed that black sheriffs should rule over the Delta Mississippi counties and that most importantly, blacks should demand Black Power. The next phrase, "We want Black Power," set the crowd into a craze as they chanted the slogan in response to Carmichael's question, "What do you want?" Although this wasn't the first time that

221

the phrase had been said publicly, it initially garnered little press coverage. The following day, upon King's return to the march, his fear of the emerging militancy of the SNCC was realized. At that evening's rally, SNCC's Willie Ricks recited the same phrase. The crowd enthusiastically chanted it back to Ricks. SCLC's Hosea Williams countered the SNCC with his own slogan of "freedom now."

Finding a Middle Ground

King was disappointed with the use of the slogan. He urged Carmichael and McKissick to refrain from using it and to consider the semantics of the phrase. He explained that he believed in a real Black Power that did not encompass separatism or racism. Instead, he explained, it was a force that focused on achieving political and economic power. Further, insisted King, the slogan moved the focus of the movement away from attacking the conscience of white Americans and left the implication of violence and separatism. King explained that the use of a slogan failed to increase Black Power. The Jewish, Irish, and Italians didn't have a slogan, instead, these groups worked hard to achieve power. Blacks, he stressed, must also work hard. Although racial pride was a positive quality, it couldn't be achieved through a slogan.

Carmichael remained unconvinced by King's analysis. While he did agree to discontinue its use in the march as long as the SCLC discontinued the use of "freedom now," he explained that the march provided a good forum for the introduction of Black Power. With King's leadership in the march, the media coverage provided an opportunity to bring national attention to the Black Power movement. In addition, he hoped to force King to take a stance for Black Power. King was dismayed with this revelation, and responded that it wasn't the first time that he had been used.

King on Black Power

To Carmichael's dismay, King remained steadfast in his disagreement with the use of the slogan. King was disappointed with the growing disunity of the march and strongly considered withdrawing. However, the media had caught on to the division, so his withdrawal would only bring more attention to the discord.

SNCC Movement Toward Black Power

The SNCC's movement toward Black Power was not a shock to King; the SNCC had increasingly moved away from nonviolent resistance. Talk of Black Power among SNCC associates outside of public earshot had grown within the organization. It had originally formed as an interracial group, but in recent years, they began to question the role of whites in the Civil Rights movement, and especially in their organization. In May 1966, Chairman John Lewis was ousted. In his place was northerner Stokely Carmichael, who was not only less religious, but he also moved the group away from Gandhi's philosophy. Instead, he emphasized the example of the violent struggles of China, Algeria, and Cuba, and was greatly influenced by Malcolm X's legacy and stance on racial separatism.

The Good and the Bad of Black Power

King later reflected on Black Power, and came to several conclusions. First, he believed that it was an expression of disappointment on several levels. The discontent had emerged as a result of the white power that had controlled blacks for centuries. It was also a response to the lengthy battle to win equality. Despite the passage of federal legislation and legal victories, the wins required continued work for the enforcement of these laws. Progress seemed far off.

THEY SAID...

" Black Power itself was something Martin disagreed with tactically....It was not Black Power that he was against, it was the slogan Black Power, because he said, 'If you really have power you don't need a slogan.' "

—Andrew Young, *Voices of Freedom*

Second, King interpreted Black Power as a reaction to the unequal distribution of power in American society. In this way, King found that it was good. Just like slaves, blacks in the ghetto were also powerless. The Black Power movement called for blacks to seek political and economic power. In addition, it advocated community unity, the election of black politicians, the use of the bloc vote, and political awareness. Third, King asserted that while federal economic aid was a possibility, Black Power called for the pooling of black financial resources.

Finally, Black Power was a "psychological call to manhood." For so many years, blacks had been led to believe that they were inferior. Finally, with the gains of the Civil Rights movement, blacks became aware of their equality. Black Power, in King's opinion, served an important role in creating a renewed sense of manhood, eliciting racial pride, and encouraging feelings of dignity and worth.

Despite the good of Black Power, it was used in a harmful way. While Black Power did have positive traits, in King's opinion, the negativity of the movement's promotion of black separatism was its greatest failure. Instead of uniting blacks and whites in favor of civil rights, it created division by alienating the black community. In addition, it worked counter to nonviolent resistance. The nonviolent method's greatest strength was in its appeal to the moral conscience of whites.

HE SAID...

" Power, properly understood, is the ability to achieve purpose. It is the strength required to bring about social, political, or economic changes. In this sense power is not only desirable but necessary in order to implement the demands of love and justice....What is needed is a realization that power without love is reckless and abusive, and that love without power is sentimental and anemic. *"*

Black Power Garners National Attention

By June 23, when the marchers reached Canton, the press had picked up the story. King was growing disillusioned with the disunity in the march. Canton failed to raise his spirits. When a group of marchers arrived early in the city, they were arrested for trespassing after erecting their tents at a black elementary school. When King, Carmichael, and McKissick arrived, they voiced their intention of putting up tents at the school. When the marchers proceeded to the school, the highway patrolmen followed. From a truck bed, King addressed the crowd. The highway patrol ordered their departure. King yelled to the crowd to stay on the school grounds, and to remain unresponsive to the violence. A succession of tear gas canisters were lobbed into the crowd. King again urged them to remain where they were. Within minutes, the marchers dispersed, and those that remained were beaten with police clubs. King, Carmichael, and McKissick retreated to a nearby church. The following day, the marchers returned to the school, where a rally was held. Upon a prior agreement with city officials and local black leaders, it was agreed that a rally could be held as long they arranged to sleep at the Catholic mission.

THEY SAID...

" Choking for breath, I could hear screams, shouts, and Dr. King calling on people to remain calm amid the sickening thud of blows. They were kicking and clubbing people lying on the ground to escape the gas. Men, women, children, it made no difference. Then they were gone, leaving us to tend the wounded.... "

—Stokely Carmichael, *Ready for Revolution*

Before long, the truce to eliminate slogans from the march soon dissipated. On June 26, the March Against Fear ended. Further disunity deepened during the last day of the 8-mile march from Tougaloo to Jackson. As King led the procession, when "Black Power" bumper stickers were seen attached to police cars, SCLC's Jim Orange led the chanting of "freedom now." The SNCC responded with "Black Power." When the marchers reached the capitol, they were not only welcomed by the thousands of black supporters, they were greeted by the loud and boisterous angry white onlookers.

King, clearly dejected by the disunity, lacked his usual charisma when he delivered his speech. After the rally, the media, fully aware of the SNCC's stance on Black Power, sought King's opinion. King reiterated his belief in achieving gains through nonviolence and stated that he was strongly in support of white involvement in the movement. It was clear to King that the slogan had taken the momentum away from the goals they sought from the march.

A further depressing fact was that calls for Black Power seemed to be emerging at lightning speed. Black Power's biggest advocate, Stokely Carmichael, had made front-page headlines when he was arrested on September 6, 1966 on the charge of inciting a riot in Atlanta. King was now unsure what the future of the movement held and whether the SNCC intended to move from their stance on nonviolence. With this new insecurity about the SNCC, King began to feel the need to distance himself from the group.

SNCC Splits the Movement

King was not alone in his feelings toward the SNCC. On October 12, Rustin, Randolph, Wilkins, and Whitney Young believed that it was time to issue a public statement voicing their opposition to Black Power in the *New York Times*. King wanted to lessen the divisions within the movement, so he decided not to sign it. However, he was caught off guard when asked by the press about whether he agreed with the statement. He replied that he did, and the press printed a headline noting his support for the statement. King was dismayed with his miscalculation and quickly clarified his position of not formally endorsing the statement.

Needless to say, their rebuke counted little to the Black Power supporters. To them, Wilkins and Young were "Uncle Toms." Despite this public rebuke, that same month, the Black Panther Party was formed in Oakland, California by Bobby Seale and Huey Newton. They believed in arming for self-defense against police brutality, and the group patrolled communities in black pants, leather jackets, and berets.

FACT

In 1967, after leaving the SNCC, Carmichael joined the Black Panther Party and served as prime minister. His commitment to Black Power intensified when he wrote the book *Black Power: The Politics of Liberation in America*. Just two years after joining the Black Panther Party, he resigned and moved to Guinea, West Africa.

Carmichael remained committed to his stance on Black Power. In an article in the *New York Review of Books*, he explained that he had embarked upon a new way of communicating for the black community. As opposed to the current leadership, he didn't act as a buffer between blacks and whites. By December 1966, the SNCC took a step toward the elimination of whites from the movement. SNCC members involved in Atlanta's Vine City project proposed and carried out the expulsion of all white members from the organization.

Black Power was also attacked in the press. King, however, was still hesitant to publicly condemn it. When riots erupted during the summer of 1966, King refused to acknowledge in his March 1967 statement that Black Power was the cause. Instead, he stated that the riots were misguided, but not meaningless. A month later, when King was on "Face the Nation," he was confronted with the issue of white backlash. Clearly, the SNCC had begun to feel the backlash as donations lessened. King, however, wasn't ready to relinquish his belief that negative reactions were increasing. When the commentator stressed that Black Power had affected further gains in racial reform, King responded that perhaps it was the other way around;

maybe Black Power and riots were the consequences of white backlash. He also declined to condemn Carmichael, and explained that Black Power should be interpreted as a sign of disappointment and despair.

Q: **Why was King hesitant to denounce the Black Power movement?**
Even though King realized that Black Power was undermining the Civil Rights movement, he was more concerned with the unity between the movement organizations.

As King fought to keep the disunity of the movement from destroying any possible gains, he continued his quest for economic equality. Despite the slow gains of Chicago, King wanted to bring the issue of poverty to the attention of the nation. President Johnson, irritated by King's continued opposition to the Vietnam War, was even more irritated by King's crusade for antipoverty programs, especially if it meant bringing the issue directly to Washington, D.C.

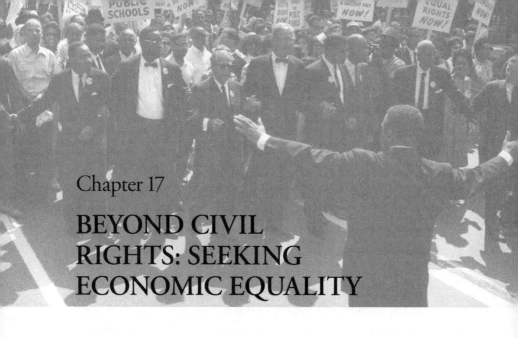

Chapter 17

BEYOND CIVIL RIGHTS: SEEKING ECONOMIC EQUALITY

THE MOVEMENT APPEARED TO be falling apart. King's commitment to ending the Vietnam War and the splintering of the Civil Rights movement were beginning to affect his popularity. Furthermore, King's own staffers were unhappy with the plan for the Poor People's March on Washington. King was determined to move forward in spite of the grumblings from associates. However, just as he had set his sights on the Washington March, he took an unplanned detour to Memphis, Tennessee.

Overcoming Disillusionment with the Movement

The Chicago campaign had done little to boost King's stamina. Some in the black community considered the agreement a sell-out. They alleged that it looked good on paper, but failed to change anything. Additionally, it was not long before the press attacked King's work in Chicago. Discrimination in housing still existed, the Housing Authority had failed to implement a new plan, and enforcement against discrimination had not taken effect.

The continued inequity in Chicago led King to make several conclusions about the struggle for black equality. He began to see that while the hard-fought battles of the North and South had been won, implementation was even harder to achieve. He concluded that while whites were outraged by the violence against protestors, many still remained committed to the status quo as opposed to justice. He resolved that the struggle, especially when related to poverty, would take time.

The status of the SCLC finances continued to plague the organization, but internal divisions moved to the forefront. Donations had substantially decreased, forcing the organization to rely heavily on large donations. This sometimes placed King in the awkward position of being urged to support the causes of the donor. By the end of 1966, internal tensions led to the resignation of four executives. The SCLC had become poorly managed. Many were overworked, like SCLC Executive Director Andrew Young, who also served as King's executive assistant. The project SCOPE, managed by Hosea Williams, rather than being noted for its success, generated rumors of scandals involving sex, alcohol, and rape. Finally, he was dismayed that President Johnson's 1966 civil-rights legislation wasn't enacted.

Renewing Opposition to the Vietnam War

The state of SCLC's struggling financial situation, along with his disillusionment over the slow pace of change, led to King's decision to take a two-month leave from the SCLC. He planned to recuperate, plot his next move, and work on his book, *Where Do We Go From Here? Chaos or Community?* Just as King set out for his vacation in Jamaica in January 1967, he came across a disturbing article about the suffering of Vietnamese children as a result of an American military action. The sight of the photos renewed King's opposition to the war. Helping him along was James Bevel, who arrived in Jamaica to tell King of his own internal urgings. God, proclaimed Bevel, had told him to work toward ending the war. In good conscience, King too determined that he could no longer remain quiet about the war. In spite of the potential financial loss to the SCLC, and even at the expense of further damaging his relationship with President Johnson, he determined to move ahead with his campaign against the war.

HE SAID...

*"*So often I had castigated those who by silence or inaction condoned and thereby cooperated with the evils of racial injustice....Had I not committed myself to the principle that looking away from evil is, in effect, a condoning of it?...I had to therefore speak out if I was to erase my name from the bombs which fall over North or South Vietnam....*"*

Taking on a Leadership Role

When King returned from his vacation, the Vietnam War became the focus of his attention. On February 25, 1967, joined by antiwar senators, King spoke vigorously about the evil of the war. His opposition stemmed from moral issues, and nonviolence was the guiding force behind his beliefs about the war. He was concerned about human suffering, the possibility that a world war would eventually erupt, and he felt that he was morally obligated to not only oppose the violence against oppressed Americans, but also to oppose violence that the American government was responsible for in Vietnam. King also observed that more blacks served in the war than whites, which was contradictory to the inequality they faced at home. King asserted that inequality in America would continue because funds for the poor were being diverted to the war. He also believed that America should serve as a moral example to the world.

At the end of March 1967, King stepped up his campaign against the Vietnam War. He returned to Chicago, where he and Dr. Spock led 5,000 protestors in an antiwar demonstration. King continued his crusade when, on April 4, he spoke at the Riverside Church in New York. In front of the crowd of 3,000, he made several demands of President Johnson. He called for the end of the bombing in Vietnam, for the government to engage in negotiations, and for the evacuation of American troops. King stressed that he was sympathetic to the Vietnamese people who were subjected to the American bombs. In addition, he encouraged those drafted to become conscientious objectors.

An Unpopular Position

King elicited a negative response from the press and other civil-rights leaders. Rustin, A. Philip Randolph, Whitney Young, and Roy Wilkins were all disappointed with his comments. Stanley Levison even criticized him for what he viewed as a poorly written speech. Levison worried that King's opposition to the war was placing him at the forefront of a fringe group. The media also took him to task for his comments: The *Washington Post*, the *New York Times*, and the *Pittsburgh Courier* interpreted his comments as irresponsible, as a tragedy, and as unsupported fact.

Despite the criticisms, King remained committed to his antiwar effort. He realized that while he was becoming unpopular, he had a moral duty to speak against the war.

He decided to take his protestations further with his commitment to speak at the April 15 demonstration organized by the Spring Mobilization Committee, an antiwar group. The rally was open to all antiwar crusaders, and Levison urged him to be careful with whom he aligned himself. Levison was especially concerned that movement toward any fringe activists, such as Dr. Spock, could increase his unpopularity on the issue. King, James Bevel, Dr. Spock, and

Harry Belafonte led 125,000 marchers to the United Nations Plaza on the day of the demonstration. King's speech, which was drafted by Levision, was more moderate, and emphasized his stance against the merging of the Civil Rights movement with the antiwar effort.

THEY SAID...

" What we had not expected to be quite so strong was the reaction among Martin's colleagues in the Civil Rights Movement.... Most of them felt that the Civil Rights Cause would be hurt by his pronouncements. Many people in the North and South felt that the two issues were going to be confused. *"*

—Coretta Scott King, *My Life with Martin Luther King, Jr.*

Rumors of His Bid for Presidency

King's antiwar crusade became somewhat overshadowed by the growing rumor that he intended to make a third-party bid for the 1968 presidency. January 1967 wiretaps recorded King's conversation with Levison on the rumor, in which he explained that while he never considered the prospects of winning, he did find the idea interesting, because such a candidacy would offer an alternative. Months later, he finally put the rumor to rest when he announced in April that he had no intention of running for president, since he wanted to remain outside of partisan politics. His explained that his commitment was to the church and the Christian ministry. With the bid for presidency laid to rest and his conscience clear on the moral issue of the Vietnam War, King set out to tackle the issue of poverty.

King on Economic Inequality

King's stance on economic inequality can be traced back to his college years. While he had never embraced Communism, he did believe that the economic system should be reformed. Capitalism, believed King, had failed the poor of all races. Further, he believed that Capitalism was beneficial to the rich. He also held a controversial admiration for Karl Marx, especially his passion for social justice. Ultimately, King believed that there was a need for the economic distribution of wealth, one that was not Communist but was a type of democratic Socialism. King, knowing full well that such a view would label him as a Communist, rarely gave this opinion in public.

Q: **What is the difference between Socialism and Communism?**
Socialism and Communism both advocate public ownership, but Socialism is the direct outgrowth of Capitalism. It is the stage between Capitalism and Communism. Communism is Socialism developed further, an advanced stage.

When King's latest book *Where Do We Go From Here? Chaos or Community?* was published in June 1967, his passion against economic inequality was evident. He offered the following proposals: an increase in elected black officials, more quality schools, an annual income, and the establishment of a program for unemployment in the ghetto. Although his ideas were attacked by critics for failing to put forth a workable solution to change society, King was undeterred from his focus on economic equality. He continued to push for an annual income in his declaration that $100 billion should be put forth in the effort to eliminate economic discrimination. Without jobs or money, King believed the gains toward equality could never be enjoyed by blacks. Now that King was more committed than ever to his antipoverty effort, he surged ahead with his next campaign to take the poverty issue straight to Washington.

The Poor People's Campaign
King's commitment to the poor ghetto dweller became his top priority when two riots in the ghettos of Newark and Detroit erupted in

mid-July, 1967. King knew that he wanted to move the SCLC into the northern cities, but he was unsure how to tackle the issues, especially with the recent violence. Despite the increasing popularity of Black Power and the more militant approach to attaining black equality, King felt that nonviolence could tackle the northern issues, in spite of the continued failure of Chicago. His search for an idea soon ended in mid-September when he spoke to civil-rights activist and attorney Marian Wright. She proposed an intriguing idea. Wright's plan was for King, a handful of poor, and labor and religious leaders to participate in a fast and sit-in in front of the office of the U.S. Secretary in Washington, D.C. The group would suffer the consequences of their actions, while the poor from around the country would converge upon Washington. This would become the second March on Washington. King liked the idea, and with the recent funding of $230,000 from the Ford Foundation, it was the perfect time to prepare for a new campaign.

The Goals of the Campaign

The goals of the new campaign were to attain an annual income, gain funds to cover the erection of at least 500,000 low-income housing units per year, achieve full employment, and eliminate black ghettos. Furthermore, the larger goal of the campaign was to change the current flawed economy to focus on people instead of profit. To enact this dramatic goal, King asserted that the demonstrations should remain nonviolent, but elicit as much attention as a violent riot. Activists, especially poor adults and students, should be trained and recruited from various cities. They would walk through Washington, camping in parks, and take control of government buildings. As opposed to the first March on Washington, King asserted that this time they would refuse to leave until President Johnson acted on their demands. It would be called the Poor People's Campaign and would take place in early April 1968.

Disunity Within the SCLC

Even though King was excited about moving the SCLC out of local protest and into a national protest, not all SCLC associates were in agreement. To many, the campaign appeared unorganized and lacking in focus. Jesse Jackson, who was still operating the successful Operation Breadbasket, pressed King on his assertion for government jobs and an annual income. He feared that such a measure would create dependency on the government. James Bevel, on the other hand, was concerned only about King's stance on the Vietnam War. He wanted to focus less on domestic issues andz move toward fighting the evil of war.

HE SAID...

" We would place the problems of the poor at the seat of government of the wealthiest nation in the history of mankind. If that power refused to acknowledge its debt to the poor, it would have failed to live up to its promise to insure 'life, liberty, and the pursuit of happiness' to its citizens. *"*

Most surprising to King was Bayard Rustin's opinion that he should first seek a victory on a small scale, since his creditability had been weakened. Rustin had predicted correctly. When King attended a National Welfare Rights Organization meeting, he was put to task for his lack of knowledge about welfare policy. He humbly admitted to his shortcoming, and requested their advisement.

In spite of the misgivings over the planned campaign, King was unwaveringly committed to enacting change for the poor. The poor included those of every race. King knew that there were more poor whites than blacks, and a multiracial demonstration could work better than one targeted at gaining wins for just blacks. His plan of taking over the Capitol was emerging as a demonstration that, through mass civil disobedience, could coerce the federal government into change. King envisioned the protestors would swarm the bridges and the hospitals, making it difficult for drivers to cross the bridge and people to seek medical care. To dramatize the effects of poverty, he visualized the creation of a shantytown, or a tented city, erected near the Capitol buildings.

THEY SAID...

"...I think that in a sense my husband was preparing himself for his fate....I think the feeling of tremendous urgency he had toward the Poor People's Campaign and the preparation that he tried to give his staff, so they could carry on without him, are indications of this. He worked as if it was to be his last and final assignment.*"*

—Coretta Scott King, *My Life with Martin Luther King, Jr.*

King's Leadership Attacked from All Sides

The disorganization of the campaign still halted the planning of the demonstration. To King's dismay, staff members continued to offer less than their full support. Bayard Rustin even declared his reservations about the demonstration to the press. Furthermore, former SNCC Chairman Stokely Carmichael and new SNCC Chairman Rap Brown were unsupportive of the effort. Although their support was unnecessary, they did promise that they would not speak out against the demonstration publicly.

President Johnson was also troubled with the campaign. Wiretaps were still being used on the phone lines of Levison and Rustin. King had escaped FBI wire surveillance on his home phone when he moved in 1965. Through the use of wiretaps and the placement of informants in the SCLC ranks, the government was aware of the lack of progress made on the campaign. Even though government officials surmised that the Poor People's Campaign would never get off the ground, they still made plans to protect the district

237

from potential chaos. The government was partly correct. Due to the lack of progress in the planning, the demonstration was postponed until April 22.

Supporting the Memphis Sanitation Workers on Strike

As King set out through the nation on a recruitment campaign in March 1968, he received a call from James Lawson, his old friend and a minister at Centenary Methodist Church in Memphis, Tennessee. Lawson asked King to make a visit to Memphis, where black sanitation workers had been on strike since February 12. The strike had begun after twenty black workers, due to weather conditions, were ordered off the job without pay. The white workers, on the other hand, were allowed to stay with pay. When officials rebuffed negotiations, 1,300 workers walked off the job and refused to return until the mayor recognized their union, AFSCME Local 1733.

FACT

Up until February 12, the union had been hesitant to engage in strikes, because there was a court injunction prohibiting it. Two weeks before the strike, two black laborers had been killed by a type of blade that had previously been reported as faulty; this incident, combined with growing dissatisfaction over the lack of wage increases and humane treatment, instigated the strike.

By March 18, when King arrived in Memphis, little had changed for the workers on strike. Their march to a black church had increased city discord when police officers used mace and clubs on them. The organization Community on the Move for Equality (COME) was formed to support the strikers, and a boycott of downtown stores began. Unlike the lack of support King was receiving for his Poor

People's Campaign, his comments and presence were enthusiastically accepted by the striking workers in Memphis. Lawson was also excited by King's reception, and asked him to return to lead the March 22 demonstration. King eagerly accepted.

The Memphis March Turns Violent

Due to snow, the Memphis march was canceled until March 28. After traveling throughout the nation in an attempt to garner recruits and financial support for the faltering Washington campaign, King made it back to Memphis in time for the 11:05 a.m. march. King and Abernathy led the marchers through city streets toward the City Hall. Without warning, a group of youths near the rear of the procession began throwing wooden sticks through store windows. Their youthful inhibitions caught on, and other young marchers followed suit and began looting the stores. The police halted the march, and as marchers walked back toward the church, the police attacked them. King was quickly whisked away to a room at the Holiday Inn.

King was both surprised and extremely upset over the violent eruption, and proposed that another march take place in order to lessen the negative publicity. Although King was certain about the next course of action, he was immensely disturbed by the violence. The Poor People's Campaign was already faltering, and the day's events, believed King, would only spread the perception that it, too, would result in violence. Not even Coretta could get him out of his mood. Only upon the urgings of Levison to get some rest was King finally able to sleep and awake somewhat renewed the next morning.

THEY SAID...

" He was terribly distressed. This was the first time violence had ever broken out in a march he was leading. Although he knew that he was not responsible, he felt he would be blamed. *"*

—Coretta Scott King, *My Life with Martin Luther King, Jr.*

King was able to get a handle on why a riot erupted when he met with the leaders of the Invaders. The Invaders were a group of young radicals who had been excluded by Lawson from the movement. They explained to King that they hadn't started the riot, even though some of their members may have participated. They argued that it occurred because they were unable to warn King of the presence of black militants, since Lawson prevented them from meeting with King on his first visit. King, while not completely convinced of their innocence, proposed that they participate and work together in the planning of the next march staged by the SCLC.

King's Anger Takes Center Stage

King was correct in his belief that the violence during the Memphis march would lead to assertions that the Washington campaign should be called off. The media quickly summed up that not only should the Poor People's Campaign be canceled, but that King's leadership in Memphis had been a failure. They asserted that rather than leaving the scene when it became violent, King should have remained and calmed the crowd. Even more hurtful to King was the continuing lack of support of his staff for the Washington campaign. They believed that if he proceeded with the second march in Memphis, the campaign in Washington should be called off. Adding to his aggravation was Jesse Jackson's lack of support and his increasing independence from the SCLC, which King viewed as a reflection of Jackson's personal ambition.

King's aggravation only increased after returning to Atlanta from Memphis. At the March 30 meeting with the SCLC, King erupted with anger when Jackson, Andrew Young, and Bevel continued to offer their lackluster support. King angrily told them that when they had a movement they were interested in, he supported them. He was just asking for the same commitment. King rose to leave the room, and asked that they come to a consensus on whether they would support him in the campaign. As he proceeded to the door, he lashed out at Jackson, who followed behind him. In an angry tone he told Jackson that if he preferred to do his own thing, then he should do it without bothering him. The surprised group of SCLC members agreed to stand behind King on both the Memphis march and the Washington campaign.

King's Last Speech: "I've Been to the Mountaintop"

Jackson, James Orange, James Bevel, and Hosea Williams went to Memphis ahead of King to make preparations for the April 8 march, and to gain the support of the Invaders. King arrived in Memphis on Wednesday, April 3, after a brief delay at the airport due to a bomb threat. He checked into the Lorraine Motel, where he learned of the temporary injunction barring marches for ten days. Memphis lawyers were soon on the job. They sought to modify the injunction to allow for a limited, well-controlled march. King planned to march regardless of the modification.

That evening, King settled into his motel room as Abernathy left to give a speech at the mass meeting at Mason Temple. King was scheduled to speak, but due to the rain, he decided that only a small crowd would be there. When Abernathy arrived at Mason, he quickly realized that King's absence was a disappointment to the crowd. He called King at the motel and requested that he come and speak.

HE SAID...

*"*I would like to live a long life—longevity has its place. But I'm not concerned about that now. I just want to do God's will. And He's allowed me to go up to the mountain. And I've looked over, and I've seen the Promised Land. I may not get there with you. But I want you to know tonight, that we, as a people, will get to the Promised Land.*"*

As he had done many times before, at Mason, King spoke about his near-death experience after being stabbed with a letter opener. He was glad that he hadn't sneezed, and that he was still alive to witness the protest movements in Albany, Birmingham, Selma, and Memphis, and he was glad to have been able to tell about his dream at the March on Washington. But now, according to King, he was unconcerned about his future, since he had been to the mountaintop.

An emotional and sweat-drenched King took his seat. Those who had heard him deliver the same speech before noted that this time King's passion exceeded all of the previous times. According to Abernathy, King's eyes were filled with tears. While it had been an emotional speech, it had also relaxed King enough for him to enjoy dinner at a friend's house, and then a brief interlude with his brother at the Lorraine Motel.

King's Assassination in Memphis

King awoke at noon the next day to the reality of the troubled Memphis demonstration. He was unsure whether the Invaders could be trusted. The SCLC promised to secure funding for their projects, and they gave their word that the march would remain nonviolent. In the meantime, court proceedings had begun over the injunction, and Andrew Young and Lawson were in court. King awaited news about the decision all day without word from either. That evening, he finally learned that the judge had agreed to modify the order. The Monday march was free to proceed.

The group had plans for dinner at Billy Kyles's house, so King went upstairs to his room to shave. Abernathy joined King as he went through his usual unorthodox shaving routine. King had sensitive skin, so he was required to use a powder to shave instead of a razor. Kyles arrived, and tried to hurry him along. King grabbed a shirt and put on a tie, and as he and Kyles made their way outside, Abernathy stayed behind in the room to put on aftershave. Awaiting them downstairs were Young, Bevel, Jackson, Williams, Chauncey Eskridge, and driver Solomon Williams. When King stepped out onto the balcony, Williams told him to bring a coat since it was getting cold. Kyles continued on toward the stairs, while King turned back toward the room. Suddenly, a loud noise was heard. It was later described as the sound of a car backfiring, but Kyles and Abernathy knew that it was the sound of a rifle blast. Kyles turned around as Abernathy quickly came outside. Both saw King on the ground, his feet hanging over the lower rail of the balcony, a large wound to his right jaw. Abernathy immediately bent down to King and saw King's eyes move toward him as he touched King's left cheek. As Abernathy spoke to him, he sensed that King could hear him, but was unable to respond. A towel was placed around his head, and Kyles tried to call an ambulance, but the motel switchboard was unresponsive. A policeman below notified them that an ambulance was on its way. Minutes later an ambulance took King, with Abernathy at his side, to St. Joseph's Hospital. The shot, which had severed his spinal cord, had caused irreparable brain damage, and the doctors were unable to save him. King was pronounced dead at 7:05 P.M. on April 4, 1968. His funeral took place on April 9, where he was eulogized by Benjamin Mays.

FACT

The Lorraine Motel was foreclosed upon in 1982. The motel was bought by the Martin Luther King Memorial Foundation at auction. They wanted to ensure that the historic site wasn't destroyed. The motel was renovated into the National Civil Rights Museum, which opened in 1991.

King's death brought happiness to many white supremacists who celebrated his murder. Blacks throughout the nation, on the other hand, erupted in anger. Stokely Carmichael only encouraged the rage when he proclaimed that King's murder meant war with white America. From April 4 to 9, riots continued throughout the nation, especially in Washington, D.C., where buildings were set on fire. When violence ended, a total of thirty-nine people were dead, and 110 cities had been affected by the riots.

A Lone Assassin or a Conspiracy?

The investigation into King's murder began immediately. Thirty-five hundred FBI agents were assigned to the case, and they quickly determined that their prime suspect was James Earl Ray. They found a rifle on South Main near the murder scene. They ascertained that Ray had purchased the rifle under an alias at a store in Birmingham. It was also determined that on April 3, Ray checked into a rooming house, where he had a direct view of the Lorraine Motel from the bathroom. Other evidence against Ray included a sighting of him leaving South Main in a white Mustang after the shooting; maps of the King home, church, and the SCLC office; and his prints on the rifle, a beer can, a newspaper, a bottle of aftershave, and binoculars, all of which were found near a store on South Main.

Months later, on June 8, Ray was arrested at the London Heathrow Airport as he attempted to take a flight to Brussels under an alias. Ray, a crook, drug dealer, and racist, was convicted of the murder and sentenced to ninety-nine years in prison. Ray later claimed that he acted at the behest of an unknown man. Over the years, it has been claimed that his actions were part of a conspiracy. Charges have ranged from King's assassination being a product of a government conspiracy to claims that Henry Clay Wilson, along with two other men, was responsible for King's murder.

In addition, a new twist to the mystery behind King's death has emerged. In a 1999 civil suit by King's family, a Memphis jury determined that defendant Loyd Jowers was part of the conspiracy to kill King. Jowers owned the restaurant below the rooming house where Ray stayed. Before the trial, in a 1983 ABC interview, Jowers claimed the mob had offered him $100,000 to find a hit man. At trial, Jowers retracted his statement, saying that although there was a conspiracy, he was unaware that King was the target. The jury ordered Jowers to pay the King family $100 in damages.

At the time of King's murder, his stance on racial equality, his opposition to the Vietnam War, and his movement toward economic equality created a multitude of enemies. In 1968, the FBI was aware of at least fifty plans to assassinate him. At the time of his death, segregationists were offering bounties on his life of $70,000 and $100,000.

Chapter 18

OTHER LEADERS OF THE CIVIL RIGHTS MOVEMENT

ALTHOUGH MARTIN LUTHER KING Jr. had a significant role in the success of the Civil Rights movement, the movement itself was the culmination of the work of many people. Many leaders, including those that held different positions than King, had a hand in the achievement of black equality. Included in the list of notables were A. Philip Randolph, Bayard Rustin, Ralph Abernathy, Ella Baker, Malcolm X, and Stokely Carmichael.

A. Philip Randolph

By the time that King stepped to the forefront of the Civil Rights movement, A. Philip Randolph's leadership had preceded him by more than forty years. With his experience as a seasoned leader, Randolph was often able to help mediate the disunity between the various civil-rights organizations. Randolph, called the prophet of the Civil Rights movement, was the son of a minister. He was born on April 15, 1889 in Crescent City, Florida. Shortly after graduating as class valedictorian from the black Cookman Institute in 1911, he moved to New York City. He set his sights on an acting career, and while he worked to attain it, he enrolled at City College.

While his goal of acting was never fruitful, he did develop a commitment to improving the lives of the black working class. New York City had a lively black activist community, so Randolph was in the company of many others committed to similar causes. His passion for the black working class led him to the Socialist Party, where his commitment to the group soon earned him the nickname "the black Lenin." It was in New York that Randolph met another socialist, Chandler Owen, in 1914. Owen and Randolph created the radical magazine the *Messenger* in 1917. The *Messenger*, at times unpopular with its controversial stance on issues, included criticisms of President Woodrow Wilson and the lack of opportunities for blacks in the military.

In 1925, Randolph began his crusade for economic equality with the creation of the Brotherhood of Sleeping Car Porters. The Pullman Company, which employed black porters to serve the white customers on the dining and sleeping cars in trains, refused to negotiate with the porters. Randolph created the union for the porters and took an active role in negotiating on their behalf. It was a long road to achieving gains with the Pullman Company, but an agreement was finally reached in 1937.

Next, Randolph set out to gain equality from the federal government. Randolph, along with the NAACP and the National Urban League, pressured President Franklin D. Roosevelt to address federal employment discrimination. After Randolph threatened to hold a mass march on Washington, Roosevelt buckled under pressure. In June 1941, Roosevelt barred discrimination in the defense industry with Executive Order 8802, which created the Fair Employment Act.

Randolph was also disheartened by the government-sponsored segregation in the military. He took his next campaign directly to blacks. Through his organization the Committee Against Jim Crow in Military Service and Training, he urged blacks to evade draft registration. Pressure from Randolph led to the issuance of Executive Order 9981 by President Harry Truman in July 1948. This order banned segregation in the military.

HE SAID...

" ...I feel that the greatest leader of these times that the Negro has produced is A. Philip Randolph, president of the Brotherhood of Sleeping Car Porters, whose total integrity, depth of dedication and caliber of statesmanship set an example for us all. "

Randolph also extended his effort toward equality beyond the economic realm when the Civil Rights movement began. However, economic equality was always his passion, and when the planning for the 1963 March on Washington began, he was adamant that it was called the March on Washington for Jobs and Freedom. Thus, the march was a combination of the quest for civil rights, as King focused on at the time, and Randolph's vision for economic equality. Several years after the march, due to his declining health, Randolph reduced his presence in the movement. On May 16, 1979, he died.

Bayard Rustin

Bayard Rustin, one of King's closest advisors, often worked behind the scenes in the Civil Rights movement due to his homosexuality and former communist ties. Rustin's ability as an organizer and his

247

immense contribution to the movement was indispensable, yet, until the 1990s, his contributions were often ignored. From recent scholarship, it has emerged that his dedication to equality was nurtured early on in life. He was born on March 17, 1912 in West Chester, Pennsylvania. His mother, an unmarried woman, left the raising of Rustin to her parents, who adopted him. He witnessed his grandmother's activism as a member of the NAACP, and she was associated with such notables as W.E.B. Du Bois, James Weldon Johnson, and Mary McLeod Bethune, who stayed in their home when visiting West Chester. It was his grandmother's Quaker teachings which led Rustin on the path to nonviolence and pacifism.

FACT

The Quakers believed in the equality of all people. They opposed the Jim Crow laws because they promoted the belief of black inequality. According to Rustin, it was the Quaker stance on racial equality, rather than him being black, that led to his participation in the Civil Rights movement.

With the seeds of protest planted firmly in Rustin's conscious, he set off for Ohio's Wilberforce University in 1932. He joined the Wilberforce Quartet, and was noted for his ability as a tenor. Within two years, Rustin left the university, and eventually made his way to New York City in 1937. He worked as a backup singer and attended City College of New York. Within a year, Rustin's concern for racial justice and peace drew him to the Young Communist League. He quickly found that with the emergence of World War II, communists lacked a strong commitment to the elimination of discrimination. Rustin's break from the group in 1941 opened up the opportunity to work with A. Philip Randolph, who had previously refused to hire him in the Brotherhood office due to his communist ties.

> Q: **Why did socialist A. Philip Randolph refuse to hire Rustin when he was a member of the Communist Party?**
> Randolph, while he was a socialist, believed that the Communist Party stance on black equality was weak.

Rustin soon fell out with Randolph, who he believed should not have called off the 1941 march on Washington. This opened a new path for Rustin. He joined the peace organization Fellowship of Reconciliation (FOR) in 1941, where he served as youth secretary, worked closely with its leader, A.J. Muste, and learned about the teachings of Gandhi. Rustin's opposition to the war led to his arrest for his failure to comply with the draft act. His noncompliance led to a three-year prison sentence in federal prison. After serving time, he returned to FOR and participated in the group's combined sponsorship with CORE of the 1947 Freedom Rides, which were planned to test the Supreme Court decision desegregating interstate buses. Rustin, one of the riders, was arrested and sentenced to thirty days on the chain gang.

Rustin's continued work with FOR, and his 1949 trip to India, served to cement his commitment to pacifism. By this time, he had become a well-known pacifist, so in 1953, when he was arrested for lewd conduct, it was publicized in the *Los Angeles Times*. Rustin's arrest led to his resignation from FOR. Two years later, when the Montgomery bus boycott began, he had already reunited with Randolph, who urged him to go to Montgomery to train King in the ways of nonviolent resistance. King, aware of Rustin's sexual orientation, accepted his mentorship. Rustin believed that success in Montgomery could lead to success throughout the South, and he was instrumental in the formation of the SCLC.

In 1965, Rustin repositioned himself in the fight for equality. He believed that economic equality was more pressing than discrimination. He became executive director of the A. Philip Randolph

Institute, which focused on economic improvements. In the 1970s, Rustin expanded his efforts to humanitarian concerns. He served as vice chairman of the International Rescue Committee, which offered refugee aid; he visited South Africa, where apartheid was taking place; and he helped to coordinate aid in 1986 through the program Project South Africa. Rustin died on August 24, 1987.

THEY SAID...

" Dr. King came from a very protected background. I don't think he'd ever known a gay person in his life. I think he had no real sympathy or understanding. I think he wanted very much to. *"*

—Bayard Rustin, as quoted in *Time on Two Crosses: The Collected Writings of Bayard Rustin*

Ralph Abernathy

Ralph David Abernathy, one of King's closest friends, was born on March 11, 1926 in Linden, Alabama. Abernathy was the son of a farmer, and a World War II veteran. Upon returning from the war, he enrolled at Alabama State University where, in his junior year, he served as president of his class. It was at the university that Abernathy got his first taste of protest. The dormitories had neither heat nor hot water, and Abernathy took a leadership role in the student demonstrations. He met with the university president, and the matter was quickly resolved. According to Abernathy, this event gave him the confidence he needed when he became involved in the Civil Rights movement. In 1950, he earned a B.S. in Mathematics.

After finishing college, Abernathy continued his education in the masters program at Atlanta University. Abernathy, although he had decided three years before to pursue a career in the ministry, chose to further his education. While at the university, he began studying the preaching styles of ministers. He often visited various churches, and on one Sunday he heard Martin Luther King Jr. speak at Ebenezer

Baptist Church. Days later, they met again, but it was years later that they became close friends.

After graduating with a M.A. in Sociology, Abernathy decided to temporarily forgo studying at a seminary, and instead, he accepted a job as Dean of Men at Alabama State. Montgomery put Abernathy in the right place. When the pastor of First Baptist Church resigned, Abernathy stepped in as acting pastor while they looked for a new minister. Shortly thereafter, to the surprise of Abernathy, this historic church offered him the position as pastor. He continued his leadership at First Baptist until 1961, when he became pastor of West Hunter Street Baptist Church in Atlanta, where King was already living by that time. Abernathy's move to Atlanta gave him greater involvement in the daily workings of the SCLC. This was especially important since he was the treasurer, and King's close friend and advisor.

FACT

Alabama State University was founded in Marion, Alabama in 1867 by former slaves. It was originally named the Lincoln School of Marion, and became known for its teacher-training program. By 1887, it had become a state school, and was moved to Montgomery, where after several name changes, it became Alabama State University in 1954.

After King's death in 1968, he became president of the SCLC. Abernathy quickly got the SCLC on track with his immediate involvement with the Memphis strike. Just one week after taking control, he led the strikers in a march. In May 1968, he continued his leadership by organizing the Poor People's Campaign. Abernathy, just like King, could not escape the internal tensions in the SCLC. Young militants within the SCLC were on the rise, and he constantly battled to continue the work of the organization through its founding principles. By 1977, the tension had become unbearable, especially with the accusations of financial mismanagement. He resigned, and returned to the ministry in Atlanta. Abernathy died on April 17, 1990.

Ella Baker

Ella Baker worked in a man's world during the Civil Rights movement, and she often paid the price. Baker, however, was not deterred. This passionate woman who sought equality was born in the South, where she knew firsthand the pain of discrimination. She was born in Norfolk, Virginia on December 13, 1903. The young Baker grew up around activism. Her mother urged other women to become involved in changing in their communities, and Baker also looked on while extended family members led their own crusades.

Baker set out on her own after graduating from Shaw University in North Carolina in 1927. She moved to Harlem, where she quickly became involved in the activist community. She became executive director of the Young Negroes Cooperative League, where she instituted consumer cooperatives in an effort to counteract the devastation of the Depression. She also worked for the Worker's Education Project as a teacher, and began involvement in trade unions such as the Congress of Industrial Organizations (CIO). Baker moved into the civil-rights realm in 1941, when she worked as a field secretary for the NAACP. In 1943, she became the Director of Branches. Baker found that the NAACP lacked the kind of involvement in the Civil Rights movement that she believed was necessary. While they used the legal system to attack discrimination, she wanted to focus on grassroots organizing.

Baker turned her attention to other groups, such as In Friendship, which she cofounded with Stanley Levison and Bayard Rustin. When the Montgomery bus boycott ended, Baker was part of the early discussions with Rustin and Levison about expanding the Civil Rights movement through the creation of the SCLC. In the beginning, Baker had a role in the SCLC as associate director under John Tilley. When Tilley left, she served as executive director from 1959 to 1960. It was not long before she became disheartened by the management of the organization. Not only was King hesitant about having a woman serving in a leadership position, the leader-centered management of the organization was at odds with Baker's belief that leadership should be group-centered. She believed that instead of depending upon one person for leadership, leadership should be expanded to include more than one leader.

THEY SAID...

"...we had a hard job with domineering women in SCLC because Martin's mother....She was never publicly saying anything, but she ran Daddy King and she ran the church and she ran Martin, and so Martin's problems with Ella Baker, for instance, in the early days of the movement were directly related to his need to be free of that strong matriarchal influence.*"*

—Andrew Young, as quoted in *Bearing the Cross*

Furthermore, Baker, unlike many who worked with King, was unimpressed by him. His refusal to treat her equally and the lack of acceptance of her ideas put a damper on their relationship. Baker left the SCLC a few months after her position as executive director ended. She took her knowledge to the newly formed SNCC, and was a constant help to the young organization. Later, Baker also became involved in the Southern Conference Education Fund, and helped establish the Mississippi Freedom Democratic Party. Baker died in New York City on December 13, 1986.

Malcolm X

Although Malcolm X's stance on the way to eliminate discrimination differed from Martin Luther King's, they did share a few commonalities. They both would die at the hands of assassins, and the activism of their fathers would serve as an example to both. Malcolm X was born in Omaha, Nebraska on May 19, 1925. Malcolm, given the name Malcolm Little at birth, was the son of Earl Little, a supporter of Marcus Garvey's black-nationalist ideology. His father was routinely harassed by white segregationists, so the family moved to Lansing, Michigan. However, they could not escape the harassment. Their home was burned down in 1929, and two years later Malcolm's father died after he was run over by a trolley. Six years later, Malcolm's mother, mentally unstable, was unable to care for him and his siblings. The children were sent to different foster homes.

FACT

The Jamaican-born Marcus Garvey rose to prominence when he came to New York in 1916. He established the organization the Universal Negro Improvement Association, which worked toward the creation of an independent black economy. To that end, he created the Black Star Line and opened grocery stores, restaurants, and a hotel.

Malcolm soon dropped out of high school and moved to Boston, Massachusetts, where he worked odd jobs. Seeking better prospects, he moved to Harlem, where his fate was far worse. He supported himself through criminal activity. By 1946, he had moved back to Boston, and his criminal behavior caught up with him when he was arrested for burglary. In prison, Malcolm experienced a religious conversion to a Muslim sect, the Nation of Islam. He changed his last name from Little, which he considered a slave name, to X. Prison provided him with the time he needed to fully immerse himself in the religion. Upon his release in 1952, the Nation's leader, Elijah Muhammad, ordained him and sent him for a tour around the country to speak out about the tenets of the religion.

Malcolm was an effective speaker, and his teachings of black pride and separatism were appealing to many blacks. As a separatist, Malcolm refused to support the Civil Rights movement's objective of integration. Instead, he called for the separation of the races. Just like King, Malcolm was a powerful speaker, and his antiwhite rhetoric and his suggestion of violent confrontation to end racism soon received the attention of the media. Membership to the Nation of Islam increased, and his divisive message caught the attention of the FBI, who infiltrated the Nation.

Malcolm's stance on civil rights also caught the attention of Martin Luther King, who disagreed with him. King perceived Malcolm's promotion of black separatism and his position on violence as a hindrance to the movement. This failed to stop Malcolm from attempting to engage in dialogue with King. Malcolm sent numerous invitations to him. Most of the time, King was unresponsive, but in one instance, he politely declined the invitation to hear Elijah Muhammad speak in Harlem. King and Malcolm, however, did meet on one occasion. They met for just a minute in March 1964 in Washington, D.C., after King's press conference about the Civil Rights Act.

While King wasn't interested in meeting with Malcolm X, the SNCC was increasingly finding his views on race relations more appealing than King's. In 1964, members of the SNCC had a meeting with Malcolm in Africa. They were impressed with him and his views. Malcolm's stance on the international struggle of blacks was especially appealing. Malcolm also emphasized that the North was just as discriminatory as the South. When King was in a Selma jail in 1965, Malcolm accepted the SNCC invitation to speak at Brown Chapel on February 4. The young members of the SNCC, just like many northern blacks, were attracted to Malcolm X's more militant leadership.

HE SAID...

" I was in jail when he was in Selma, Alabama. I couldn't block his coming, but my philosophy was so antithetical to the philosophy of Malcolm X that I would never have invited Malcolm X to come to Selma when we were in the midst of a nonviolent demonstration. This says nothing about the personal respect I had for him. *"*

By the time of the SNCC meeting with Malcolm, he had left the Nation of Islam. He was disheartened by Muhammad's extramarital affairs. When Malcolm spoke publicly about President Kennedy's death as the "chickens coming home to roost," this prompted Muhammad to silence Malcolm for ninety days. Malcolm left the Nation of Islam in March 1964 and established the Muslim Mosque, Inc. His view of separatism changed when he traveled to Mecca, where he saw that black and white Muslims coexisted. It was then that he adopted his stance on "true brotherhood" and cross-racial alliance. He returned to the United States, where he discontinued his message of separatism, but continued to advocate Black Nationalism. Just days after his trip to Selma, his home was firebombed. On February 21, 1965, while on stage at the Manhattan Audubon Ballroom, he was shot by three Nation of Islam members.

Stokely Carmichael

Stokely Carmichael was among those in the SNCC who was influenced by Malcolm X. Carmichael, a native of Trinidad who was born in Port of Spain on June 29, 1941, began to hear about him when he arrived in New York City in 1952. One of the first stories he heard about Malcolm was how he stopped his car one day after driving by a group of black men shooting craps, and pointed out the futility of what they were doing. The young Malcolm, who was in the process of organizing Muhammad's Mosque #7, informed the men that behind them sat the Schomburg building, which housed one of the largest collections of black-history documents. This story inspired Carmichael to visit the Schomburg regularly.

Carmichael took his studies further when, in 1960, he left New York for Washington, D.C., where he began his studies at Howard University. Carmichael quickly became caught up in the Civil Rights movement. He was a participant in the 1961 Freedom Rides. In 1964, he graduated from Howard and took on the role of the SNCC director of a voter-registration drive in Mississippi. In 1966, after becoming Chairman of the SNCC, he popularized the slogan "Black Power." He started to move away from the movement's stance on nonviolence, and was instrumental in the 1966 organization of the political party the Lowndes County Freedom Organization, which worked to register voters. The group adopted the black panther as their emblem. In October 1966, in Oakland, California, the Black Panther Party was created. One year later, Carmichael left the SNCC to join the Black Panther Party. He served as prime minister until 1969, when he moved to Guinea, West Africa. He changed his name to Kwame Ture, and spent many years promoting Pan-Africanism. On November 15, 1998 he died of prostate cancer.

Chapter 19

KING'S PERSONAL LIFE

WHILE EQUALITY BECAME KING'S mission, his life reflected little of the satisfaction that he should have received. His constant traveling, exhaustion, and depression at times put a damper on his enthusiasm for the accomplishments of the Civil Rights movement. There is nothing new about these facets of King's life, but recent scholarship has uncovered that King was a man who had failings as well. He was unfaithful to his wife, and plagiarism has been revealed in many of his writings.

Life on the Road

After the Montgomery bus boycott ended, King spent the majority of his life traveling throughout the nation giving speeches to earn money for the SCLC. On average, he traveled four times per week, and it was typical for him to give more than one speech per day. According to King, he was able to endure this grueling schedule because he only needed four hours of sleep. Nevertheless, King's constant travels drove him to exhaustion. Naturally, the pressure eventually led to the necessity of several days of rest.

A Life of Exhaustion

Exhaustion led King to consider other alternatives for his life. On several occasions he contemplated a temporary leave from the SCLC, but he declined to do so until 1967, when he took a two-month sabbatical. This, however, failed to provide him with the rest he needed. King also contemplated another career. During the last few months of his life, he considered taking a sabbatical, teaching temporarily at New York's Union Theological Seminary, or even moving out of the country to Switzerland or Africa to retire from public life. He weighed the reasons for such a move, but ultimately he concluded that he could not run from his responsibilities.

HE SAID...

"...at times I have felt that I could no longer bear such a heavy burden, and was tempted to retreat to a more quiet and serene life. But every time such a temptation appeared, something came to strengthen and sustain my determination....God has been profoundly real to me....In the midst of outer dangers I have felt an inner calm."

Counting on God for Strength

King often turned to God for strength. Time after time, he relied on his memory of the occasion in his kitchen during the Montgomery bus boycott. King was comforted by his belief that God was his constant companion. It was also his belief that his life and purpose was guided by God, and this gave him strength. It was this knowledge that always drew him back into the movement and away from his own desire to live an ordinary life. For King, it was more important to do God's work than to fulfill his own desires. According to associates, King realized that his purpose had been defined by God, and that it was a divine calling.

THEY SAID...

" I think that Martin always felt that he had a special purpose in life and that that purpose in life was something that was given to him by God, that he was the son and grandson of Baptist preachers, and he understood, I think, the scriptural notion of men of destiny. *"*

—Andrew Young, as quoted in *Bearing the Cross*

The Death Threats

As King became increasingly famous, dealing with the death threats, especially while on the road, became a common part of his life. At first, the threats burdened him emotionally, but he eventually adjusted. While he was well aware that the threats should be taken seriously, King refused to have bodyguards. For King, life was worthless if he had to live in constant fear. His own death was something he had come to accept as far back as 1957, when Montgomery withstood a series of shootings after the bus boycott ended. King proclaimed to a reporter that if death was the cost of dedication to the cause, it was worth dying for.

As the death threats increased, he regularly discussed his own death. When President Kennedy was assassinated, King told Coretta that he anticipated that his end would come in the same way. The violence in society disturbed him, and he believed that because society was sick with a tendency toward violence, he too would be murdered. Months later, in January 1964, King reiterated his belief to Coretta and a friend when they were forced to evacuate a plane after a bomb threat was made. His friend discouraged such talk, but King responded that he was just being realistic.

HE SAID...

"If I were constantly worried about death, I couldn't function. After a while, if your life is more or less constantly in peril, you come to a point where you accept the possibility philosophically....I feel, though, that my cause is so right, so moral, that if I should lose my life, in some way it would aid the cause."

King again faced the possibility of death when he toured Mississippi in support of the MFDP's door-to-door campaign in July 1964. He was keenly aware of the death threats by the Klan, but went anyway. His friends were fearful, and so was President Johnson, who took the unusual step of ordering FBI Director J. Edgar Hoover to send agents to protect him. King, despite the unusual circumstances, continued with the tour as if nothing was out of the ordinary. By this time, King's attitude about his own immortality was indifference. When Malcolm X died, the press was quick to ask King about his concern over his own death. He responded that he was used to the weekly and sometimes daily threats that he received. In addition, he stated that he was prepared. He had named Ralph Abernathy as his successor to the SCLC. Furthermore, it was more important to stand up against evil than to harbor a fear of death.

King also freely discussed his impending death in public. It was customary, especially near the end of his life, for King to incorporate comments about his mortality in his sermons. In his last speech in Memphis he spoke about his readiness to die, the same speech he had delivered many times before. King's lack of concern over his potential death was also noted by his friends, who viewed his intense preoccupation with it as morbid. When King and Abernathy returned from their vacation in Jamaica, a month before King's involvement in the Memphis strike, King told Abernathy that when he died, his desire was to be remembered as a "drum major for justice." However, King also spoke of his desire to live, and not be a martyr for the cause. At a speech to a Chicago crowd, he proclaimed the he desired to live, but that he knew he probably wouldn't.

Fighting Depression

King's preoccupation with his own death only added to his bouts of depression. Early on, his depression stemmed from the constant stream of demands for speaking engagements. Through the years, he struggled to combat his depression, which only seemed to worsen when he received less-than-adequate rest. His depression, however, reached its peak during the last year of his life. As King's leadership in the movement began to falter, he struggled with confidence in his own abilities.

Dealing with Self-Doubt

His increased opposition to the Vietnam War and the public rebuke of this position only intensified his feelings of self-doubt. In a state of depression, he told Coretta that even though he was expected to have all the answers, he didn't, and he no longer wanted to speak to people. Shortly thereafter, King expressed his misgivings about his abilities to the Ebenezer congregation. He confessed that people often develop inferiority complexes, feel insecure, lack confidence, and experience a sense of failure.

THEY SAID...

" Few people know how humble this giant was. And even fewer knew how troubled he was, and even tortured, because he doubted his own capacity to be unerring in the fateful divisions thrust upon him. *"*

—Harry Belafonte and Stanley Levison as quoted in *My Life with Martin Luther King, Jr.*

Even King's associates and friends saw the change in King during the last year of his life. Roger Wilkins of the Justice Department's Community Relations Service perceived that King was tired and discouraged. Abernathy noted that after returning from a brief vacation, he saw a complete change in King. King was weary, sad, depressed, and appeared to be a different person. Andrew Young noted that King's depression was much different from his earlier depression. He didn't sleep, he talked often about death, spiritually he was drained, and he lacked direction in the Poor People's Campaign. Young interpreted the cause for his depression as less physical than emotional fatigue. He described King as having the disposition of bull: He had the strength when things were working, but in the times when clarity and direction were lacking, King found it challenging. According to Young, King was having feelings of self-doubt.

A Stressful Home Life

Those close to King had another perception as to why King suffered from depression—his home life. According to SCLC executive director William Rutherford, while he recognized that Coretta Scott King bore the entire burden of raising their children, he believed that Coretta also resented King's insistence that she stay home rather than have a larger role in the movement. It was King's persistence, according to Rutherford, that caused a lot of tension. Rutherford described their relationship as tense and at times unpleasant due to these differences. According to staff members, Coretta was a widow before King died.

A Lonely Life

King's friends also sensed an increasing loneliness in King. They described King's personality as typically formal and reserved with a hint of shyness in public. To his friends, he was a good-humored man who liked to joke around. One of the most notable qualities about him was his extraordinary ability to accurately mimic people. His friends noted the many times King entertained them with this talent. Although he was constantly surrounded by people, he had few close friends. King expressed his desire for more friends like Ralph Abernathy, with whom he could discuss his deepest feelings, burdens, and weaknesses. His friends noted that the man they had known was slowly changing into a lonely person.

King and Coretta's Marriage

Two years after King and Coretta married, King began his work in the Civil Rights movement. With barely a honeymoon phase, King left his new wife and young baby to pursue endeavors that would take him far from home. Coretta, while supportive of King's crusade for equality, found her own life with King put aside. King spent most of his time away from home. However, when he was home, his time was often spent on the phone. Coretta, therefore, was charged with making the decisions regarding the children without input from King. For example, Coretta recalled that on one occasion when she was deciding which school their oldest daughter should attend, King told her that those concerns were her domain and she should make the decision.

FACT

Yolanda King also remembered her mother taking charge of the household as a result of her father's absence from the home. King acknowledged that he was away from home, and credited Coretta with the raising of the children. He also believed that although his children were young, they understood the importance of his work.

Coretta was also torn by her own desires to extend her realm beyond the home. Prior to marrying King, she had wanted to become a professional singer. Although she realized her marriage to a man with old-fashioned views of women would dictate that she remain home, she still desired more. She expressed to one reporter that she had been unable to participate in many of the marches due to her husband's desire she stay home with the children. Andrew Young explained that King felt that at least one of them had to be home for the children.

Coretta understood her husband's commitment to the movement, and most of the time she remained quiet about her dissatisfaction with it. Nevertheless, despite her understanding, at times the lack of attention he gave to the family was overwhelming. During the St. Augustine campaign, an FBI wiretap recorded an angry Coretta telling King that she was displeased with the lack of time he spent at home. Coretta became increasingly agitated with King's neglect when, months later, he forgot to call and check on Marty and Dexter, who had undergone operations to remove their tonsils.

Allegations of Extramarital Affairs

The allegations of extramarital affairs began after the Montgomery bus boycott. In October 1957, the nationally circulated newspaper the *Pittsburgh Courier* published a story that a southern preacher involved in the Civil Rights movement should be careful about his conduct. The story further noted that segregationists had hired private detectives to catch this preacher in a compromising position with a woman who wasn't his wife.

A Cautionary Warning

Just one year later, King received another warning. This time, it was from family friend and Reverend J. Raymond Henderson, who had heard of the violent attack on Abernathy by the husband of the woman he allegedly had an affair with. Henderson was concerned for King's reputation, and cautioned him about the importance of avoiding the appearance of wrongdoing. He further noted that because of King's prominence, he would become the target of those seeking to discredit him. Women, wrote Henderson, could very well become his downfall if he failed to resist this temptation.

THEY SAID...

" During our whole marriage we never had one single serious discussion about either of us being involved with another person....If I ever had any suspicions....I never would have even mentioned them to Martin. I just wouldn't have burdened him with anything so trivial...all that other business just didn't have a place in the very high-level relationship we enjoyed. *"*

—Coretta Scott King, *My Life with Martin Luther King, Jr.*

King failed to take Henderson's warning, and those that came later from associates. By the time he won the Nobel Peace Prize of 1964, his relations with women outside of his marriage were far from secret. Wiley Branton decided to approach King about the subject when he was unable to ignore the rumors. He told King that colleagues had expressed concern over his behavior and were worried that he was going to get hurt, but King was unresponsive. The topic again came up with another friend, and this time King responded that because he was away from home the majority of each month, sex served as a way to reduce his anxiety.

Promiscuity in the Movement

King's sexual proclivities were common among other civil-rights activists. The movement itself and the leadership position King was in seemed to harbor an environment where it was acceptable for movement leaders to engage in extramarital affairs. According to activist Michael Harrington, King's behavior was typical. James

Bevel, who was married to activist Diane Nash, was known for his womanizing behavior, and Hosea Williams had gained a reputation for his sexual escapades during his leadership of the SCOPE project. Further, SCLC's William Rutherford noted his shock at hearing about a SCLC party in Atlanta in which a prostitute was hired. When newcomer Rutherford brought up the rumors at a meeting, the rest of the staff, including King, laughed.

King, as a nationally recognized leader, had even more access to woman than other associates. Harrington later recounted that he witnessed women throwing themselves at King. William Rutherford also came to know this other side of King. He saw that King had an interest in women in general. According to Rutherford, while King did engage in one-night stands, he had three relationships that were longstanding. In one relationship, he saw the woman daily for years and developed an emotional attachment to her.

A Guilt-Ridden Man

It's hard to say how King justified his extramarital affairs that were in direct conflict with Christian principles. Perhaps his sexual escapades during his college years had numbed his sensitivity to his behavior. It is clear that he was keenly aware of the scriptural prohibition against this behavior. In an interview, King described sex as sacred when not abused. King stated that God created sex for the marriage relationship, and sex shouldn't be abused, as is so often done when it is engaged in casually.

King's sermons to the Ebenezer congregation were a telling reflection of his understanding of sin and his own guilt. He believed that it was human nature for all men to sin. He also believed that in each person there was the duality of Dr. Jekyll and Mr. Hyde. It was even common for him to speak about himself as a sinner who made moral mistakes, because he wanted his congregation to view him as a sinner and not a saint. Ultimately, he wanted to be a good man who God would accept in his Kingdom because he had tried.

A Humble Man

King's humility may help explain the reason behind his extra-marital affairs. King's friends and close associates all noted that King was intensely humble. The snobbishness that Reverend William E. Gardener had found in King during his time at Crozer was non-existent during his leadership in the Civil Rights movement. King never hesitated to speak with people from even the most humble background. According to his friends, he made everyone feel important, and took the time to talk with anyone who approached him. According to David J. Garrow, it may have been King's own belief in his unworthiness that was the cause of his promiscuity; it was a way for him to throw off the robe of sainthood.

Coretta's Knowledge of Affairs

Coretta has stated that she had never discussed the issue of affairs with King. According to William Rutherford, one of his visits to the King home turned into an uncomfortable situation. When he arrived at their home with associate Chauncey Eskridge, they were greeted by Coretta. Eskridge asked if King was home, and she responded that he was at a meeting at Rutherford's house. An uncomfortable Rutherford was caught off guard. He responded with hesitancy that his presence at the meeting was unnecessary. According to Rutherford, Coretta gave him a "penetrating glance."

This wasn't the first time that Coretta had encountered the unpleasantness of King's behavior. She had heard the 1965 FBI tape in which King allegedly engaged in sexual activity with another woman. When asked later about the recording, she said that she was unable to decipher its content. Other associates also experienced this same type of avoidance from Coretta.

King's Financial Support of the Movement

While King had a hard time resisting sexual temptation, the temptation to profit from his fame was by no means a temptation for him. He had never been influenced by the prospect of making money. In fact, while in college he had developed an opposition to his father's concern with money. King felt that his father, like many people, was overly concerned with making money. His lack of desire for material possessions increased after he visited India. Coretta sensed a change in him. She said that his growing selflessness had led to his increasingly dismissive attitude toward his clothing and appearance, which up until then he had taken pride in. Since his college years at Morehouse, King had enjoyed nice clothing. Even his college friends noticed this, and gave him the nickname "Tweed."

King's selflessness also affected the financial status of the SCLC. When he won the Nobel Peace Prize, he donated the prize money to the group, despite the objection of Coretta. She wanted to put some of the money aside for college for their children, but King insisted that the money go in full to the SCLC. Later, when two board members suggested that he accept a salary from the organization, King declined the offer. He explained that his income from Ebenezer Baptist Church and the sum that he kept from speaking and writing was enough to support his family.

FACT

King believed that he should not profit from the Civil Rights movement and he was horrified at the thought of leaving substantial wealth behind upon his death. The only salary he accepted from the SCLC was $1 per year. According to King, this was only so that he could participate in the employee's group insurance plan.

King was also concerned with even the slightest appearance of greed. His family lived in a modest rented house until they finally bought one in 1965. Long before, Coretta had urged him to buy a home, but King had always been reluctant to own a house because of his philosophical beliefs about acquiring wealth. When he finally did agree, they purchased a home for $10,000 in a modest area in southwest Atlanta. He also agreed to have it renovated, and once finished, he was dismayed because he considered it too nice. He was so troubled in fact, that his friends were subjected to his constant inquiries about whether the house was too big and too nice. According to Coretta, to him the house seemed like a mansion.

Plagiarism Uncovered

In the 1970s, Professor Ira Zepp discovered that in *Stride Toward Freedom*, King had replicated and paraphrased exact portions from several sources. According to an unpublished study by Zepp, King took phrases, sentences, and paragraphs from the books *Basic Christian Ethics* by Paul Ramsey and *Agape and Eros* by Anders Nygren. In all cases, King had failed to note his reference to either source.

THEY SAID...

" Even as we became more and more aware of the extent to which King relied upon the words of others, we also came to the somewhat paradoxical conclusion that King's academic writings—and certainly his later writings and speeches as a public figure—were reliable expressions of his persona. *"*

—Clayborne Carson, "Editing Martin Luther King, Jr.: Political and Scholarly Issues"

Plagiarism was discovered again in 1988, when Clayborne Carson and the staff at the King Project came across more plagiaries when conducting research for an upcoming book of King's academic work, writings, and speeches. After investigating whether this was a general pattern of King's work as a college student and public personality, it was affirmed that King had in fact engaged in plagiarism on numerous occasions. In June 1991, the findings of the King Project research staff were published in the *Journal of American History*. After years of research, they determined that King had consistently plagiarized in his work, including material in his dissertation, speeches, and sermons.

Chapter 20

MARTIN LUTHER KING'S LEGACY

THE MEMORY OF MARTIN Luther King's life and work has become ingrained in the nation's consciousness. He has come to symbolize the time in American history when black citizens sought something more than separate and unequal. His legacy is that of a crusader for justice, equality, and peace. It was his work and leadership in the Civil Rights movement that helped move society toward creating a more just and equitable nation.

Impact on Society

King undoubtedly had a hand in changing the social fabric of America during the 1950s and 1960s. Yet, it has been said by scholars, participants in the movement, and even King himself, that if Martin Luther King had remained absent from the Montgomery bus boycott of 1955, the Civil Rights movement would have continued without him. According to Ella Baker, it was the Civil Rights movement that made King, not King who made the Civil Rights movement.

King neither disputed nor disagreed with these statements. Prior to his leadership, groups such as the NAACP had been attacking segregation through legal methods for years. In addition, many southern black communities were active in fighting for equality, and had even achieved gains at the local level. In fact, the Montgomery bus boycott was initiated by Rosa Parks's refusal to move from her seat, and it was originally orchestrated by local leader E.D. Nixon. In addition, one of the most substantial gains came nationally with the NAACP's legal victory in the 1954 Supreme Court decision *Brown v. Board of Education*. Gains, especially in the legal realm, would have come, and did come, without King.

An Oratory Gift That Moved a Nation

Even so, King did possess a unique gift that distinguished him from other movement leaders. His greatest asset was his oratory abilities. It was this skill that placed him at the forefront of the movement. King utilized this ability to the fullest by traveling throughout the country making speeches, leading marches, and at his most nationally televised speech at the March on Washington, he used it as a forum to urge the nation to see the wrong and evil of segregation. Especially on that day, but on numerous other occasions, King's style of expression was more appealing than any other black leader that came before him. He used the skill that he had developed for a career in the ministry to help institute a plan for social change.

A Drum Major for Justice

On countless occasions, King voiced his desire that if he was remembered for nothing else, he wanted to be called a "drum major for justice." King's first priorities were voting rights and desegregation. In 1964, the passage of the Civil Rights Act was momentous. Not since 1875 had the government made any substantial move toward civil-rights legislation. At that moment in time, King had a hand in working toward its enactment. King helped to draw attention to the injustice from a moral standpoint that not only led to the enactment of additional civil-rights legislation, but also changed the hearts and minds of many white Americans. With King at the forefront, it was the combined efforts of civil-rights groups and activists that led to the change in America.

HE SAID...

" Yes, if you want to say that I was a drum major, say that I was a drum major for justice. Say that I was a drum major for peace. I was a drum major for righteousness....I won't have the fine and luxurious things of life to leave behind. But I just want to leave a committed life behind. *"*

King's commitment to serve others led him beyond the fight for racial and political equality, and into the realm of economic equality. The last years of his life were focused on his belief that poverty should be stricken from American society. By using the same method of nonviolence as he had done to effect change in the South, King attacked the inequity the poor faced. King believed the northern cities required his attention just as much as the South. The Poor People's Campaign was the beginning of his crusade to attack the poverty faced by all races.

King, a Nobel Peace Prize winner, was committed to peace at all levels of society. Since his leadership of nonviolent resistance had won him the prize, King felt a strong passion to speak out against the Vietnam War. He was consistent on his stance for peace not only domestically; he wanted America to act peacefully toward other nations as well. Despite the unpopularity of his opinion on the war, King believed it was better to stand up alone for what he believed in than remain silent.

King's Leadership

Martin Luther King is often categorized as a leader for blacks, but this is far from the truth. King was a moral leader who brought the country out of a dark time in American history. His leadership was twofold: He was able to mobilize blacks, while at the same time appealing to the consciences of many whites. King's appeal as a leader to blacks was unique. Roy Wilkins, A. Philip Randolph, and the Urban League's Whitney Young all had a following, but far less than King's. There had never been a black leader, until King, that was able to appeal with such force. King's influence was a result of several factors. For African Americans, his background was rooted in the black community, he was a Baptist preacher, and his academic training combined with his religious faith provided the leadership skills he needed. To white America, he was an African American with an extraordinary ability to convince them of the evil of segregation. His words carried a powerful punch that, while what he said about segregation was not new, stirred a moral awakening. Cementing his position was his leadership through nonviolent resistance, which appealed to decency and the commonality of humanity that, until then, had been ignored.

In addition to the charisma of his leadership, King had clear strategies for achieving goals. He believed that besides the use of legal tactics, the federal government was a necessary ally. Through his studies of Reinhold Niebuhr, King concluded that because of man's sinfulness, a restraining force was needed. King agreed with Niebuhr that it was the government that could counteract collective evil. King's ultimate goal in many of his campaigns was to force the federal government to act. Time after time, his strategy worked.

Initially, King was disappointed with federal intervention, which only encompassed protection, but soon the federal government responded with the enactment of civil-rights legislation. By utilizing the federal government, in combination with nonviolent resistance, King's role in the Civil Rights movement was instrumental in securing longstanding change.

THEY SAID...

// Martin Luther King died as he lived, fighting to his last breath for justice. In only twelve years of public life he evoked more respect for black people than a preceding century had produced. //

—Harry Belafonte and Stanley Levison, as quoted in *My Life with Martin Luther King, Jr.*

King's Courage

King's legacy also exemplifies something else: courage. King believed that when fighting oppression, the participant must willingly give his life for the cause. His dedication to justice in the face of death is an example of his immense courage. He placed his own safety in jeopardy in the numerous marches he led and in his tours throughout the country speaking out for the cause of civil rights. Despite the danger he faced, he was committed to achieving justice for black Americans. King threw his fear aside and set out to achieve justice in a nation that had continually been unjust.

King the Theologian

King's work as a social reformer is one of his greatest contributions. However, King's role as a theologian has received less attention. As early as May 3, 1968, King was recognized as a theologian by Herbert Richardson in his unpublished article, "Martin Luther King—Unsung Theologian." Richardson argued that King was the greatest theologian of his time because of his perception of the problem of evil.

Theologian James Cone contends that King was fundamental in the development of black theology. According to Cone and James Evans, King's theological perspective has its roots in the black church. While King studied the work of white theologians, his thought was rooted in the black community. Evans notes that evidence of this appears in the SCLC's connection to the church and King's service as a minister. Thus, King was committed to the black community and formulated his theology from this perspective.

THEY SAID...

"The bedrock of King's theology was not laid at Crozer Theological Seminary or at Boston University, but in the Afro-American Baptist Church of his youth, and at Morehouse College....King's dream grew out of the spirituality of the Afro-American tradition."

—James Evans, "Keepers of the Dream: The Black Church and Martin Luther King, Jr."

While King drew from theologians, he also expanded on their conclusions. Other scholars have asserted that King was aware and influenced by the method of theology and chose to use it as a tool to sustain the Civil Rights movement. The scholarship of Noel Leo Erskine has noted that King drew from theology when he wrote the "Letter from Birmingham Jail," in which he applied the theological concept of not confirming or affirming church practice, but instead criticizing and revising church practice. The letter to the ministers was intended to expose their support of unjust laws and challenge them to seek justice.

According to Erskine, King took theology beyond just concept, and applied it to human experience. While most theologians use the Bible and tradition for the purpose of communicating about culture, King took it a step further. He questioned a particular situation—the segregation of African Americans—and was able to relate the gospel of Jesus to that situation. He determined that the gospel could be used in a social context as well as in a personal context. It is through this distinction that King was able to draw the justification to challenge oppression from Christianity. For King, salvation wasn't just a personal commitment; it was also a commitment to seek social change. Thus, religion and social concerns couldn't be separated.

King also believed that reconciliation was both the goal and at the center of the struggle for equality. Reconciliation would lead to a restored and beloved community. Throughout his leadership, he continuously stressed that the goal was not to shame the white man, but to turn him into a friend. King had been astounded when he went to India and saw that nonviolent resistance had brought reconciliation between the former European leaders and the new Indian government. King remained impressed by this, and taught that for a beloved community to be built, reconciliation must be the goal. Love, asserted King, was central to the concept of a reconciled community. Love insists upon justice within relationships. Neither love nor justice could be separated from the other. It was the combination of love and justice that forced a person to see how power operates in society, according to King. Reconciliation was necessary because human beings were part of a moral community, and God was a part of the struggle.

Later in King's life, he expanded his focus from racial inequality to economic inequality. King believed social justice was not enough. As sons and daughters of God, economic and political justice was required in order to change society. King's last campaign, the Poor People's March, was an attempt to attack society's oppression of the poor. In his final book, *Where Do We Go From Here? Chaos or Community?*, King reiterated his long-held belief that capitalism created a large gap between the rich and the poor. The church, he believed, should have a large part in seeking equity between the rich and poor. It was the duty of the Church, just as Jesus helped the poor, to help the oppressed.

THEY SAID...

" There was no doubt in King's mind that Christian faith required the combining of a deeply religious faith with an intense social involvement. He refused to separate the religious and the ethical, the spiritual and the secular, and the personal and the social. *"*

—Noel Leo Erskine, *King Among the Theologians*

King's Legacy Continues: The Poor People's Campaign

In death, King would finally get the support he wanted for the Poor People's Campaign. The former opposition to it by King's associates was put aside in an effort to carry out the legacy of their slain leader. Despite King's death, leaders in Washington were still unhappy about the march. They anticipated that just like the violence that had spread throughout the nation over the past few years and had recently erupted due to King's death, the march would cause bloodshed. What Washington's politicians did support was the passage of the 1968 Civil Rights Act. Just days after King was murdered, it was signed into law by President Johnson. This act, also known as the Fair Housing Act, banned housing discrimination and provided more protection for civil-rights workers.

To launch the protest, Ralph Abernathy, the president of the SCLC, led a Memphis rally on May 2. On May 11, Coretta Scott King, in the wake of her husband's death, took on a leadership role and became directly involved in the movement, leading welfare recipients in the Mother's Day march. On May 13, the first phase of the demonstration got underway when the building of "Resurrection City" began. Abernathy launched the event when he hammered the first nail into one of the wooden homes. The community was expected to encompass brotherhood and love, and would exemplify the poverty experienced by America's poor.

Abernathy and the SCLC quickly found that King's leadership was sorely missed. Among the interracial group that had come to Washington for the demonstration were gang members. The media, who covered the event twenty-four hours a day, was subjected to constant taunting and harassment by the young gang members. Such hostile behavior only intensified the negative media coverage of the campaign. In addition, the Solidarity Day rally had to be postponed from May 30 to June 19, due to the slowed building of Resurrection City. To make matters worse, it rained for eleven days.

FACT

Although officials were less-than supportive of this second march on Washington, the SCLC encountered very little resistance during the planning of the demonstration. When they requested a permit to occupy specific areas for six weeks, their request was speedily granted. The Attorney General concluded that it was better to grant the request than to deal with the aftermath a denial would bring.

By the time that planning for Solidarity Day began, things only got worse. Abernathy requested that Bayard Rustin plan the events of the day. Rustin, believing that the campaign desperately needed to define their goals, took the matter into his own hands. A problem emerged when the campaign leaders realized that the goals had been reduced. Rustin was forced to resign on June 7. On June 13, a revised statement of goals was issued. It called for the expansion of welfare, education, jobs, and health programs. Despite the glitch to the movement, Solidarity Day proceeded as planned on June 19. While it was far from as stirring as the first March on Washington, and had only 50,000 participants, a surprising twist emerged. Jesse Jackson, one of the first to object to King's Poor People's Campaign, delivered a memorable speech that encompassed many of King's beliefs. He spoke of the disparity between the rich and the poor and of the evil of a war that took resources away from providing an annual income and jobs for all Americans.

Despite Jackson's speech, Solidarity Day ended with a whimper. As participants left for home, Resurrection City remained a hideaway for the gangs. Days later, tension with the police reached a heightened level. On June 24, Resurrection City was cleared away as Washington, D.C. got back to business.

Coretta Continues King's Legacy

After King's death, Coretta Scott King became determined to have the legacy of her husband carried on. She became a spokesperson for justice, nonviolence, equality, and peace. She continued to stay involved in demonstrations, she traveled worldwide speaking out against social and economic injustice, and she helped create the Black Leadership Forum, the Black Leadership Roundtable, and the Full Employment Action Council. Her dedication encompassed more than the justice and equality that her husband had died for. She dedicated her life to ensuring that King's memory was carried on for generations through the creation of the Martin Luther King Nonviolent Center for Social Change, and she became committed to the establishment of a Martin Luther King federal holiday.

MLK Nonviolent Center for Social Change

The King Center was founded by Coretta Scott King in 1968. It is located in the Martin Luther King National Historic Site in Atlanta, which houses King's childhood home and Ebenezer Baptist Church. This twenty-three-acre national historic park is a living memorial to Dr. King's legacy. Included on the site is the tomb of Dr. King, located next to Freedom Hall and his birth home. The King Center includes a library of archives and exhibits. In 1977, the site was declared a National Historic Landmark, and three years later it was named a National Historic Site. The chairman of the center is Dr. King's son, Dexter Scott King. Under his leadership, the center has taken on the new goal of using Dr. King's philosophy of nonviolence to achieve a beloved community.

The tomb of Martin Luther King Jr. located next to Freedom Hall and a reflecting pool.

Martin Luther King Day

The call for a federal holiday to celebrate the work of Dr. King began in the House of Representatives, with the introduction of a bill by Congressman John Conyers four days after King was murdered. Success was evasive in 1968, but ten years later, Congress again faced the issue when the National Council of Churches urged the creation of a national holiday in honor of King. Shortly after his assassination, various northern states had already created a state holiday, but the federal government still resisted the passage of legislation.

In October 1983, after years of Coretta Scott King campaigning for a national holiday, the Senate passed legislation creating a Martin Luther King Jr. holiday and a Martin Luther King Jr. Federal Holiday Commission, which would oversee the implementation of the first observance on January 20, 1986. When the bill was signed into law by President Ronald Reagan, Coretta Scott King was there for the occasion. Mrs. King served as chair of the commission until the first celebration. In 1994, Congress passed a bill making the Martin Luther King holiday a day of service in celebration of his legacy.

Martin Luther King Jr. National Memorial

The four-acre Washington, D.C. Martin Luther King Jr. National Memorial is located on the National Mall. The Memorial, which is in the process of being built, held a groundbreaking ceremony on November 13, 2006. The expected completion of the project is in 2008. At the center of the Memorial will be the 30-foot statue called the "Stone of Hope." The grounds will include a stone wall with excerpts from his speeches, and a tribute to his beliefs of democracy, justice, and hope will be reflected throughout the Memorial. The purpose of the Memorial is to honor Martin Luther King Jr. and to share the significance of his contributions to visitors.

Has His Dream Been Fulfilled?

Has Martin Luther King's dream of equality been achieved? Progress has been made, especially in the realm of Dr. King's original goals of desegregation and voting rights. There have also been considerable steps forward in politics. During King's lifetime, Thurgood Marshall, the director of NAACP's Legal Defense and Education Fund, became the nation's first black U.S. Supreme Court Justice in 1967. One year later, Shirley Chisholm became the first African American woman elected to Congress, and in 1990 Lawrence Douglas Wilder became Virginia's first black elected governor. Most recently, in 2001 Colin Powell became the first black Secretary of State, and Condoleezza Rice became the first black female Secretary of State in 2005.

Improvements in educational opportunities for African Americans have also been realized through special programs. Affirmative Action, for instance, has led to the increased population of blacks on college campuses around the nation. Affirmative Action has become a widely debated issue, and challengers to the program have often enlisted the name of King in support of their opposition. They claim that King wouldn't have wanted a program that sorted out college applicants by the color of their skin. However, according to proponents of affirmative action, there is evidence that King would have supported this program. It is argued that his own insistence on the creation of special programs, such as economic reform and compensation to blacks for past wrongs, supports the belief that he would have favored the program.

Q: **When was the Affirmative Action program created?**
Affirmative Action was incorporated into the 1964 Civil Rights Act. One year later, an executive order extended the Act's reach to apply to federal contractors, in order to ensure that they didn't discriminate. A revised order in 1970 expanded it to include education.

While Affirmative Action has led to gains at the college level, primary and secondary schools in black communities have often been left behind. Even though the decision in *Brown v. Board of Education* dismantled public-school segregation, many schools in minority areas are unable to provide students with a quality education. Typically, schools are financed with local tax money. As a result, in predominately minority areas in the slums, black students often receive below-standard instructional materials, equipment, and school facilities.

Economic reform was another issue that King was deeply concerned with. Since his death, the type of reform he envisioned hasn't been implemented. There is no guaranteed employment nor is there an annual income, and the disparity between the rich and the poor still exists. Poor blacks in the ghetto still feel the devastating effects of poverty. The black ghetto has seen a rise in drug addiction, unemployment, and violence. On the other hand, the African American middle class has continued to grow as greater educational opportunities have provided blacks with new avenues. The rise of upper-class blacks has markedly increased, especially among athletes.

FACT

In 1992, Los Angeles police officers were put on trial in federal court for violating Rodney King's civil rights. Two officers were convicted and two were acquitted. In response to the King incident, the Secretary of State headed up a commission to investigate the Los Angeles police department. It was determined that the police department was plagued by both racism and sexism.

Though gains have been made, racial tensions continue to plague the nation. In 1999, the governor of New Jersey acknowledged that highway-patrol officers regularly engaged in stopping black motorists based only on their race. The Los Angeles police have also played a role in the tension between blacks and the law. In 1991, an observer caught the beating of Rodney King by white officers on tape. When the case went to trial one year later, a jury acquitted the officers of all charges. Los Angeles's black community erupted in violence. For four days, the city was in chaos as rioting, looting, and fires caused substantial devastation in the black community.

Since King's death there have been both gains and failings in regard to the accomplishment of his dream. The end of poverty and implementation of peace are still unrealized, and discrimination, while no longer in the form of segregation, still plagues society to a certain extent. However, America has come a long way from the racial tension that existed prior to the Civil Rights movement. The battles waged by King and others during the Civil Rights movement are still being waged by those who believe in the fulfillment of his dream.

King's family has chosen to use his legacy to effect change throughout the world. It is through such efforts as the Martin Luther King Nonviolent Center for Social Change, the King Memorial in Washington, D.C., and the Martin Luther King Jr. holiday that his legacy as a "drum major for justice" will continue.

Appendix A

GLOSSARY

Affirmative Action
It gives preferences in social benefits and educational opportunities to minorities and women as a way to remedy past discrimination.

beloved community
Occurs following the aftermath of non-violent resistance.

Black Codes
These laws were enacted during Reconstruction to restrict the freedom of blacks.

Black Panther Party
They believed in armed self-defense and patrolled black communities carrying weapons, legal references, and recorders.

black power
This was a movement during the Civil Rights era that sought social, political, and economic equality. The movement is associated with the black radical activists of the Civil Rights movement.

Capitalism
The economic system where production, distribution, and property are privately owned.

civil disobedience
Nonviolent protest of governmental laws or policy used to change these laws.

Civil Rights Act of 1964
It prohibits racial discrimination in employment, schools, and public facilities.

Civil Rights movement
The movement began in the late 1950s and was led mostly by black leaders. The main objective was to dismantle the system of segregation in the South and to eliminate discriminatory voter registration.

Communism
Communism is an economic theory that promotes the idea that society should control the production of goods. Ideally, it was a classless society without a government structure.

Congress of Racial Equality (CORE)
An interracial organization that attacked racial segregation using nonviolent resistance by conducting sit-ins, Freedom Rides, and voter-registration drives.

Fellowship of Reconciliation (FOR)
It was a pacifist organization in America that promoted the use of nonviolent resistance.

Fifteenth Amendment
It declared that the right to vote could not be infringed upon due to one's race.

Fourteenth Amendment
It gave blacks citizenship and established that all laws would apply equally to blacks and whites.

Freedmen's Bureau
The bureau was established during reconstruction to help former slaves. It provided food and medical services, helped with settlement, managed

289

abandoned lands, regulated labor, and established schools.

freedom ride
Freedom rides were used to challenge racial segregation on buses in the South. Participants, both white and black, rode interstate buses throughout the South in 1961.

integration
Equal and unrestricted access of all racial groups to public facilities and other amenities.

Jim Crow
The phrase Jim Crow emerged in 1828, when minstrel performer Thomas Dartmouth "Daddy" Rice popularized it with his performance as a crippled slave named Jim Crow.

Jim Crow Laws
Also known as segregation laws, these regulations prevented blacks in the South access to public facilities, schools, restaurants, hospitals, and many other amenities.

Ku Klux Klan (KKK)
A white supremacist group that has used lynching and other mechanisms of violence to intimidate blacks.

National Association for the Advancement of Colored People (NAACP)
The original goals of the organization were male suffrage, the elimination of segregation, and equality in education. Later, it became known for its legal success at challenging segregation laws.

National Urban League
Created in 1911, the group focused on economic issues for blacks.

nonviolent resistance
The method of peaceful resistance against a government.

pacifism
The belief that war or violence is unnecessary in the resolution of disputes.

reconciliation
To re-establish a relationship.

Reconstruction
This was known as the time of political restructuring in the South. It began after the Civil War and ended in 1877.

segregation
Laws that regulate based on one's race or ethnicity.

Socialism
Socialism, like Communism, advocates public ownership. Socialism is the direct outgrowth of Capitalism.

Student Nonviolent Coordinating Committee (SNCC)
A civil-rights group organized by students involved in the lunch-counter sit-ins.

Voting Rights Act of 1965
The act prohibits the discriminatory practice of literacy tests.

Appendix B

RESOURCES

Books

Abernathy, Ralph David. *And the Walls Came Tumbling Down: An Autobiography.* New York: Harper & Row, Publishers, 1989.

Ansbro, John J. *Martin Luther King, Jr.: Nonviolent Strategies and Tactics for Social Change.* Lanham, Maryland: Madison Books, 1982.

Branch, Taylor. *At Canaan's Edge: America in the King Years, 1965–68.* New York: Simon & Schuster, 2006.

——— *Parting the Waters: America in the King Years, 1954–63.* New York: Simon & Schuster, 1988.

——— *Pillar of Fire: America in the King Years, 1963–65.* New York: Simon & Schuster, 1998.

Carbado, Devon W., and Donald Weise (Editors). *Time on Two Crosses: The Collected Writings of Bayard Rustin.* San Francisco, California: Cleis Press, 2003.

Carmichael, Stokely. *Ready for Revolution: The Life and Struggles of Stokely Carmichael (Kwame Ture).* New York: Scribner, 2003.

Carson, Clayborne (Editor). *The Autobiography of Martin Luther King, Jr.* New York: Warner Books, 1998.

——— "Editing Martin Luther King, Jr.: Political and Scholarly Issues." In *Palimpsest: Editorial Theory in the Humanities,* edited by George Bornstein and Ralph G. Williams, 305–316. Ann Arbor: University of Michigan Press, 1993.

——— "King Advocated Special Programs That Went Beyond Affirmative Action," *San Jose Mercury News,* October 27, 1996.

——— "Martin Luther King, Jr., and the African American Social Gospel." In *African American Christianity,* edited by Paul E. Johnson, 159–177. Berkeley: University of California Press, 1994. Reprinted in *African American Religion: Interpretive Essays in History and Culture,* edited by Tomothy E. Fulop and Albert J. Raboteau. New York: Routledge, 1997.

———*The Papers of Martin Luther King, Jr., Volume I: Called to Serve, January 1929–June 1951.* Berkeley: University of California Press, 1992.

——— *The Papers of Martin Luther King, Jr., Volume II: Rediscovering Precious Values, July 1951–November 1955.* Berkeley: University of California Press, 1994.

——— *The Papers of Martin Luther King, Jr., Volume III: Birth of a New Age, December 1955–December 1956.* Berkeley: University of California Press, 1997.

——— *The Papers of Martin Luther King, Jr., Volume IV: Symbol of the Movement, January 1957–December 1958.* Berkeley: University of California Press, 2000.

————*The Papers of Martin Luther King, Jr., Volume V: Threshold of a New Decade, January 1959–December 1960.* Berkeley: University of California Press, 2005.

Erskine, Noel Leo. *King Among the Theologians.* Cleveland, Ohio: Pilgrim Press, 1994.

Garrow, David J. *Bearing the Cross: Martin Luther King, Jr., and the Southern Christian Leadership Conference.* New York: Harper Perennial Modern Classics, 1999.

Hampton, Henry, Steve Fayer, and Sarah Flynn. *Voices of Freedom: An Oral History of the Civil Rights Movement from the 1950s through the 1980s.* New York: Bantam Books, 1990.

King, Coretta Scott. *My Life with Martin Luther King, Jr.* New York: Henry Holt and Company, 1969.

Lewis, John. *Walking with the Wind: A Memoir of the Movement.* New York: Simon & Schuster, 1998.

Ling, Peter J. *Martin Luther King, Jr.* New York: Routledge, 2002.

McWhorter, Diane. *Carry Me Home: Birmingham, Alabama: The Climatic Battle of the Civil Rights Revolution.* New York: Simon & Schuster, 2001.

Washington, James M. (Editor). *A Testament of Hope: The Essential Writings and Speeches of Martin Luther King, Jr.* New York: Harper Collins, 1991.

Wofford, Harris. *Of Kennedys & Kings: Making Sense of the Sixties.* Pittsburgh, Pennsylvania: University of Pittsburgh Press, 1980.

Web Sites

African American World

A timeline of the Civil Rights movement.

✎ *www.pbs.org/wnet/aaworld/time line/civil_01.html*

Google Video: I Have a Dream

The full version of Martin Luther King's "I Have a Dream" speech.

✎ *http://video.google.com/videoplay? docid=1732754907698549493*

The King Center

This Web site provides information about the King Center, Dr. King, and Coretta Scott King.

✎ *www.thekingcenter.org*

Martin Luther King Jr. Birth Home Virtual Tour

A virtual tour of the birth home of Martin Luther King Jr.

✎ *www.nps.gov/archive/malu/Birth HomeTour*

Martin Luther King Jr. National Historic Site

Information about the location, hours of operation, and tours of the King home and Ebenezer Baptist Church.

✎ *http://martinlutherkingjr.areaparks. com*

Martin Luther King Jr. Papers Project

A large collection of King's sermons, speeches, and writings.

✎ *www.stanford.edu/group/King/ mlkpapers*

Voices of Civil Rights

Includes a timeline, a photo gallery, and personal accounts by lesser-known participants.

✎ *www.voicesofcivilrights.org*

We Shall Overcome: Historic Places of the Civil Rights Movement

Information about segregation, the participants of the movement, the various campaigns, and historic civil-rights places.

✎ *www.cr.nps.gov/nr/travel/civilrights/ index.htm*

INDEX